THE
UNITED STATES
OF AWESOME

Fun, Fascinating and Bizarre Trivia
about the Greatest Country in the Universe

JOSHUA MILLER

 Ulysses Press

Published by:
Ulysses Press
P.O. Box 3440
Berkeley, CA 94703
www.ulyssespress.com

ISBN: 978-1-61243-113-0
Library of Congress Catalog Number 2012940433

Printed in the United States by Bang Printing

10 9 8 7 6 5 4 3 2 1

Acquisitions editor: Keith Riegert
Managing editor: Claire Chun
Editor: Jessica Benner
Proofreader: Elyce Berrigan-Dunlop
Interior illustrations: Valentin Ramon
Interior clip art: flag © Vector pro/shutterstock.com, eagle © abrakadabra/shutterstock.com, strip of stars © Christophe BOISSON/shutterstock.com
Cover design: what!design @ whatweb.com
Cover artwork: space capsule © James Steidl/shutterstock.com; Liberty Bell © James Steidl/shutterstock.com; hot dog © Paul Johnson/istockphoto.com; mitt and ball © eurobanks/shutterstock.com; Vegas sign © trekandshoot/shutterstock.com; bear © Dennis Donohue/shutterstock.com

Distributed by Publishers Group West

PROLOGUE
★ ★ ★ ★ ★ ★ ★ ★ ★

"The United States themselves are
essentially the greatest poem."
—*Walt Whitman*

"You cannot spill a drop of American
blood without spilling the blood of the
whole world...We are not a nation,
so much as a world."
—*Herman Melville*

"What's the difference between the
United States and a cup of yogurt?
If you leave a cup of yogurt to sit
for 200 years, it will develop a culture."
—*a drunk Englishman
this author encountered
in a London pub*

Awesome is a word that has lost most of its original meaning in recent years through casual overuse. Once a weighty
bit of vocabulary used to describe towering cathedrals and
erupting volcanoes, the word is now uttered by most of us
on a daily basis. Does the "awesome" sandwich you just
made actually inspire such admiration that it is intimidat-
ing, or leave you with a sense of apprehension, even fear?
Probably not. That would be one serious sandwich. The
title of this book is meant to convey both the classic and
current meanings of awesome. US history can be great,
fun, funny, inspiring, horrifying, and completely ridiculous,

if not all those things at once. And there is a daunting amount of it. The *United States of Awesome* shall attempt to present the United States's truly awesome history in the casual and digestible manner of an awesome sandwich.

But before we dive into the roughly five hundred years of shenanigans that make up the American narrative, we might as well be thorough and jump all the way back to the beginning for some context…

A craton is what those who know what they're talking about call the stable blocks of the Earth's crust that form the nucleus of a continent. A little over a billion years ago, a plucky new craton named Laurentia was born, becoming the ancient geologic core of what is currently North America. Citizens of the United States are among the latest of the great many tenants that have squatted atop Laurentia as it floats around our planet's ever-shifting surface, periodically bonking into other cratons, getting into relationships, and having messy break-ups. Briefly, Laurentia and the other cratons decided to form something akin to a band, all squashing together into the supercontinent Pangaea. As happens with a lot of bands, eventually the continents decided to part ways. North America got to keep the Appalachian Mountains, which formed when Laurentia crashed into Eurasia and are now among Earth's oldest mountain ranges. So it wasn't a total waste of time.

The newly single Laurentia now headed out West with its share of the dinosaurs, discarding Greenland along the way and eventually making a leisurely connection with South America. Laurentia also made an even more leisurely connection with the northeastern portion of Eurasia. During the Pleistocene glaciation, or Ice Age, ocean levels dipped far enough to expose that connection and create the Bering Land Bridge between modern Russia and Alaska. Turned out that since Laurentia had last spoken with the other continents, an aggressive and ambitious new species had spread like wildfire across the remnants of old Pangaea—*Homo sapiens*. Some of these sneaky humans quickly scuttled into North America before the ebb and flow of Mother Nature sent the Bering Land Bridge back beneath the waves. As things went back to business as usual for Eurasia, North America's new residents busied themselves propagating across the choice new real estate and killing off all the cool giant sloths and mastodons, and Eurasia forgot all about the place.

North America forgot all about Eurasia too. Which made things a little awkward when the Eurasians known as the Vikings showed up on the shores of present-day Newfoundland about on thousand years ago. The Vikings were not known for their friendliness, so, even though the relatively beardless North Americans were presumably quite impressed with the size and thickness of the Vikings's beards, it didn't take long for the North Americans to escort their unwanted houseguests to the door. Luckily for the North Americans, no one liked the Vikings much back in Eurasia either, so tales of this "New World" didn't get far. And everyone forgot once more.

For a handful of centuries, the North Americans got to keep Laurentia all to themselves, until the king and queen of a western Eurasian country paid a guy to find a faster way to get to eastern Eurasia. This guy thought he could accomplish this task by sailing westerly around the planet, but he didn't realize there was a whole other craton with a bunch of stuff on top of it blocking his path. Unfortunately for the North Americans, this guy immediately sailed back to Eurasia and blabbed to everyone about what he found.

Okay, that brings us up to speed.

PRODIGAL SON

William Franklin was the illegitimate son of Benjamin Franklin. Though his mother's identity is unknown, Benjamin and his common-law wife, Deborah Read, raised William as a natural son. And William at first seemed to be following in his father's impressive footsteps. In his early twenties, William assisted Benjamin in his famous kite experiment. He fought in King George's War, obtaining the rank of captain. In 1763 he became the governor of New Jersey and signed the charter for Queen's College (now Rutgers University). But when the American Revolution reared its head, William enraged his father by becoming a Loyalist to the British Crown. In 1776, the Provincial Congress of New Jersey arrested William and he spent two years in incarceration. Then, in 1782, he departed for Britain, never to return.

After the war, William tried to make peace with his father, but Benjamin could never forgive William for his choices. Benjamin held the grudge to the bitter end, evening referencing it in his will—he left William very little, spitefully adding for emphasis: "The part he acted against me in the late war, which is of public notoriety, will account for my leaving him no more of an estate he endeavoured to deprive me of."

 ## A FLYING DISC BY ANY OTHER NAME

In 1871, William Frisbie founded a pie company in Bridgeport, Connecticut. It is uncertain just how delicious Frisbie's pies were, but at least one part of his product became quite popular with local college students: the pie tin. Frisbie's pie tins formed the basis for a game in which the tins were thrown, sailing through the air, from person to person. In the 1940s, California inventor Walter Frederick Morrison came up with a similar game, using a popcorn lid to play catch with his

girlfriend. Morrison took the game a step further, modeling a plastic creation he initially called a Whirlo-Way—then the Flyin-Saucer, then the Pluto Platter. In 1957, Morrison sold the Pluto Platter to the Wham-O toy company, who soon discovered that Connecticut college students were calling the Pluto Platter a Frisbie. Liking the sound of this name better, in 1958 Wham-O decided to tweak that spelling to the trademarkable Frisbee. The rest is toy history.

▤ McNixon

By the end of the 1960s, inflation was raging in the United States, exceeding 6 percent in 1970. So in 1971 President Richard Nixon imposed price controls, a freeze on wages and consumer goods. Yet McDonald's raised the price of its Quarter Pounder cheeseburger from fifty-nine cents to sixty-five cents. Some found this fishy when it was revealed that Ray A. Kroc, chairman of the board of McDonald's, had contributed $200,000 to Nixon's reelection campaign. Not only that, but the Price Commission originally denied McDonald's a price increase on May 21, 1972. Then, when McDonald's reapplied in September, the Price Commission granted the increase. Oh, and Kroc made his donation to Nixon's campaign in three installments—paid in June, July, and August.

It was suspicious enough that these details were included in the Specification of Charges (Bill of Particulars) of the Articles of Impeachment against Richard Nixon. Too bad Nixon resigned; otherwise this factoid could have been about the only president to get fired, in part, for raising the price of a cheeseburger.

THE CURSE OF THE PHARAOHS

In 1979, the famed *Treasures of Tutankhamun* international exhibition tour concluded the last leg of its American stint at the M. H. de Young Memorial Museum in San Francisco. Just seven days before the exhibit was to close, fifty-six-year-old Lt. George E. LaBrash suffered a stroke while guarding King Tut's 3,300-year-old mask. LaBrash survived, and blamed the stroke on the legendary Curse of the Pharaohs, referring to the hex ancient Egyptians believed that Osiris, god of the dead, placed on all those who should dare to disturb the dead. Modern believers claim the curse has been responsible for dozens of deaths since King Tut's tomb was rediscovered in 1922. LaBrash felt that the city of San Francisco had acted in reckless negligence by displaying these accursed artifacts. So he sued the city for $18,400 in disability pay, saying, "I firmly believe that King Tut's curse is as good an explanation for what happened to me as any."

At 6 feet 4 inches, Abraham Lincoln was the TALLEST president. At 5 feet 4 inches, James Madison holds the record for the SHORTEST.

A MAJOR JINX

Major General John Sedgwick was the highest-ranking Union casualty of the Civil War, and also the most ironic. Having survived a bout with cholera and three bullet wounds during the Battle of Antietam, Sedgwick may have thought himself invincible. Unfortunately for him, at the Battle of Spotsylvania Courthouse, Virginia, on May 9, 1864, he found out just how far luck could take a man.

Standing above his ducking men, the Major General shouted, "What? Men dodging this way for single bullets? What will you do when they open fire along the whole line? I am ashamed of you. They couldn't hit an elephant at this distance." He then repeated, "They couldn't hit an elephant at this distance…" At which point, he was promptly shot through the left eye.

 ## CASTRO'S CRAPPY WELCOME

On January 1, 1959, the communist revolutionary forces of Fidel Castro overthrew the Cuban dictator Fulgencio Batista. Four months later Castro visited the United States on invitation from the American Society of Newspaper Editors. If Castro nursed any illusions that America would greet him with open arms, his illusions were quickly dispelled when President Dwight D. Eisenhower left for a golfing trip to make sure there was no chance the two men might cross paths. Instead, Vice President Richard Nixon was left to meet with Castro. Nixon hoped he could sway Castro away from communism, but he left the meeting concluding that Castro was "either incredibly naive about communism or under communist discipline. My guess is the former." After Castro returned to Cuba, President Eisenhower had the CIA start arming and training a group of Cuban exiles to reclaim Cuba, which culminated in the disastrous Bay of Pigs snafu during the Kennedy administration.

Despite Nixon's feelings regarding Castro's naiveté, on April 19, 2011, when Castro stepped down as leader of Cuba's Communist Party, he had ruled for nearly fifty-two years—the longest reign of power for a nonroyal national leader in modern history.

 ## THE HUDSON MUTINY

In 1609, the Dutch East India Company hired English explorer Henry Hudson to find the elusive Northwest Passage, a sailable connection between the Atlantic and Pacific Oceans. He didn't find it. Instead he wound up exploring the modern New York metropolitan area. The following year he made another attempt, exploring what is now Hudson Bay in Canada. But when winter pounced on Hudson and his crew, their ship became trapped in the ice, forcing them to spend a rough winter ashore. When the ice finally thawed in the spring, Hudson wished to continue exploring. Most of the crewmen weren't exactly into this idea anymore, so they mutinied, placing Hudson, his teenage son, and seven other non-mutinous sailors into a small boat and then setting them adrift. Hudson and his fellow castaways were never heard from again.

Not a great way to go out. But on the upside, Hudson wound up with a lot of things named after him in America—the Hudson River, the Henry Hudson Bridge (which connects the Bronx with the north end of Manhattan), Hudson County, New Jersey, and the town of Hudson, New York.

WHITE ANIMAL HOUSE

After Thomas Jefferson was sworn in as president, he began a tradition of hosting a post-inauguration party in the White House. On March 4, 1829, Andrew Jackson kept with that tradition. After Jackson's swearing-in ceremony, he retreated to the White House with a throng of partygoers made up of politicians, celebrities, and regular citizens—*some 20,000 of them*. What had formerly been a staid and dignified event was now a riotous party, as Jackson's revelers proceeded to trash the White House, standing on furniture, breaking things, and grinding food into the carpet under their many feet. Fearing that the presidential headquarters would be completely ruined, the serving staff filled a series of washtubs with whiskey and juice on the White House lawn in order to draw the horde out of the building.

The party tradition officially ended in 1885 when partypooper Grover Cleveland decided to have a celebratory parade instead.

 ## NICE SHOT, MAN

The Grumman F-11 Tiger has the dubious honor of being the first jet aircraft to ever shoot itself down. On September 21, 1956, during a test flight, pilot Tom Attridge fired two cannon bursts during a shallow dive. But as he continued his dive, the

Tiger ultimately caught up with its cannon rounds, destroying the aircraft and forcing Attridge to crash land.

America may be associated with hamburgers and hot dogs but it's the CORN DOG that truly encapsulates the innovative spirit of the U.S. of A. Purportedly created for the TEXAS State Fair in 1942, the original easy-eatin' meat Popsicle has since been joined by the fair's other deep-fried delights: mac and cheese, bacon, Coke, JAMBALAYA, butter, and, for dessert, cotton candy. To your health!

THE FIRST MONUMENT

In January of 1776, the Continental Congress authorized what would become the United States' first national memorial in honor of Brigadier General Richard Montgomery, who had been killed on the battlefield in Quebec on December 31, 1775. Benjamin Franklin was entrusted with the memorial's creation, for which he hired King Louis XV's personal sculptor, Jean-Jacques Caffieri. Completed in 1778, the Montgomery memorial was officially installed in 1788 beneath the portico of New York City's St. Paul's Chapel, which had served as George Washington's church during his time in the city.

OOPS, OHIO

In 1803, Ohio formally became the seventeenth state admitted into the United States. In 1953, the Ohio government was preparing festivities to celebrate the state's sesquicentennial, so their congressional delegation decided it would be cute to borrow the formal resolution that declared Ohio's admission to the Union from the National Archives. When the National Archive went to retrieve the document, they made a peculiar discovery—*they found nothing*. It seems that, for whatever reason, back in 1803, Congress never quite got around to formally adopting the Buckeye State. Oops. Perhaps there is credence to that persistent urban legend that many of the Founding Fathers smoked marijuana? In any case, upon this embarrassing discovery, Congress swiftly passed a resolution declaring Ohio's admission, and did what any American does when writing an overdue document…they predated it "1803."

SORRY, STONERS

As to that Founding Father pot smoking rumor—while it is true that many prominent revolutionaries, such as George Washington, grew hemp, there is little reason to believe that any of them used cannabis for recreation. Given the frequency with which the Founding Fathers referenced and praised alcohol in their correspondence, and considering that marijuana was not illegal until the twentieth century, it is conspicuous that none of them seem to mention getting high—if they were in fact lovers of weed.

Speaking of inaccuracies about the Founding Fathers, including their praise of alcohol, one of the most quoted quotes from Benjamin Franklin, "Beer is proof that God loves us and wants us to be happy," is also erroneous. Sorry beer drinkers, the actual statement, from a 1779 letter addressed to French philosophe André Morellet, was regarding wine:

> *Behold the rain which descends from heaven upon our vineyards, there it enters the roots of the vines, to be changed into wine, a constant proof that God loves us, and loves to see us happy.*

In 1919, two million gallons of MOLASSES burst from a tank and flooded a neighborhood in Boston. The molasses SURGED through the streets at 35 miles per hour, KILLING twenty-one people and injuring a great many more. It took weeks to clean up and the SMELL of molasses persisted for years.

SOME SERIOUS BALLS IN THE BULGE

The Battle of the Bulge—so named in the press because of the way the Allied front line *bulged* inward on war maps—proved the biggest and bloodiest battle for America in World War II, with nearly ninety thousand casualties and roughly twenty thousand deaths during a fight that raged through a densely forested region of Belgium from December 16, 1944, to January 25, 1945. The German plan had been to split the American and British Allied line in half, then surround the Allied armies, forcing peace treaty negotiations in the Nazis' favor. And by December 21, the plan was working. The Germans had surrounded two American divisions in the town of Bastogne and, as might be expected, the Germans requested that the encircled Americans surrender.

The acting commander of the American forces, Brigadier General Anthony McAuliffe, responded with a single word: "Nuts!"—which, in 1940s slang, basically meant, "Eat shit!" A Colonel Harper was sent to deliver the typed note to the Germans, who received it with total bafflement. Harper explained the note's meaning and then added his own personal badass panache, saying: "I will tell you something else. If you continue to attack, we will kill every goddamn German that tries to break into this city." The American forces at Bastogne took on "Nuts!" as their rallying cry and held their ground until General George S. Patton's Third Army came to the rescue. Purportedly, when Patton first heard of McAuliffe's snarky reply, he said, "A man that eloquent *has* to be saved!"

SHORT BUT SWEET

Despite remaining one of the more famous chapters in American history, the celebrated Pony Express mail service was only operational for an objectively insignificant eighteen months. William H. Russell, Alexander Majors, and William B. Waddell opened the service in 1860 to expedite communication across the ever-growing country. Messages were carried by riders on horseback through an impressively staged system of relay stations, where fresh riders with fresh horses were waiting to continue the journey. It was a dangerous job that involved venturing into the untamed reaches of the American West—so dangerous in fact that the Pony Express job ad ended with "Orphans Preferred." Sad to say, the horse lost out to technology. On October 26, 1861, the Pony Express announced it was hanging up its saddle for good, just two days after the transcontinental telegraph line became operational.

NOW IT IS AGAINST THE LAW?

Between the time that George Washington became the first president of the United States and the death of President John F. Kennedy in 1963, there were six notable assassination attempts made on a president's life—three of which were successful. Yet despite the fact that the president commands the federal government, killing the president was not a federal crime. For example, in 1901, when anarchist Leon Czolgosz assassinated President William McKinley in Erie County, New York, he was tried and executed by the Erie County court system. Only after Kennedy's assassination did killing, kidnapping, or otherwise harming a president or vice president become a federal felony (as did even attempting to do any of those things).

IT WAS JUST THE WIND

On July 8, 1680, a servant in Cambridge, Massachusetts, named John Robbins became the first officially documented American fatality of a tornado—a natural force that baffled witnesses could only identify as a terrifying "whirl-wind." Robbins succumbed to wounds caused by broken bones and overall body bruising.

DEAR SMALL POX, THANKS FOR THE REAL ESTATE

While modern Americans are inclined to feel at least some awkward guilt over the fact that our ancestors stole North America from the Native Americans, we are also inclined to feel that the Native Americans were doomed to conquest in the face of our superior weaponry and civilized technology. Hell, Americans even felt a bit weird about it back in the late nineteenth century, when scholars estimated that the Indian population had been upward of ten million before the arrival of Columbus in 1492. Here's the thing though: current estimates place the pre-Columbian Native American population somewhere over fifty million, possibly even as high as one hundred million (which was larger than the population of Europe at the time). Sure, we had guns and horses and bitchin' beards, but the truth is that disease did the bulk of the conquest for us…long before most English settlers arrived.

Smallpox is believed to have arrived in the Americas in 1520, carried by an infected African slave on a Spanish ship sailing from Cuba. Native Americans had never encountered smallpox, measles, or even flu before. For the Indians it was an all-out plague. When the Pilgrims stepped on Plymouth Rock in 1620 they probably thought, "Wow, this area is so spacious!" What they didn't realize was that almost the entire indigenous population of Massachusetts died from illness before the Pilgrims even thought about moving to the New World.

It is estimated that upward of 90 percent of the total pre-Columbian population died from infectious European diseases. For context, the famous Black Death (or bubonic plague) bumped off between 30 and 60 percent of Europe's population in the fourteenth century. There are less precise figures regarding the Native American devastation, but even in estimated form it ranks as one of the most catastrophic epidemics in global history.

THE SUPEREST SUPER TORNADO

The Tri-State Tornado that roared through Missouri, Illinois, and Indiana on March 18, 1925, holds several records. Aside from being the deadliest tornado in American history, with 695 fatalities, it set global records for the longest path length (219 miles), longest uninterrupted duration (3.5 hours), and fastest forward speed for a major tornado (73 miles per hour).

THE LITTLE SURE SHOT OF THE WILD WEST

In 1875, Francis E. Butler, a traveling exposition marksman, rolled into Cincinnati to earn some money the way he always did, by showing off his shooting skills. He bet a hotel owner $100 that he could best any shooter in town.

Butler was surprised when the hotel owner presented him with his competitor, a fifteen-year-old girl named Phoebe Ann Moses. Much to Butler's dismay, the girl kept up with him, hitting target after target until finally Butler missed his twenty-fifth shot. The girl did not and claimed her $100. A year later, Butler married her and they became a marksman (and markswoman) duo. Moses adopted the stage name Annie Oakley.

In 1888 the couple joined Buffalo Bill's Wild West Show and Annie became a star. Her most famous trick was being able to split a playing card, edge-on, with a .22 caliber rifle from a distance of 90 feet. She toured Europe, performing for various world leaders. So deadly accurate was her aim that the newly crowned German Kaiser Wilhelm II allowed her to shoot the ashes off his cigarette... while it was between his lips.

I BEG YOUR PARDON?

When Gerald Ford assumed the presidency—after Richard Nixon resigned in the wake of the Watergate scandal—he made the controversial decision to give Nixon an unconditional pardon for any crimes he may have committed against the United States. For those who had hoped to see Nixon prosecuted for any wrongdoing, the pardon would prove to be the lasting memory of Ford's otherwise uneventful presidency.

Less remembered is the fact that Ford also pardoned a man who had posed a substantially more dire threat to the United States than Nixon ever did—Confederate General Robert E. Lee. Nixon may have been sending young men to die in Vietnam, but at least he wasn't commanding the Viet Cong.

When the Civil War ended, Confederate soldiers were given the opportunity to apply for a pardon and have their citizenship restored. Robert E. Lee did just that. He appealed to his former adversary, General Ulysses S. Grant, who forwarded Lee's appeal to the secretary of state. And that is where the process stopped. Lee's appeal never reached President Andrew Johnson, and Lee died several years later. Then, in 1970, an archivist at the National Archives rediscovered Lee's appeal. Apparently Secretary of State William H. Seward did not think Lee deserved legal forgiveness, so he gave Lee's amnesty application to a friend as a souvenir. On August 5, 1975, President Ford accepted Lee's appeal and restored his US citizenship, 105 years after Lee's death.

Ralph and Carolyn CUMMINS of Clintwood, Virginia, had five children between 1952 and 1966. All were born on February 20.

SIBLING RIVALRY

Edwin Thomas Booth was considered by many critics to be the finest American actor of the nineteenth century. His most famous role was that of Hamlet, which he played for a record-setting one hundred performances at The Winter Garden Theatre in 1864 (a record that held until John Barrymore broke it in 1922). But Booth's legacy became overshadowed on April 14, 1865, when his younger brother and fellow thespian John Wilkes Booth assassinated President Lincoln. Unlike John, Edwin was a loyal Unionist, and the stain left to his family name after the assassination would trouble him for the remainder of his life.

In an almost unreal moment of cosmic connection, less than a year before the assassination, Edwin saved the life of a young man who fell from the platform of a Jersey City,

New Jersey, train station. The young man was Robert Lincoln, the president's son.

 DYING BY EXAMPLE

During the Civil War, generals on both sides had the somewhat peculiar habit of literally leading their troops into battle—a rare tactic in modern warfare, for good reason. Thus, generals were 50 percent more likely to die in combat than privates.

LIKE A HOLE IN THE HEAD

On September 13, 1848, twenty-five-year-old Phineas Gage was working as the foreman of a crew cutting a railroad bed in Cavendish, Vermont. While he was using a tamping iron to pack explosive powder into a hole, the powder accidentally detonated, propelling the 3.5-foot-long, 13-pound rod up through Gage's left cheek, into his brain, out the top of his skull, and high up into the air before landing several paces away.

Miraculously, when Dr. Edward H. Williams arrived on the scene, Gage was sitting up and speaking clearly. Williams later recorded: "Mr. Gage, during the time I was examining this wound, was relating the manner in which he was injured to the bystanders. I did not believe Mr. Gage's statement at that time, but thought he was deceived. Mr. Gage persisted in saying that the bar went through his head....Mr. G. got up and vomited; the effort of vomiting pressed out about half a teacupful of the brain, which fell upon the floor."

Gage lived for another twelve years and he displayed personality changes due to the horrendous damage done to his frontal lobe. Yet his lasting fame came less from his remarkable survival and more from the telephone-game of exaggerations that his story took on as it was retold over the decades. For example, Gage is often said to have gone from being a forthright and kind man to a drunken cad who routinely beat his wife and children. But he never had a wife or children. The reality, while less melodramatic, is that Gage's personality changes were mild—probably proportionately less dramatic than those of an average brain trauma victim, considering the man's skull got Swiss-cheesed by a giant metal pole.

THE FIRST PRESIDENT

In 1781, the Continental Congress ratified the Articles of Confederation, an agreement among the thirteen colonies that legally established the United States of America as a union of sovereign states and also served as the first constitution. Shortly afterward, John Hanson, a delegate from Maryland, was elected the ninth president of the Continental Congress, following more famous Johns like John Hancock and John Jay. The position was almost entirely ceremonial, consisting mostly of signing official documents and performing other mundane office tasks. All in all, it was an unglamorous job, and one that Hanson found tedious.

But because Hanson was the first to be elected after the Articles of Confederation were ratified, down the road some people—notably one of Hanson's grandsons—suggested the idea that Hanson was technically the first president of the United States, not George Washington (who was elected president in 1789). There was a fairly big difference between being the president of the United States and the president of the Continental Congress, but this notion was at least intriguing enough to earn John Hanson a place as one of two statues representing Maryland in the National Statuary Hall of the US Capitol building.

WHO ELECTED THESE GUYS?

In 1973, after Vice President Spiro Agnew resigned in disgrace over charges that he accepted bribes, President Nixon appointed Gerald Ford vice president. Then in 1974, Nixon also resigned in disgrace over charges related to the Watergate scandal, which left Ford as President. Ford then appointed Nelson Rockefeller vice president. So for the next two years, until Ford lost the 1976 election to Jimmy Carter, the country was run by a president and a vice president that the public did not elect to office.

John F. Kennedy was the FIRST president born in the twentieth century.

THE ULTIMATE CONGRESSIONAL HIDEAWAY

In the 1950s, as Cold War psychosis flamed hot, Americans across the country built themselves bomb shelters. So did the government. In 1957, the luxurious Greenbrier Hotel in White Sulphur Springs, West Virginia, announced plans to build a new wing. What they didn't announce was that the new wing was a front for the construction of a secret bunker designed to house Congress—one hundred senators, 435 congressmen and around five hundred staffers—in the event of an all-out Soviet nuclear attack. The subterranean facility was 112,000 square feet on two levels and was made up of 153 rooms, including eighteen dormitories, a hospital, a power plant, and even a TV studio. The concrete walls were 5 feet thick, and the entire structure was buried under 20 feet of dirt.

Fortunately, Congress never had reason to use the bunker. And, ironically, on the one occasion when they probably should have been used it—the Cuban Missile Crisis (1962)—they didn't. Why? Because the government was astute enough to realize that the very act of evacuating Congress from Washington, D.C., would have been seen as an indication to the Soviets of an upcoming war.

GERONIMO'S SKULL

The famed Apache leader and warrior Geronimo battled against US and Mexican expansion in the Southwest for nearly three decades until he was finally captured in 1886. He died of pneumonia on February 17, 1909, a prisoner of the United States and was buried at Fort Sill, Oklahoma.

During WWI, six members of Yale's prestigious secret society, Skull and Bones, including Prescott Bush—father of George H. W. Bush, grandfather of George W. Bush—were serving as army volunteers at Fort Sill. It is claimed that Bush and his compatriots mischievously dug up Geronimo's grave and plundered it of several items, including the warrior's skull. Those looking to reclaim the items have never been able to prove that Skull and Bones was behind the theft, and no Skull and Bones member has ever publicly admitted to it. But supposedly the skull still resides inside the society's windowless clubhouse in New Haven, Connecticut.

INVOKING THE 25TH

The 25th Amendment was adopted in 1967 and laid out clear instructions for the succession of power in the event that the president should be incapacitated by illness or other medical impediments. The amendment has only been invoked for that purpose on three occasions. The first was in 1985, when Vice President George H. W. Bush took over for President Ronald Reagan while the president underwent surgery to remove a lesion discovered during a colonoscopy. Oddly enough, the second and third instances occurred in 2002 and 2007 when Vice President Dick Cheney took over for Bush's son, President George W. Bush, when W. Bush underwent two colonoscopies.

GHOST SHIP

The *Baychimo* was a 1,322-ton steel cargo steamer built in 1914 and operated by the Hudson's Bay Company. On October 1, 1931, she became trapped in pack ice off the northern shore of Alaska, forcing the crew to leave the ship and travel over a half mile of ice to the town of Barrow. When they returned two days later, the vessel had broken free from the ice and vanished. Eventually it was located with the help of local Inuit fishermen, but the ship's captain determined the *Baychimo* was no longer seaworthy and it was abandoned to sink into the briny deep. But the *Baychimo* had other ideas. She did not sink. Instead the ghost ship bobbed around the Alaskan coast for several decades, being spotted and sometimes boarded by other vessels nearly a dozen times. The *Baychimo* was last sighted in 1969, once again frozen in pack ice.

PULLING THE LONG CON ON GERMANY

As WWII wore on, it became clear to the United States and our allies that victory would be impossible until we broke the Nazis' lock on Western Europe. We knew that France was the key to that lock. We knew that the Germans knew this too. But we also knew that the German high command presumed we would cross from England to France at Pas-de-Calais, the narrowest section of the English Channel. So it was time to come up with something that we didn't *both* know. The Allies needed to believably threaten Pas-de-Calais, which would force the Germans to keep their reserves in place and away from the actual attacks in Normandy (several hundred miles to the west). So the Allies crafted Operation Fortitude, one of the greatest con jobs in the history of war.

When the First US Army Group (FUSAG) was redesignated as the Twelfth Army Group, FUSAG continued to exist in name only as Operation Fortitude's facade. To lend FUSAG plausibility, General George S. Patton, who was both feared and respected by the German commanders, was given command of the fictitious army. A base was constructed for the phantom force in Dover, England, and populated by a threadbare number of real soldiers. Tents were set up and parking lots were filled with fake tanks and jeeps constructed of cloth and wood. Scripted radio transmissions were broadcast and double agents were used to help beef up FUSAG's image. Allied intelligence even went as far as printing letters in local English newspapers pretending to be from irate citizens complaining about the rowdy behavior of the troops.

The elaborate subterfuge continued on D-Day, with a number of real battle ships left behind to mingle with dummy ships near Pas-de-Calais. The masterstroke came when an Allied double agent gave a radio transmission regarding fake troop movements so believable that the message made its way to Hitler himself, who not only withdrew an order to send the Pas-de-Calais forces to Normandy, but actually rerouted reinforcements *away* from Normandy and sent them to Calais instead.

 ## LONELY TOWN

America's least populous town is Buford, Wyoming. The town was founded in 1866 during the construction of the First Transcontinental Railroad and named in honor of Union cavalry officer Major General John Buford. At its peak of prosperity it had a population of two thousand, but by the time Don Sammons purchased Buford in 1992 the only residents were Sammons, his wife, and their son. Then, after his wife died in 1995, and his son moved away in 2007, Sammons became the town's sole citizen. But being a town of one gets lonely, so in April of 2012 Sammons put Buford up for sale. It was purchased for $900,000 by two Vietnamese men.

BRITISH COMMANDER WASHINGTON

When George Washington was a teenager, he came extremely close to gaining an appointment in the British Royal Navy, but his mother put the kibosh on the whole thing after learning how physically demanding it would be for her lil' man.

Years later, during the French and Indian War (1754–1762), Washington served as colonel of the Virginia Regiment, the first full-time American military unit in the colonies (as opposed to temporary American militias or the permanent British army). Washington hoped that a successful showing of his leadership skills would earn him a commission in the British army. He commanded his men as a disciplinarian and led them through numerous battles, but ultimately retired from the Virginia Regiment in 1758 when no commission in the British army presented itself. He would not serve in the military again until 1775, when called to lead the colonial forces *against* the British.

Had his mother allowed him to join the Royal Navy, or had he received a commission from the British army, the course of US history may have turned out very differently. Or possibly not turned out at all.

The world's oldest still-functional LIGHT BULB was first switched on in 1901 in a fire station in Livermore, California, where it still SHINES light today. It is known as the "Centennial Light."

A REALLY TERRIBLE INTERMISSION

On the night of January 28, 1922, several hundred movie-goers braved their way through the largest snowstorm in Washington, D.C., history to the Knickerbocker Theatre for a showing of the silent film comedy *Get-Rich-Quick Wallingford*. The Knickerbocker was the newest and largest movie house in D.C., but as the storm raged on outside, eventually the theater's roof had all the snow it could take. During the film's intermission the ceiling collapsed, killing ninety-eight people and hospitalizing another 133. Some have theorized that the lasting memory of the disaster led the Knickerbocker's architect, Reginald Wyckliffe Geare, and its owner, Harry Crandall, to commit suicide. The men took their own lives in 1927 and 1937 respectively. This is of course purely speculation.

HARRIET THE SPY

Escaped slave Harriet Tubman is remembered for leading other slaves to freedom in the North along the Underground Railroad prior to the abolition of slavery after the Civil War. But Tubman also played an important role *during* the Civil War. Espionage!

Initially Tubman joined the Union camp at Port Royal, South Carolina, in the spring of 1862 to teach freed slave women skills that would help them earn wages in the army. But soon she was gathering intelligence of the Confederate army from the slaves she met. On June 1, 1863, Tubman and Col. James Montgomery took three hundred black Union soldiers and swept through nearby plantations, burning Confederate homes and freeing enslaved men, women, and children. In that single mission, 720 slaves were liberated, ten times the number of slaves Tubman had freed during her entire run on the Underground Railroad. The mission also marked the first raid led by a woman during the Civil War.

Dolphin Veterans

Perhaps you have heard the urban legends about the US military's classified weaponization of dolphins? And perhaps these wild images of dolphins strapped with bombs or lasers have led you to assume that the whole thing is an utter fabrication. But the United States does indeed have dolphins in the armed forces—just not the badass assassin kind.

The US Navy Marine Mammal Program (NMMP) began in the 1960s as a way for scientists and engineers to improve hydrodynamics and sonar by studying dolphins and sea lions. Over time the navy found other uses for their aquatic subjects. Military dolphins were deployed in the Gulf Wars to help detect mines in the Persian Gulf.

The Greatest Cowboy

These days the term "cowboy" tends to conjure images of lone drifters and gunslingers. But originally it was a job title. The country's expansion into the untamed western territories of the United States was motivated in part by the rise of the cattle industry and the need for land on which to raise said cattle. Cowboys were simply the men who worked with cows, branding them and herding them (though most probably preferred the less demeaning title of herder or rancher). So it may be disappointing to learn that the man once hailed as the "Greatest Cowboy" never got in a gunfight in his life.

Born in Texas in 1870 of African American and Cherokee descent, Bill Pickett became famous for a technique he called "bulldogging." Inspired by watching a bulldog pull down a steer by biting its face, Pickett (for some reason) thought, "That looks fun!" While other cowboys would lasso a cow, Pickett would jump from his horse, grabbing the animal by the horns, often biting its lip, and wrestling it to the ground. Obviously far too dangerous to be practical, bulldogging was nonetheless incredibly entertaining to watch.

Pickett became a popular staple of rodeos, county fairs, and Wild West shows, and even starred in a couple motion pictures. After a lifetime of surviving pissed-off bulls, Pickett died in 1932 when he was kicked in the head by a horse. But bulldogging is still performed in rodeos today.

THE LONG AND SHORT OF IT

The Persian Gulf War was America's shortest war, with the main offensive, Operation Desert Storm, barely lasting over forty days in 1991. The Spanish-American War was a close second, lasting only five months in 1898. America's longest war? Well, that depends on how you look at it.

The War in Afghanistan began in 2001, and, at the time of this book's publishing, the conflict is still going strong at eleven years old, making it the official champ. Then again, there is some disagreement among war historians regarding the exact start date of the Vietnam War. The war ended in 1975, and its officially accepted kick-off date is August 1964, with the Gulf of Tonkin incident. But since Congress never formally declared war against Vietnam, some think the start date should be placed in November 1955, when the Military Assistance and Advisory Group was established in Saigon. If you believe the latter argument, this would mean the Vietnam War lasted twenty whopping years. But then there is the strange case of the Korean War. In 1953, America signed a ceasefire with North Korea, ending the three-year conflict. But no formal peace treaty was ever signed—both sides simply stopped shooting at each other. Which means, technically, the war is still going on today.

SETTING A PRESIDENT PRECEDENT

The term length for president and vice president has always been four years, but the Founding Fathers never bothered to put restrictions on how many terms an individual could serve. George Washington likely could have served for forty years if he had so desired (and had lived that long), but he grew weary of the responsibilities and declined to run again after only two terms. Since Washington was the model president (quite literally), no one wanted to be the asshole who thought he was better than ol' George.

A precedent had been set. Though any man could legally run for however many terms he liked, for almost one hundred years nobody had the balls to try it. Ulysses S. Grant possessed those balls. He became the first president to make the attempt when he sought the Republican nomination for a third term in 1879. But he lost the nomination to James Garfield.

As Grant learned, it is hard to maintain the level of popularity necessary to get elected to three terms after you've likely been pissing off half of the population for eight years. But such popularity is exactly what Franklin D. Roosevelt had. He had taken over the presidency while the country floundered in the Great Depression and, though he had his share of haters among the establishment, many viewed him as something of a savior. And with Europe in the grips of World War II, Roosevelt felt confident that voters might welcome him to stick around a while longer. And they did. Roosevelt made history in 1940 when he was elected to a third term. Then he made history yet again when he was elected to a fourth term in 1944. He probably could have kept going into a fifth term had he not died in 1945.

Meanwhile, Roosevelt's enemies were aghast that he had broken the unspoken rule. They claimed that Washington's retirement was a clear indication that the Founding Fathers never intended anyone to serve so long. In reality, Washington's farewell address indicated that he was leaving due to his age (he died just two years later), and numerous presidents after Grant had *attempted* a third term; they just weren't successful. Regardless, in 1947

Congress passed the 22nd Amendment, which bars any individual from being elected president more than twice, or more than once if that individual already served more than half of another president's term.

▤ LAST PIGEON STANDING

At the beginning of the nineteenth century the passenger pigeon could be counted as one of the most successful species in North America as far as sheer population numbers were concerned. By the dawn of the twentieth century not a single passenger pigeon existed in the wild. The pigeon had the misfortune of becoming a wildly popular and affordable food source for slaves and the lower class, and they were hunted in staggeringly high numbers. In 1878, the motivated citizens of Petoskey, Michigan, killed roughly fifty thousand birds *every day* for five months.

In the twentieth century, attempts were made to keep the species going in captivity, but the caged population was simply too small to carry on. The species' last hope was Martha (named for George Washington's wife). She lived at the Cincinnati Zoo, where she was paired with the only two remaining male pigeons. Sadly, the males both died, and for four years Martha was Earth's sole passenger pigeon. In 1914, when her spirit finally went to the big flock in the sky, her body was frozen and sent to the Smithsonian museum, where it was stuffed and put on display until being retired in 1999.

There are 293 different ways to MAKE CHANGE for a US dollar.

On the Wings of Destiny

As Christopher Columbus crossed the Atlantic searching for Asia, he was sailing due west. Then Martín Alonso Pinzón, captain of the *Pinta*, spotted birds flying southwest and suggested that their ships follow the flock. This led them to the Bahamas. Had they continued on their previous path they would have hit Florida, and Spain's early colonies would likely have spread along the eastern coast of North America instead of the Caribbean Islands and Central America, setting the New World on a radically different path. Spanish Catholics would have dominated North America, and the English Protestants would have been left to settle in Central and South America.

 ## The What House?

The White House finished construction in 1800. But the earliest recorded evidence of its popular nickname didn't appear until 1811. The residence had initially been referred to by many names, including: the President's Palace, the Presidential Mansion, and just the President's House. Even after the nickname caught on, "Executive Mansion" was used in all official contexts until President Theodore Roosevelt decided to put "White House, Washington" on his stationery in 1901.

The Not Quite War

The aptly named Quasi-War (sometimes known as the Franco-American War or Half-War) was a naval conflict fought between the French Republic and the fledgling United States from 1798 to 1800. French support had been instrumental to the colonists' success during the American Revolution. When the French Republic was declared in 1792 during the French Revolution, the new government presumed America would have their backs. Not so much. By the Founding Fathers' reasoning, they had borrowed money from the French monarchy, and that debt had been removed at the same time as King Louis XVI's head (he and Queen Marie Antoinette were beheaded by the revolutionaries, in case you're fuzzy on your French history).

When the United States signed the Jay Treaty with Great Britain, which resolved a lot of smoldering issues America still had with its former parent country, the French Republic got all pissy and started seizing American ships trading with Britain. So President John Adams built up a new American navy and started pissing back. It became known as the Quasi-War because neither side ever officially declared it a war. Fighting ceased when Napoleon Bonaparte decided he might make a decent emperor of France.

SORE LOSERS

Needless to say, Britain wasn't too stoked about losing the Revolutionary War—especially when they found themselves at war with France shortly thereafter and desperately needed men to fill their war ships. So the Royal Navy turned to the honored tradition of impressment, which is a more innocuous sounding term for abduction and enslavement.

The Royal Navy did not recognize the right of a British citizen to relinquish his or her status as a British subject. In other words, in the eyes of the Crown, just because America successfully gained its independence, that didn't make British-born individuals living in America actually American. So the Brits began stopping and searching US merchant ships looking for these "deserters." The Founding Fathers weren't especially pleased to discover that Britain didn't think they had the ability to naturalize foreigners. This, among other economic vexations, led President James Madison to declare war on Britain yet again—ushering in the War of 1812.

THIS WHALE ISN'T MOBY-DICKING AROUND

The *Essex* was a whaleship based in Nantucket, Massachusetts. On August 12, 1819, Captain George Pollard Jr. and his crew left port for a two-and-a-half-year voyage to the whaling grounds off the west coast of South America on what would prove to be a journey fraught with misfortune (though there is an element of just deserts to the *Essex's* downfall). On November 20, 1820, a pod of sperm whales was sighted. Pollard and several other men pursued the whales in three smaller whaleboats. While they were away, another sperm whale foolishly swam close to the *Essex* and was harpooned. In the whale's struggle, its thrashing tail opened a seam in the ship, forcing the sailors to cut the animal free and attend to repairs.

As they were repairing the ship, the crew observed yet another whale, but something was different about this one. Massive, much larger than an average sperm whale, the lone beast sat motionless in the water, facing the ship from a distance. Then, it mainlined directly for the ship, swiftly picking up speed. Unaccustomed to such a predator/prey role reversal, the sailors didn't realize what was happening until it was too late and the irate monster rammed the *Essex*. At first the beast seemed stunned by the collision, slowly swimming away. Then, much to the men's horror, the whale turned itself around and charged back to finish what it had started. Its second blow was lethal, completely smashing the ship's bow. Satisfied that justice had been served, the whale swam off, never to return.

Amazingly, when Pollard returned to find the *Essex* destroyed, none of his men had died…*yet*. Their lengthy trip back to the mainland in the small whaleboats proved even unluckier. Half the men perished during the journey, and the other men resorted to eating the dead to survive. Afterward, Pollard returned to work and would outlive *two*

more wrecks before he was deemed a "Jonah" (jinxed), ending his seafaring career.

Author Herman Melville was inspired to write his classic *Moby-Dick* based on the story of the *Essex*.

INVADING AMERICA

These days the idea of a foreign enemy successfully invading the United States capital seems like a preposterous movie premise. But on August 24, 1814, during the War of 1812—which, despite what its name implies, lasted until 1815—British Major General Robert Ross not only occupied Washington, D.C., he set the damn place on fire, burning down several government building, including the White House. Though, in all fairness, it should be mentioned that Ross's desecration of the nation's capital was actually revenge for the American troops' destruction of the Parliament buildings in Upper Canada the previous year. Tit for tat.

President John Quincy Adams liked to begin each day by swimming NAKED in the Potomac River.

SMOOCHING ROYALTY

There is no formalized or obligatory way to greet British royalty, but bowing or handshaking is what generally occurs. Not if you're President Jimmy Carter though. The American press had a field day when Carter did an interview in 1976 with *Playboy* magazine in which he notoriously said that he had "looked on a lot of women with lust," and had "committed adultery in my heart many times." While the quotes revealed only that Carter was a very honest, forthcoming, and entirely normal man, the following year Carter's famously lusty thoughts came to light in an unexpected way.

Carter was in London for an economic summit, so, as is standard protocol, he paid a visit to Buckingham Palace to say 'ello to Queen Elizabeth II. For whatever reason, as Carter was exchanging greetings with the Royal Family, he decided to kiss the Queen Mum, Queen Elizabeth II's mother, smack on the lips. For the pathologically proper Brits, this was extremely uncool. The Queen Mum wasn't too happy either. "Nobody has done that since my husband died," she said. Even decades later (she lived an impressive 101 years), she wasn't too happy with Carter. Having apparently sensed the president's sexy intentions, the Queen Mother later said, "I took a sharp step backwards—not quite far enough."

Oopsy-Daisy

Residents in Albuquerque, New Mexico, were enjoying a lovely spring day on May 22, 1957, when the ground shook violently and suddenly, as though a bomb had gone off nearby. It had. And they had no idea how close they came to being completely obliterated. A B–36 military aircraft was transporting a nuclear weapon from Texas to New Mexico when, for reasons still unknown, the device fell out the bomb bay doors. The impact detonated the device's conventional explosives, making a crater 12 feet deep and 25 feet across. Fortunately the nuclear capsule had been separated from the conventional explosives before the flight. The only casualty of the blast was a single luckless cow.

Liver-Eating Johnson

The exact details of John Garrison's life between his birth, sometime in 1824 somewhere in New Jersey, and when he joined the Union army in St. Louis (the first official record of his existence) in 1864 are the thing of legend, in all meanings of the word. As the tale goes, he adopted the name Johnson after striking an officer while in the navy and then fleeing into the wilds of the untamed West to avoid punishment. Here is where Johnson's legend grows more legendary.

Johnson took a Native American for his wife. When Crow Indians killed her, Johnson embarked on a blood-thirsty vendetta that lasted over two decades. The Crow people ate the livers of the animals they killed, believing they could absorb a creature's life force. So, to add insult to injury, Johnson purportedly ate the livers of the Crow warriors he slew, earning himself the heinous moniker "Liver-Eating" Johnson. In time, the Crow made peace with Johnson, possibly seeing the wisdom in turning their great mountain-man foe into a friend, if for no other reason than to protect their livers.

THE KENTUCKY CANNIBAL

Speaking of cannibals, aspects of Liver-Eating Johnson's legend have often been confused with the far more nefarious legend of Boone Helm.

Born 1828 in Kentucky and raised in Missouri, Helm had *unique* responses to stress and conflict. Everyone gets mad when a friend cancels travel plans, but when Helm's close friend Littlebury Shoot flaked on their plans to move to California, Helm stabbed him in the chest, killing him instantly. Now wanted by the law, Helm embarked on a bloody rampage into the West, killing, robbing, and, yes, eating his unfortunate victims.

In October of 1858, while fleeing robbery charges in the Oregon Territory, Helm and several companions were robbed themselves by a band of Indians. Still on the run from the law, Helm's group had no choice but to continue forward without any provisions. When the men needed food, they killed and ate their horses one by one, eventually leaving them without any mounts. Straggling men were left to die, until only Helm and a man named Burton were left. Helm claimed that eventually Burton committed suicide, at which point Helm ate one of Burton's legs, then cut off the other leg and wrapped it up as leftovers. Subsisting on Burton's leg, Helm was eventually found and saved by a friendly traveler who took Helm to Salt Lake City—where Helm was soon run out of town on two new murder charges.

Helm was eventually hanged in front of a crowd of six thousand people in Virginia City, Montana, on January 14, 1864. His final words were "Let 'er rip!," which he said before jumping from the hangman's box before the executioner could do the honors. Or so the story goes.

One Cent for One Hundred Years

Prior to 1909, no American coin featured the likeness of an actual person. President Teddy Roosevelt started the current tradition when he introduced the Lincoln penny—or one-cent piece, if you want to be technical—to commemorate the one hundredth anniversary of Abraham Lincoln's birth.

A Cause Worth Slaughtering For

John Brown was a fanatical Christian who believed that the Second Coming of Christ was only being held back by America's fondness for slavery. So he was a tad more serious about the issue than your average abolitionist. Though in his mid-fifties, when Brown's sons informed him of rising proslavery shenanigans in Kansas, Brown loaded up a wagon with guns, gunpowder, and swords—that's right, swords—and moved there.

In May 1856, when a slaver mob sacked the antislavery town of Lawrence, Kansas, to make a statement, John

Brown decided to make a statement of his own and went completely medieval. Or as he put it, he inflicted "a radical retaliatory measure." With four of his sons and a few other men, Brown snuck into the proslavery settlement at Pottawatomie Creek in the middle of the night, dragged five sleeping settlers from their cabins, and hacked them to pieces with those aforementioned swords. And that was just the beginning. The proslavery side retaliated for Brown's retaliation, which Brown retaliated against once again, and so on. Two hundred people died in the guerilla conflict over the next three years, only ending when Brown was finally captured in 1859, tried for treason, and executed as a terrorist.

Lewis "Lew" Wallace was a Union GENERAL in the Civil War and a governor of the New Mexico Territory. But he is best remembered today for one of his hobbies: WRITING. Wallace's most famous book is *Ben-Hur: A Tale of the Christ*, which has been adapted into a MOVIE four different times, most famously in the 1959 version starring Charlton Heston.

 ## HITLER IS ALIVE AND WELL

On April 30, 1945, with Soviet troops just blocks away from the Reich Chancellery in Berlin, Adolf Hitler knew the end was nigh. He also knew that the previous day fellow evil fascist dictator Benito Mussolini had been captured, then shot, kicked, spat on, hung upside down from a meat hook, and presented to angry citizens to be pelted with stones. Hitler presumably didn't think that sounded very appealing, so he and his wife, Eva Braun, committed suicide instead.

Because Hitler had instructed that their bodies be burnt before the Allies arrived, conspiracies soon abounded that maybe it had all been a clever ruse. Maybe Hitler lived! Ever diligent, the FBI kept a massive file of leads and supposed Hitler sightings. Some ranged from the vaguely plausible, like Hitler having escaped to Argentina aboard a submarine, to the plain ridiculous, like Hitler living in disguise in the suburbs of Madison, Wisconsin.

SIT DOWN, GET COMFORTABLE

Death by electric chair is incredibly gruesome. Ironically, its invention was the result of an 1881 attempt by the state of New York to find a new and more humane method of execution to replace hanging. The winning idea came from a dentist named Alfred P. Southwick. Southwick was under the false impression that having enough electricity run through your body to kill you would be painless (an impression he deduced from a story about a drunk who died touching an exposed power line). Being a dentist, Southwick was used to working with patients in a chair. And sitting in a chair *seemed* relaxing. Southwick's painless death-chair was eventually made a reality by employees of Thomas Edison, and then put to work on August 6, 1890, in New York's Auburn Prison.

The first victim was murderer William Kemmler, who needed to be electrocuted more than once to get the job done. Kemmler's veins exploded on the second try. Everyone who witnessed the event agreed that it seemed far, far worse than being hanged.

PRESIDENT FOR A DAY

On the statue of Senator David Rice Atchison in Kansas City, Missouri, an inscription reads, "David Rice Atchison, 1807–1886, President of the United States [for] one day."

The US Constitution states that the vice president is also the president of the Senate, despite not being an actual member of the body. And the Senate elects a *president pro tempore* to preside over proceedings when the V.P. is absent. By chain-of-command, this puts the president pro tempore third in the line of succession to the presidency, after the V.P. and the Speaker of the House of Representatives. During the time of Atchison, who served in the US Senate from 1843 to 1855, the president pro tempore was second in line. Atchison, a proslavery Democrat, was elected president pro tempore thirteen times.

Up until the 1930s, presidential terms began at noon on March 4. In 1849, that date fell on a Sunday (i.e., church time), causing newly elected President Zachary Taylor to delay his inauguration until the next day. Postponing the ceremony had no impact on when Taylor and his V.P. Millard Fillmore's terms technically began, but those in government often seem to have a poor understanding of how government works, so many in Washington felt that the postponement made Atchison president during the interim. What did President Atchison do with his brief moment of glory? Well, it turned out God wasn't the only one who rested on Sundays. Atchison slept for most of the day. But for the rest of his life he enjoyed bragging, with a wink, that his presidency was "the honestest administration this country ever had."

ONE WORD: PLASTICS

Yonkers resident Leo Baekeland entered into the burgeoning field of synthetic resins looking for a replacement for shellac, which is used for making varnish. Shellac was and is made from the excretion of lac beetles, and the beetle extraction process is not an easy one—it takes around sixteen thousand beetles six months to make just a single pound of shellac. What Baekeland came up with during his experimentation was a hard moldable synthetic plastic: polyoxybenzylmethylenglycolanhydride, or Bakelite. He officially announced his revolutionary new product in 1909 at an American Chemical Society meeting in New York, thereby kicking off the Age of Plastic. But Baekeland's plastic took a while to enter the consumer marketplace; even though plastic was initially a luxury product, not a single item preserved in the 1912 wreck of the *Titanic* is synthetic plastic.

 ## A POOR RETORT

On May 20, 1856, Senator Charles Sumner of Massachusetts made a vitriolic speech against slavery on the Senate floor. In the speech he compared slavery to prostitution and those who supported slavery to pimps. One of the men he insulted was South Carolina Senator Andrew Butler. Butler was not in attendance that day, but Congressman Preston Brooks, Bulter's relative and fellow South Carolinian, was.

Brooks took umbrage with Sumner's tone. Two days later, Brooks jumped Sumner and beat him within an inch of his life with a metal-tipped cane. It took Sumner three years to recover enough to return to the Senate. Not only was Brooks never prosecuted or even reprimanded for the assault, his constituents promptly reelected him and sent him replacement canes to show their support.

 ## FRANKLIN MINTING TERMS

Benjamin Franklin was a major figure in the American Enlightenment, an intellectual and humanist period in the eighteenth century leading up to the American Revolution. His discoveries and theories regarding electricity helped shape the modern world. Every school child knows the iconic tale of Franklin's kite experiment, in which he used a kite to draw lightning during a storm, but his legacy lives on more intimately than most know. Because the field of electrical studies was such undiscovered territory during Franklin's time, he was forced to invent numerous terms to help describe his theories and findings. Some of the electrical terms that Franklin coined include: battery, charge, condenser, conductor, plus, minus, positively, and negatively.

A Popular Place to End it All

San Francisco is a draw to people around the country for a variety of reasons, some cultural, some touristic, some *macabre*—the city's Golden Gate Bridge is the most popular end-of-the-road destination in the world for the suicidal.

Since the bridge's completion in 1937, an estimated 1,600 people have leaped to their doom from its edge into the San Francisco Bay. And that figure is not taking into consideration the number of bodies never recovered or the countless number of jumpers that authorities manage to catch before they leap. The Golden Gate's most popular year for jumpers was 1977, with a recorded forty suicides. The city of San Francisco is not fond of this custom, and has done much—to little avail—to foil jumpers, even putting forth an initiative to construct a giant net below the bridge.

THE JEFFERSON GOSPEL

Thomas Jefferson is well remembered for his scientific enthusiasm. But he was also an enthusiastic Christian, in his own Jeffersonian way. Jefferson believed strongly in the teachings of Jesus Christ, yet he did not find Mark, John, Luke, and Matthew (the claimed authors of the four gospels of the New Testament) to be entirely trustworthy sources.

So, in 1820, six years before he died, Jefferson did what any enterprising maverick genius would do—he took a penknife and chopped up dozens of Bibles written in Greek, Latin, French, and English, removing the passages he liked and pasting them together to make his own version of the New Testament that corrected what he called "the corruption of schismatizing followers." Jefferson bound his eighty-three–page gospel in red leather and titled it *The Life and Morals of Jesus of Nazareth*. So what kind of bible did the man whose opponents had labeled a "howling atheist" create? In keeping with his philosophical outlook, Jefferson excised all the elements he found "contrary to reason." So no walking on water, no feeding multitudes with two fish, and, probably of the most consequence, the Jefferson Bible concludes with the crucifixion. In other words: no resurrection. Jefferson viewed Jesus as a great philosopher, not a divine being.

On November 4, 2008, Barack Obama was elected the forty-fourth PRESIDENT of the United States, but there have technically only been 43 presidents. Grover CLEVELAND was elected to two nonconsecutive terms (1885 and 1893) and is thus counted TWICE, as the twenty-second and twenty-fourth president.

THANK FRANCE

Americans delight in pointing out that we bailed snooty and condescending France out of two World Wars. But without France's support—both financially and militarily—American independence never would have happened.

The Statue of Liberty, officially named *Liberty Enlightening the World,* was conceived as a symbol of that original bond. The project was a joint effort of American and French fundraising, the brainchild of French politician Édouard René de Laboulaye and French sculptor Frédéric Bartholdi. It is quite possible our Lady Liberty might have turned out looking slightly different if Ismail Pasha, Khedive of Egypt, had followed through with Bartholdi's proposal to build a giant lighthouse at the entrance to the Suez Canal in the late 1860s—Bartholdi's design for the lighthouse was in the form of a woman, holding up a torch. But it was not to be. So Bartholdi refocused his energy on an American monument.

The statue itself was to be a gift from France, with America securing the location and building a massive pedestal for it to stand upon. Many Americans balked at the idea of having to pay for the statue's pedestal (what kind of *gift* is that?!). But on March 3, 1877, his final day in office, President Ulysses S. Grant signed a joint resolution okaying the proposal, and on October 28, 1886, the completed *Liberty Enlightening the World* received her official welcoming ceremony.

THAT'S ONE SALTY PIRATE

In 1808, the US government began to enforce the Embargo Act of 1807, which was intended to weaken the British economy by forbidding American ships from docking in foreign ports. Great Britain didn't seem to care, but the act nearly crippled the American merchant class. New Orleans merchants were particularly annoyed, since New Orleans had only become a US territory three years earlier. The pirate Jean Lafitte had a clever way around this—create your own port!

Lafitte created a smugglers' paradise on a private island in Louisiana's Barataria Bay from which he could bypass the navy and customs officials by secreting goods through the bayou swamps to eager buyers. This made Lafitte a popular figure. When Louisiana governor William Claiborne offered a reward for the pirate's capture, within days handbills were posted all over New Orleans offering a reward for the arrest of Claiborne!

During the War of 1812, which the Embargo Act had been intended to avert through economic means, the British made Lafitte an offer—work for them and they would give him a generous amount of land in what they intended to be their reclaimed American colony. They threatened to destroy Barataria if Lafitte refused. Apparently Lafitte preferred being an American criminal to being a British citizen, so he promptly informed the United States of Britain's intentions. Lafitte and his men temporarily joined forces with the U.S., playing a pivotal role in the Battle of New Orleans. Afterward, General (and future president) Andrew Jackson even went to the trouble of ensuring that Lafitte and his men received full pardons for all their crimes.

 ## PRESIDENTIAL SHAVING HABITS

John Quincy Adams (1825–1829), with his excellently bushy sideburns, was the first US President to have notable facial hair. Abraham Lincoln (1861–1865) was the first president with a beard. Then for a while it seemed like Lincoln set a facial hair trend—after him all but two presidents wore either beards or mustaches, up through mustachioed William Taft (1909–1913), who was sadly to be the last facially hairy president.

All the presidents with beards were Republicans.

 ## NOT SO SAVAGE

Precolonial Native Americans are generally thought of as noble savages, living like backward hippies, petting trees and pray-

ing to buffaloes, but the truth is that long before Christopher Columbus bungled his way to the New World, Native Americans were doing pretty well for themselves on the civilization front. Around the year 600 AD, the Mississippian Indians built a city known as Cahokia (near where European colonists eventually put St. Louis). It was a walled city covering 5 square miles, including an impressive structure now known as Monk's Mound. Made of earth, the man-made mound stands ten stories high, with a base larger than any of Egypt's pyramids. Cahokia peaked at a population of forty thousand residents around the year 1200—a size that rivaled Europe's largest cities during the same period.

By the time European settlers arrived in the area, the city had been long abandoned, leaving behind a mind-boggling array of over a hundred ceremonial mounds.

▰▰ Decatur's Duel

Born in 1779, Stephen Decatur became a captain in the US navy at the age of twenty-five and still holds the record for the youngest man to ever hold the rank. He was America's first major war hero of the post–Revolutionary War era, fighting in the Quasi-War, the First and Second Barbary Wars, and the War of 1812, and he has subsequently had five naval ships named in his honor. He was famous for achieving daring feats with extremely small crews. During the First Barbary War, while fighting near Tripoli, he learned that a Tripolitan captain had killed Decatur's younger brother James. Despite having just successfully overtaken another vessel, Decatur immediately sought vengeance. He hunted down the enemy ship, and though outnumbered five to one, he and ten other men boarded the Tripolitan vessel. Decatur zeroed in on the corsair captain who had killed his brother and engaged the man in battle, killing the hell out of the corsair. In fact, Decatur and his men killed almost the entire enemy crew.

Yet, despite all his crazy battle victories, Decatur died on dry land at the age of forty-one in a pointless duel with fellow naval officer James Barron. Years earlier, Decatur had partaken in the court-martial that found Barron guilty of "unpreparedness," and Barron held a grudge. Both men succeeded in shooting the other. Barron lived. Decatur did not.

GOOD TASTE

John Adams was our second president, and by prevailing accounts he was not a great one. This also made him the first single-term president and damaged his post-Revolution legacy. But during the Revolution Adams may have in fact been the most important Founding Father. When the war ended, George Washington was unanimously picked to be the first president, but it was Adams who had first suggested forming a Continental army and who had recommended Washington to be its commander. And Thomas Jefferson gets all the love for writing the Declaration of Independence, but it was also Adams's idea to assign the eloquent Jefferson the task of writing it in the first place.

Adams's son John Quincy Adams would follow in his father's footsteps—he became the sixth president of the United States…and the second president to lose a reelection bid.

In 1878, Alexander Graham Bell installed the first TELEPHONE exchange in New Haven, Connecticut. The first phone book was a single page and contained only fifty names.

THE COST OF WAR

Usually when people say "the cost of war" they're referring to human casualties, but a lot of dollars get killed in wars too. Here's a breakdown of America's major military conflicts, adjusted for modern inflation. These figures do not include collateral economic costs or postwar costs.

American Revolution (1775–1783): $2.4 billion
War of 1812 (1812–1815): $1.55 billion
Mexican-American War (1846–1848): $2.38 billion
Civil War (1861–1865): $79.74 billion
Spanish-American War (1898–1899): $9.04 billion
World War I (1914–1918): $334 billion
World War II (1941–1945): $4.1 trillion
Korean War (1950–1953): $341 billion
Vietnam War (1965–1975): $738 billion
Persian Gulf War (1990–1991): $102 billion
Afghanistan War, Iraq War, and other War on Terror operations (2001–present): $1.3 trillion

For contrast, here are the price tags on some other government spending, again adjusted for inflation.

Louisiana Purchase (1803): $220 million
Panama Canal (1904–1914): $8.9 billion
Hoover Dam (1931–1935): $700 million
The New Deal (1933–1938): $500 billion (estimated)
Marshall Plan (1948–1952): $115.3 billion
Race to the Moon (1958–1969): $237 billion

WHITE HOUSE WEDDING

Grover Cleveland entered the White House in 1885 as a bachelor, with his sister Rose essentially filling the role of First Lady. But Cleveland also had a blossoming relationship with a young lass named Frances Folsom. The backstory on their relationship now seems a bit creepier, and less storybook, than it once did.

Cleveland was twenty-seven years Frances's senior and he had been a close friend of the Folsom family. Purportedly, he even bought newborn Frances her first baby carriage. While Cleveland was governor of New York and Frances was in college, he received Frances's mother's permission to court the young lady. And on June 2, 1886, the two were married in a ceremony at the White House, making twenty-one-year-old Frances the youngest First Lady in history. Despite moving into the White House midway through Cleveland's first term, Frances went on to become one of the most beloved First Ladies.

 ## REMEMBER THE RAISIN

Before "Remember the Alamo," America's most famous rallying cry was "Remember the Raisin." In January of 1813, during the War of 1812, American forces suffered their most devastating loss of the war near the River Raisin in Frenchtown, Michigan Territory (present-day Monroe, Michigan). Of the roughly one thousand American soldiers that battled the British and their Indian allies at River Raisin, only a few dozen avoided being killed or captured. The battle accounted for 15 percent of all American combat deaths during the war. But the rallying cry was born after the battle, when Indians attacked sixty-five wounded American prisoners. Sure, the attack was a reprisal for the odious things Americans had been doing to the Indians, but Americans didn't really see it that way. The massacre was heavily exaggerated in the press and the "Remember the Raisin" rallying cry refocused bitterness toward the British. And doubly so toward the Indians. Memories of the River Raisin Massacre fueled the rapid postwar expulsion of Indian tribes east of the Mississippi.

WHAT'S THAT PASSWORD AGAIN?

During the height of the Cold War, Robert McNamara, secretary of defense to both Kennedy and Johnson, built up an arsenal of Minuteman intercontinental ballistic missiles (ICBM) to serve as the backbone of our strategic deterrence against the Soviets. Since just one of those missiles held the power to start a nuclear war, McNamara had special locks, or "Permissive Action Links," placed on all the individual Minutemen to prevent unauthorized launches. Or so he thought.

In a masterly idiotic move, the powers that be at Strategic Air Command (SAC) in Omaha were far less worried about unauthorized launches than they were about the incompetence of their own staff during a moment of crisis. What if the launch officer forgot the combinations?! So they came up with the nice and easy-to-remember combination of 00000000...*for all the Minuteman missiles.* Moreover, the combinations were kept at 00000000, meaning that all the missiles were ready to be fired at all times. And they stayed that way until 1977 when someone finally suggested they actually turn those locks into, well, *locks.*

Nine presidents never attended college: George WASHINGTON, Andrew Jackson, Martin Van Buren, Zachary Taylor, Millard Fillmore, Abraham LINCOLN, Andrew Johnson, Grover Cleveland, and Harry TRUMAN.

IT WAS JUST AN OKAY GUNFIGHT

Guns blazed in the Gunfight at the O.K. Corral on October 26, 1881, in Tombstone, Arizona Territory. The altercation turned Wyatt Earp into a legend, and remains history's most famous gunfight. Yet it lasted about thirty seconds, it claimed only three lives, and Earp's motivations in the fight had more to do with personal gain and shady grudges than they did with law enforcement—at the time some even considered the Earp brothers and Doc Holliday the villains of the fight. On top of that, Wyatt was only a temporary assistant marshal serving under his brother Virgil. So how did things turn around so favorably for Wyatt? Well, for one, it helped that Wyatt outlived Virgil and every other participant in the gunfight. It also helped that he lived long enough to have some influence on his biographers. But more than anything else, movies are probably to blame. Hollywood loves saintly heroes, and Wyatt Earp had many friends and admirers in the industry by the time he died in 1929 at the age of eighty. And so history followed entertainment into the popular consciousness.

THE FIRST FIRST LADY

The exact origins of the term "First Lady" are fuzzy. Legend says that President Zachary Taylor posthumously referred to Dolley Madison as the "First Lady" in his eulogy at her funeral in 1849. Sometime later the title entered Washington, D.C., social circles. Some referred to Mary Todd Lincoln as the "First Lady in the Land." The term didn't gain public recognition until 1877 when a newspaper journalist used it to refer to Lucy Webb Hayes while reporting on the inauguration of Rutherford B. Hayes. The frequent reporting on Lucy Hayes's activities helped spread use of the title outside Washington. Yet it still didn't gain its current mainstream usage until the 1930s.

BABY ON BOARD

During the three-month-long Mayflower *voyage that brought the Pilgrims to America in the fall of 1620, Stephen Hopkins and his wife Elizabeth welcomed a baby boy, delivered as the ship bounced along the waves of the Atlantic Ocean. In honor of the baby's unusual birthplace, the Hopkins named the boy Oceanus.*

AGE AIN'T NOTHIN' BUT A NUMBER

The median age of a newly elected president is fifty-four years. The youngest person to assume the office was Theodore Roosevelt, who at age forty-two upgraded from vice president to commander in chief following the assassination of William McKinley. But John F. Kennedy holds the record for the youngest elected president, at forty-three years of age. On the opposite end of the scale, sixty-nine-year-old Ronald Reagan was the oldest elected president. Kennedy also has the unfortunate record for shortest-lived president, dying at age forty-six. Gerald Ford, who died at ninety-three, was our longest-lived. James Polk was the shortest-lived president to die of natural causes, at age fifty-three.

Barack Obama is the fifth-youngest person inaugurated as president, behind Theodore Roosevelt, John F. Kennedy, Bill Clinton, and Ulysses S. Grant, in that order.

FREE LOVE IN 1872

Virginia Woodhull became infamous in her time for promoting "free love," though Woodhull's definition of the term was rooted in the championing of women's rights, not the LSD-fueled sex jamborees of 1960s counterculture.

In Woodhull's time, divorce was not an option available to most women, and those few who did have the right, and elected to use it, were scandalized and ostracized. Yet society tolerated married men taking mistresses and committing other dalliances. Woodhull called shenanigans on all this—women should have the right to leave a lousy marriage. And commit their own dalliances too. She cofounded a radical newspaper that espoused "crazy" things like women's suffrage, vegetarianism, sex education in schools, and licensed prostitution, as well as printing the first English version of Karl Marx's *Communist Manifesto*.

In 1872, the Equal Rights Party nominated Woodhull for president to run against the incumbent, President Ulysses S. Grant, which many believe makes her the first woman to run for president. But Woodhull didn't have a chance in hell of winning. Not only was she a radical preaching sex topics during a time when stuffy Victorian ideals pervaded the English-speaking world, but her running mate was former slave and black rights leader Frederick Douglass (though he never officially accepted the nomination). Oh yeah, and she was a *woman*, which meant that she couldn't even vote for herself on Election Day. Was the world ready? We'll never know because the government chivalrously declined to put her name on the ballot.

🇺🇸 VOLUNTEERS NEEDED

The *H. L. Hunley* was a primitive submarine built by Horace Lawson Hunley for the Confederate navy during the Civil War. Though it was not the first submarine built by either side during the conflict, it ranks in history as the first submarine to successfully sink an enemy ship. The *Hunley* demonstrated the possibilities of the submarine in naval warfare. It also demonstrated how super crazy dangerous submarines were. Built in July 1863 and originally named the *Fish Boat*, the submarine was 40 feet long and held an eight-man crew who powered the vessel by a hand-crank system. Being one of those crewmen quickly proved a questionable gig. On August 29, five men died when the submarine sank during a training exercise. Undeterred, the Confederate navy salvaged the vessel and resumed testing. On October 15, during another training exercise, it sank yet again, this time killing the entire crew, including Horace Lawson Hunley. Still undeterred, the Confederate navy salvaged the death-bucket once more.

Renamed the *H.L. Hunley*, in honor of its newly deceased creator, the submarine made her first and only attack on February 17, 1864, against the USS *Housatonic*. The *Hunley* attached a barbed spar torpedo to the *Housantonic's* hull, which quickly sank the Union ship upon detonation. But the victory was short lived. Surely shocking absolutely no one by that point, the *Hunley* sank before it could return to base, killing the entire crew.

 ## A PRESCIENT NOVEL

Morgan Robertson was an American novelist whose best-known work was the novella *Futility*, which tells the disastrous tale of a massive British passenger liner called the *Titan*. Hailed as unsinkable, the liner carried an insufficient number of lifeboats. The ship sets sail in April through the North Atlantic and meets a chilling fate when it hits an iceberg. You may think that Robertson was rather uncreatively retelling the story of the *Titanic*, which was also a massive British passenger liner hailed as unsinkable that killed nearly all its passengers due to having insufficient lifeboats when it hit an iceberg in April in the North Atlantic. Only Robertson's story was published in 1898, fourteen years before the *Titanic* sank.

 ## SILENT CAL

President Calvin Coolidge had an image as a reticent man. A popular story from his era has it that a young woman walked up to Coolidge at a party and informed him that she had just made a bet with her friend. The friend had claimed that the

young woman couldn't get Coolidge to say more than two words to her. When she informed Coolidge of these terms he responded coolly, "You lose," revealing that his reserved persona had little to do with a lack of wit.

A PENNY PINCHED IS A PENNY EARNED

Born in 1892 in Minneapolis, Minnesota, J. Paul Getty would become the richest man in America and the richest private citizen in the world by the mid-twentieth century. After he died in 1976, his name would live on in the myriad of art institutions and programs funded by the J. Paul Getty Trust.

But during his lifetime he was far more famous for being a stingy miser. For example, after feeling that his houseguests were abusing their phone privileges, Getty installed a pay phone in his mansion.

His most notorious moment of Scroogery came in 1973 when his sixteen-year-old grandson, John Paul Getty III, was kidnapped in Rome and ransomed for $17 million. Getty Sr. refused to pay. In his defense, many in the family believed the whole thing was a prank perpetrated by the rebellious Getty III. When a second ransom note arrived with the teen's severed ear inside, now demanding a reduced $3.2 million, Getty Sr. acquiesced, agreeing to pay $2.2 million (the maximum that would be tax deductible). The remainder of the amount was a loan to his son, Getty II, carrying with it a 4 percent interest to be repaid. Getty III was freed, and in 1977 he had reconstructive surgery to rebuild his ear.

RED FLAG ON THIS FLAG STORY

Betsy Ross is widely credited as the creator of the first American flag. But there is no evidence that Ross (who worked in the upholstery business) ever made an American flag, much less the very first American flag. The Ross Flag story didn't appear until 1870, thirty-six years after her death, when Ross's grandson William J. Canby presented it to the Historical Society of Pennsylvania. The story was quickly picked up by a generation of Americans hungry for new tales from the Revolution as they approached the United States' hundredth birthday. To Ross's credit, while there is no evidence that she designed the first flag, there is also no evidence that she herself ever claimed to have designed it.

JUNEAU, Alaska, has a population of thirty-one thousand people, but it covers an AREA of 3,000 square miles, which is bigger than either Rhode Island or Delaware, and almost as BIG as the two states COMBINED.

ONE GIANT HOAX

October 16, 1869, two laborers were digging a well on the farm of one William Newell in Cardiff, New York, when they uncovered the petrified remains of a perfectly pre-served man—a man who would have stood 10 feet tall dur-ing his living days! Newell put up a tent around what soon became known as The Cardiff Giant and charged curious visitors twenty-five cents to gaze upon it. Scholars called it a hoax. Christian fundamentalists saw it as validation of Genesis 6:4, which in the *King James Bible* begins: "There were giants in the earth in those days…" Circus mogul P. T. Barnum tried to buy the giant from Newell, and when

Newell refused, Barnum simply created a fake version to display himself, claiming that the original Cardiff exhibit was in fact the fake.

They were of course *both* fakes. The Cardiff Giant was an extremely elaborate and expensive prank perpetrated by Newell's cousin George Hull. Hull, a successful tobacconist and strident atheist, had been inspired to spend $2,600 ($42,000 today) of his own money to have the giant built and buried after getting into an argument with a group of Methodists over the presence of giants in the Bible. By the end of the year, Hull, satisfied that his prank had done its job, revealed the truth to the press.

The Cardiff Giant can still be seen today at the Farmers' Museum in Cooperstown, New York.

First to Fly

Everyone agrees that the Wright Brothers hold the record for the first successful manned airplane flight, though some disagree that they *deserve* to hold that record. A decent number of aviation historians contend that a German immigrant named Gustave Whitehead beat them to it, possibly even as early as 1899—four years before the Wright Brothers' famous flight in Kitty Hawk, North Carolina. Unfortunately for Whitehead, though a smattering of news articles exist from the period documenting his flights, his story disappeared from the public landscape until being rediscovered in the 1930s, by which point the lack of photographs and verifiable witnesses threw the validity of those news pieces into questionable light.

The city of Bridgeport, Connecticut, where Whitehead lived, considers itself convinced. In 2012 they dedicated a fountain to Gustave with the inscription, "First in Flight"—a jab at the motto proudly featured on North Carolina's license plates.

THE RELIGION OF POLITICS

Historically, the most common religious affiliation among presidents is Episcopalian. That makes Episcopalians rather disproportionately represented in the White House, considering they make up less than 2 percent of the current US population. Conversely, the country's largest religious denomination is Catholicism, making up a whopping 25 percent of the population. Yet there has been but one Catholic president (John F. Kennedy). There has never been a Lutheran president. The primary factor here is that prior to the American Revolution, the Episcopal Church had been the Church of England, which was the official religion in many states, such as early presidential headsprings like New York and Virginia (the first seven Episcopalian presidents were all born in Virginia).

THE SHORT-LIVED FOURTEENTH STATE

At the conclusion of the Revolutionary War, North Carolina found itself in a minor pickle. Many of its citizens had moved into its western territory and were now demanding that the state help defend them against hostile Indians and outlaws. Attempting to rid itself of the problem in the laziest way possible, North Carolina simply ceded the area to the Continental Congress to let them worry about it. This didn't sit well with the western North Carolinians, particularly John "Nolichucky Jack" Sevier (his nickname was a reference to the Nolichucky River).

In 1784, the area declared itself the independent Republic of Franklin (named after Benjamin Franklin), with Nolichucky Jack as its first governor. Dismayed, North Carolina promptly tried to reclaim the territory, but it was too late. The Republic of Franklin then sought admittance to the Union as the fourteenth state and came incredibly close, receiving support from seven of the states, but lacking the two-thirds majority needed. Spain even tried acquiring the republic, which would have had disastrous results for the fledgling nation. In 1788, after four years of struggle, Jack and his compatriots realized the futility of their situation. Their republic had no currency (Jack's salary as governor was a thousand deer hides a year). So Jack turned the territory back over to North Carolina, who once again turned it over to the Continental Congress, who then turned it into Tennessee. The new state's first governor was Nolichucky Jack.

 ## THANKS FOR ALL THE MUSIC, ENGLAND

In 1814, after witnessing the British Royal Navy blow the H-E-double-hockey-sticks out of Fort McHenry during the War of 1812, thirty-five-year-old lawyer and wannabe poet Francis Scott Key wrote a poem titled "Defence of Fort McHenry." Later on, Key's words were set to the tune of "To Anacreon in Heaven," a popular British song by John Stafford Smith. This new song was titled "The Star-Spangled Banner." Though the song gained popularity throughout the 1800s, it was not officially made the national anthem until 1931. Oddly enough, prior to 1931, "My Country, 'Tis of Thee" was often used as the US anthem. That song also reuses the music from a popular British song—the British national anthem.

AN UNFITTING END FOR A BADASS

General George S. Patton, who had the charming nickname Old Blood and Guts, is now remembered as one of the greatest American military icons of the twentieth century. This would no doubt please him greatly, as he had been obsessed with the military since childhood. Patton came from a long, long line of military men on both sides of his family; his ancestors included generals and colonels in the American Revolution and the Confederate side of the Civil War. His mind was consumed with the philosophy of war and he was good at it. During WWII, Patton's famed Third Army became operational on August 1, 1944, and was in continuous combat for the next 281 days of its existence. With around 250,000 to 300,000 men, Patton's Third advanced faster and farther than any army in military history. They killed, wounded, or captured roughly 1.8 million enemy soldiers, while suffering around 140,000 casualties and missing-in-action losses themselves—a ratio of nearly thirteen to one in their favor.

While the rest of the Allied command rejoiced at the conclusion of the war, Patton wanted to turn against their former Russian allies and keep the good times going. On December 9, 1945, before Patton was to return to the United States, his chief of staff took him on a pheasant hunting trip near Mannheim, Germany, meant to cheer Old Blood and Guts up. While en route, Patton's Cadillac got into a low-speed crash with a large truck. None of the other passengers sustained injuries, but Patton was mortally wounded. Paralyzed and intermittently unconscious, Patton lived for another twelve days. When informed of his woeful state during one of his conscious moments, Patton commented, "This is a hell of a way to die."

FREEDOM SUIT

In 1781, Bett, an illiterate female slave of the Ashley family of Sheffield, Massachusetts, heard the Massachusetts Constitution read aloud in a public forum. A passage beginning with the words, "All men are born free and equal," left a particular impression on her. Soon after, she showed up at the door of a young lawyer named Theodore Sedgwick, inquiring if he could get the law to set her free. Sedgwick agreed to represent Bett and another Ashley household slave named Brom, and the case of *Brom and Bett vs. Ashley* went before the court. In a history-changing verdict, the court awarded Bett her freedom, making her the first slave to legally obtain her independence in a court of law and setting the legal precedent that eventually ended slavery in Massachusetts. Bett then changed her name to Elizabeth Freeman and accepted a paying job in Sedgwick's home.

Harvard counts more presidents as alumni than any other university, with seven in total: John Adams, John Quincy ADAMS, Theodore Roosevelt, Franklin Roosevelt, John F. KENNEDY, George W. Bush, and Barack OBAMA. Yale is a close second, with five presidents as alumni: William Taft, Gerald FORD, George H. W. Bush, Bill Clinton, and George W. Bush again.

PRESIDENTIAL BOOZE

After he gave up on the presidency in 1797, George Washington returned to life as a private citizen. Since speaking tours and big payday autobiographies weren't yet a part of the typical post-office lifestyle for an ex-president, Washington needed to figure out how to generate profits from his plantation at Mount Vernon. He considered liquor essential to the health of a man (we're talking about a guy who named his four coonhounds Drunkard, Taster, Tipler, and Tipsy), so he built a whiskey distillery. Washington's rye whiskey turned out to be relatively popular, selling nearly 11,000 gallons in one year, but shortly after his sudden death in 1799 the distillery was shut down.

Recently historians and whiskey makers joined forces to recreate Washington's rye whiskey recipe. Unlike modern whiskey, Washington's blend wasn't aged, which gave it a taste and bite more similar to moonshine. But by all accounts, it gets the job done.

 ## A SHAMELESS EXTROVERT

George Smathers was a Democratic senator for the state of Florida from 1951 to 1969. But his most noted achievement is probably a speech he never actually gave. While running against incumbent senator Claude Pepper in the Democratic primary, it was reported that Smathers gave a speech saying, "Are you aware that Claude Pepper is known all over Washington as a shameless extrovert? Not only that, but this man is reliably reported to practice nepotism with his sister-in-law, and he has a sister who was once a thespian in wicked New York. Worst of all, it is an established fact that Mr. Pepper before his marriage habitually practiced celibacy." But it turned out that this speech was nothing more than the whimsical fantasy of an unidentified and apparently bored reporter. Smathers even offered a $10,000 reward to anyone who could prove he ever said those words. No one ever claimed it.

 ## WHO GOES THERE?

Confederate General Thomas "Stonewall" Jackson (so nicknamed for his stubborn resistance at the First Battle of Bull Run in 1861) is widely considered one of the most brilliant tactical commanders in US military history. Which was bad news for the North during the Civil War. Fortunately for the Union, Jackson's men weren't that brilliant. On May 2, 1863, after Jackson had just made a stunning victory during the Battle of Chancellorsville, he and his staff were returning to their camp when the 18th North

Carolina Infantry mistook them for the enemy and opened fired without verifying who they were even firing at. When Jackson's staff desperately tried to identify themselves, the geniuses in the 18th determined it was a "Yankee trick" and kept shooting, wounding Jackson's arm. The camp's chief surgeon had to amputate the arm in an attempt to save Jackson's life, but the general caught pneumonia and died from the complications. The loss of Jackson was both a strategic and emotional blow to the Confederacy. If he had lived, the outcome of the Civil War could have turned out very differently.

Surprisingly, Major John D. Barry, the man who ordered the soldiers of the 18th to fire on Jackson, was not punished for the screw-up, and when the Battle of Chancellorsville ended…he was promoted.

DON'T MESS WITH JIM BOWIE

On September 19, 1827, Samuel Levi Wells III and Dr. Thomas Harris Maddox met for a duel on a sandbar near Natchez, Mississippi, with over a dozen other men acting as supporters or witnesses. Both duelists fired two shots, and both men missed. They then shook hands, resolving their conflict. But before the two parties could part, Maddox supporter Robert Crain fired his gun at an old enemy, Samuel Cuny, who was there in favor of Wells. Crain missed and hit a young slave smuggler named Jim Bowie who had been supporting Wells. Displeased with being erroneously shot, Bowie pulled out his trusty knife and attacked Crain. Crain then bashed Bowie over the head with his gun, breaking it. Major Norris Wright, another Maddox supporter, decided to stab Bowie in the chest with a sword to end the sparring.

Despite having a sword sticking out of his chest, Bowie's rage only grew more acute. He grabbed Wright and killed the man with a deft placement of his knife. Bowie was then shot and stabbed yet again by two other members of the opposing party. Bowie removed Wright's sword from his chest and continued his knife-wielding offensive until enough people were finally dead for things to calm down. The fracas became known as The Sandbar Fight and made Bowie an instant folk hero. His doctor was reported as saying, "How he lived is a mystery to me, but live he did." Not only did Bowie become famous, but so did the knife he used during the fight. The model is still known as a Bowie knife.

★★★★★★★★★★★★★★★★★★

Looking at the average map of the contiguous United States, MAINE appears to be the northernmost state (this is not including Alaska). But this is an ILLUSION created by the warped appearance of most maps. In reality, the summit of the U.S. is the nub at the top of MINNESOTA, known as the Northwest Angle—or simply as the Angle to locals—which reaches north past the forty-ninth parallel into Canada.

★★★★★★★★★★★★★★★★★★

DE WAAL STRAAT

In 1614 the Dutch Republic established a fur trading settlement on the southern tip of Manhattan, which by 1625 had become New Amsterdam. To protect the settlement against British invaders and hostile Native Americans (unhappy with their land being poached), the Dutch built a wall along the northern boundary of the city. When a street was built along the wall, they gave it the uninspired name "Wall Street." When the British acquired the city in the 1660s, they renamed it "New York," after the English Duke of York and Albany. As the city expanded, the Brits did away with the Dutch wall, but Wall Street's name has remained intact.

I THINK YOU FORGOT SOMETHING

Before his death, Thomas Jefferson left explicit written instructions regarding his burial. He supplied a sketch of the marker he wanted as his monument (a small obelisk), and the epitaph to be inscribed upon it. The epitaph, he explained, would be a testimonial to the things that "I wish most to be remembered."

> *Here was buried*
> *Thomas Jefferson*
> *Author of the Declaration of American Independence*
> *of the Statute of Virginia for religious freedom*
> *Father of the University of Virginia*

You'll note that he makes no mention of having been vice president or president.

AMERICA'S SHERLOCK HOLMES

William J. Burns possessed a natural proclivity for detective work rivaled only by his talent for publicity. As the head of the William J. Burns International Detective Agency, Burns promoted an image that earned him the nickname America's Sherlock Holmes.

In 1910, the city of Los Angeles hired Burns to catch the arsonists who burned down the Los Angeles Times building. He succeeded. In 1921, he was appointed director of the Bureau of Investigation (predecessor of the FBI), but the thuggish tactics that had served him well on the hardboiled streets of private investigation embroiled Burns in scandal almost at once. He was replaced with J. Edgar

Hoover in 1924. Burns descended further into scandal during the Teapot Dome Scandal, which involved the secret leasing of navy petroleum reserves to private companies. Burns was hired by oil industrialist Harry F. Sinclair to "investigate" the jury hearing Sinclair's case. Burns and several other members of his agency were convicted of tampering with that jury. Always the showman, Burns then retired to Florida where he published numerous stories detailing heavily exaggerated versions of his detective exploits.

HORSE BOMB

At noon on September 16, 1920, a horse-drawn wagon stopped in front of J. P. Morgan bank headquarters at 23 Wall Street, the Financial District's busiest corner. The driver abandoned the wagon, and shortly thereafter 100 pounds of dynamite exploded over 500 pounds of iron shrapnel into the crowded area, killing thirty-eight people, injuring over a hundred more, and causing extensive damage to the Morgan building. Though a note was left at a nearby post office, reading, "Remember, we will not tolerate any longer. Free the political prisoners, or it will be sure death for all of you," and signed, "American Anarchist Fighters," the crime was never solved. Damage from the blast is still visible on the exterior of 23 Wall Street.

PRESIDENTIAL ZOO

The White House has been home to many pets. In recent decades most of the First Pets have been dogs, like Ronald Reagan's Rex (a Cavalier King Charles Spaniel) or Barack Obama's Bo (a Portuguese Water Dog). But as we move farther back in time the species get a bit wilder…

George Washington had a donkey. Thomas Jefferson had two grizzly bear cubs. James Madison had a parrot. John Quincy Adams was gifted two alligators, which, for a time, he kept in the White House bathtub. James Buchanan had an eagle. Both William Henry Harrison and

Benjamin Harrison had a goat. William Taft had a pet cow named Pauline. Of the myriad of species that Theodore Roosevelt kept, the most famous was Josiah the badger, who was just as ornery as Teddy himself.

Calvin Coolidge comes in as a close second to Roosevelt for biggest animal lover, but he takes first place for being the owner of the weirdest animal—Billy, a pygmy hippo. Billy was a gift to Coolidge from tire tycoon Harvey Firestone, at a time when most Americans had no idea that a pygmy hippo was even a real thing. But "pygmy" hippo is a somewhat misleading name, given that Billy weighed around 600 pounds. The adorable animal's size forced Coolidge to donate him to the National Zoo. So rare were pygmy hippos in America that Billy got to live out the rest of his life as a swingin' stud. Almost all the pygmy hippos currently in captivity in the United States can trace their ancestry directly to Billy.

 ## CONNING SCARFACE

European con-man Victor Lustig is best known for selling the Eiffel Tower as scrap metal to some improbably gullible Parisian businessmen (more than once), but after one of his Eiffel sales was discovered by authorities, Lustig hightailed it to America to seek new devious fortunes. As it was the 1920s, America had a thriving criminal ecosystem thanks to Prohibition, and Lustig fit right in. As the story goes, Lustig convinced the gangster Al Capone to invest $50,000 in a phony stock deal. Lustig sat on Capone's money for a couple months, then returned it in full explaining that the deal had fallen through. Impressed with Lustig's loyalty, Capone gave him $5,000 for his troubles. This had been Lustig's goal all along, of course.

In 1935, Lustig was arrested for counterfeiting, and sentenced to twenty years in Alcatraz, where, oddly enough, Al Capone was already serving time. Both men died in prison in 1947.

Jimmy Carter is the only president to give an interview to *PLAYBOY* magazine.

A PAINE IN THE ASS

Thomas Paine was an Englishman, but he earned a prominent place in American history when he anonymously published the pamphlet *Common Sense* in January of 1776. The pamphlet was an astute and passionate argument for an American break from British rule, and though it had only minor influence on the Continental Congress's decision to declare independence, the pamphlet spread like wildfire among the public, radically changing the mood in the colonies in favor of colonial sovereignty.

But, always the rabble-rouser, after America gained its independence, Paine bounced around Europe and the States, making political enemies everywhere he went. When he died at the age of seventy-two in 1809, one of his obituaries read, "He had lived long, did some good and much harm." A vocal deist (belief in the intellectual concept of a creator, but not a creator who intervenes in the universe), Paine was not particularly popular with the religious crowd either. No Christian cemetery would receive his remains for burial, so he was buried under a tree on his farm in New Rochelle, New York. Only six people attended his funeral.

In 1819, English journalist William Cobbett dug up Paine's bones and brought them back to England for a proper burial. But apparently Cobbett got distracted. When Cobbett died twenty years later, the bones were still among his effects. No one is quite certain where Paine is now, though in the 1980s an Australian businessman claimed that he purchased Paine's skull while on vacation in London.

The Kooky Mrs. Lincoln

Abraham Lincoln's diminutive wife, Mary Todd, was renowned in her time for being feisty and eccentric. She also possibly suffered from bipolar disorder. She was prone to outbursts and manic spending sprees, which only got worse after her husband was assassinated and her financial resources dried up. Despite her economic misfortunes, she often still purchased multiples of single items, like ten pairs of gloves or twelve pairs of curtains. Her only living son, Robert, eventually had her committed. At her insanity trial, a doctor testified that he had witnessed her "possessed with the idea that some Indian spirit was working in her head and taking wires out of her eyes." But Mary Todd convinced her doctors that she was not insane and was released after just six months.

In 1882, in response to Mary Todd's vigorous lobbying, Congress finally passed a bill increasing her pension to $5,000 a year, plus $15,000 in back payments. Sadly, she died of a stroke before she could collect a penny of it.

 ## Big in Russia

*Science fiction author Ray Bradbury (*Fahrenheit 451*, The Martian Chronicles*) *was one of the most popular foreign authors in the Soviet Union, boasting fan clubs in most major Soviet cities at a time when American literature was frowned upon.*

 ## Two-Drink Minimum Justice

Judge Roy Bean was a Texas saloon owner and justice of the peace in the later decades of the 1800s who touted himself as "The Law West of the Pecos." But Bean's concern for the law wasn't as keen as his concerns for his booze business. He operated his court out of his saloon and stocked his juries with his customers, fully expecting them to purchase drinks during recesses. Since he had no jail, he dealt almost entirely with fines as punishment, and the fines were usually determined by how much money the guilty party had in his pocket.

One legend holds that Bean tried the case of an Irishman named Paddy O'Rourke who had shot a Chinese laborer in a dispute. When a mob of angry Irishmen surrounded the courtroom, threatening to lynch Bean if O'Rourke was not freed, Bean examined his trusty law book and declared that "homicide was the killing of a human being. However, I can find no law against killing a Chinaman."

 ## Horse Power

On June 9, 1973, nearly 100,000 people came to Belmont Park near New York City to see if Secretariat would become the first horse in twenty-five years to win the coveted Triple Crown (victories at the Kentucky Derby, the Preakness, and the Belmont Stakes). And he did. Secretariat also broke the record for fastest finish and biggest lead. Ron Turcotte, who jockeyed Secretariat, even claimed that he had lost control of the horse toward the end of the race and that Secretariat piloted himself to his record-setting victory. An autopsy done on the horse after his death in 1989 revealed that Secretariat's heart was 2.5 times larger than that of the average horse.

Hanging President

George W. Bush has received criticism for the number of executions carried out by the state of Texas while he was governor, but Bush never executed any of the prisoners himself. The twenty-fourth president, Grover Cleveland, can't say the same.

In the 1870s, Cleveland served as sheriff of Erie County, New York. As sheriff, when it came to capital punishment, he had two options: carry out the execution himself, or pay a deputy $10 to pull the lever. Feeling that it was dishonorable to coerce another man to perform his duty, Cleveland opted to carry out the executions himself. He served as executioner at the hanging of Patrick Morrissey in 1872, and John Gaffney in 1873.

WHEN THE LEVEES BROKE

The worst flood in US history occurred in 1927 along the Mississippi River. When accumulated rainwater broke the levees at Mounds Landing, Mississippi, more than double the water volume of Niagara Falls spilled out. The river broke out of its levee system in 145 places, flooding some 27,000 square miles across Arkansas, Illinois, Kentucky, Louisiana, Mississippi, Missouri, Tennessee, Texas, Oklahoma, and Kansas. Fourteen percent of Arkansas was eventually covered by floodwaters. In the aftermath, the Flood Control Act of 1928 was passed, and the world's longest system of levees was built along the Mississippi. The disaster would prove to have lasting effects for the nation too.

Many African Americans from the region were fed up, having been left to fend for themselves during the flood while whites were promptly rescued. This, in part, helped fuel the Great Migration of African Americans to northern cities. It also fueled the political career of Secretary of Commerce Herbert Hoover, who was in charge of flood relief operations. The national attention he received during the flood set the stage for his election to the presidency in 1928.

THE FOUNDING HYPOCRITES?

Annoying taxes were the political snowball that rolled into the avalanche that was the American Revolution. The British Crown needed more money to support their many wars and interests around the globe. Colonists didn't appreciate being asked to pay for it, especially when they had no formal representatives in Parliament. So they rebelled. But the rebellion put America in considerable debt. In 1791 to pay off the debt, Alexander Hamilton, the first secretary of the Treasury, implemented a tax on domestically distilled spirits. What became known as the whiskey tax was the first tax levied by the national government on a domestic product, and as is still the case today with new taxes, some people felt it was completely unacceptable. Western Pennsylvania resisted the tax, going so far as to attack the home of a tax inspector. So President George Washington sent the army in to show that the government wasn't messing around. The Whiskey Rebellion demonstrated that the revolutionary spirit of the revolution just wasn't going to fly anymore.

SATANIC FOOD POISONING

In a 1976 issue of *Science*, Professor Linnda Caporael wrote an article that proposed a very different interpretation of what led to the Salem Witch Trials in 1692 and 1693. The trials resulted from accusations made by several young girls after they began exhibiting unusual and frightening behavior. To the Salem Puritans, the culprit was surely witches in league with the devil!

Modern theories have always held that the accusers were simply full of shit and that their scheming stemmed from a variety of petty motivations. But Caporael theorized that the truth was neither deception nor Satan. She proposed that the girls may have been suffering from ergotism, which is caused by the ingestion of a fungus that infects rye and other cereals. The symptoms include seizures, spasms, diarrhea, vomiting, paresthesias, itching, and mental effects including mania, psychosis, and hallucinations similar to those produced by LSD—all similar to those symptoms exhibited by the young Salem girls.

ESCAPE FROM ALCATRAZ

The prison on Alcatraz Island was designed to hold the worst of the worst from federal penitentiaries around the country. Known as "The Rock," the prison was billed as escape-proof, and in the twenty-nine years of its operation (1934–1963), Alcatraz claimed that no prisoner ever successfully escaped. But that statistic is more of a technicality than it is a truth.

On June 11, 1962, after over a year of hard work, Frank Morris and brothers Clarence and John Anglin most certainly escaped. Along with another inmate named Allen West, the men chiseled away the concrete from around air vents leading to an unguarded utility corridor, using spoons and a drill improvised from a stolen vacuum cleaner motor. They even fashioned dummy heads using soap, toilet paper, and their own collected hair in order to fool passing guards that they were sleeping in their beds. On the night of their escape, West was unable to successfully make it out of his cell. But Morris and the Anglin brothers floated out into the dark, icy waters of San Francisco Bay using a raft they made from raincoats. A nationwide manhunt ensued, but the men were never apprehended. Despite the fact that their corpses were never found either, the prison was able to hold onto its record by proclaiming that the men must have drowned.

Legend held that Frank Morris and the Anglin brothers would return to Alcatraz on the fiftieth anniversary of their breakout. On June 11, 2012, a group of hopefuls, including some of their surviving family members, waited for them. But they never came.

 # WINNING FACIAL HAIR

Ambrose Burnside earned himself a reputation as one of the most incompetent generals of the Civil War due to disastrous defeats in the Battle of Fredericksburg and Battle of the Crater. He would surely have been forgotten by time were it not for his unusual and distinctive facial hair. Burnside had massive, bushy strips of hair extending from his ears to his mustache, with a clean-shaven chin. People described the unique style as "burnsides." Over time the word was inverted to sideburns.

PSYCHOANALYZING WILSON

Though the two men never met, in the 1930s Sigmund Freud, the father of psychoanalysis, published *Woodrow Wilson: A Psychological Study*, a biographical analysis of former President Woodrow Wilson. In the book Freud posited that Wilson suffered from personality defects that inhibited his ability to be an effective president. He diagnosed Wilson as a neurotic who had been dominated by his father and overprotected by his mother, which Freud claimed had prevented Wilson from having the masculinity needed to carry out his desires and his political will. Freud also proclaimed that Wilson suffered from a savior complex and the need to be worshipped. Freud's book posited that it was for these reasons that Wilson failed to achieve many of his loftier political endeavors—most notably his goal of coercing the Senate into entering the United States in the League of Nations.

The book was not published in American until the 1960s, and was met with a wave of critical derision. Many found it suspect that the book was cowritten by William Christian Bullitt Jr., who had briefly served under Wilson, and supposedly left the Wilson administration with many disgruntled feelings toward the president.

A HISTORIC CALL

There is some controversy over whether or not Alexander Graham Bell deserves the title "Inventor of the Telephone." His detractors believe Bell stole key ideas from inventor Elisha Gray. Both men filed for patents on the same day, February 14, 1876, but Bell's patent was subsequently given primacy after he succeeded in getting his phone to work on March 10.

As the story goes, Bell and his assistant, Thomas A. Watson, were working in separate rooms containing the telephone prototype when Bell spilled polishing liquid on himself. Bell then spoke the first words ever transferred via telephone: "Mr. Watson, come here, I want to see you." In 1915, Watson and Bell paid homage to their historic moment during the inauguration of the first transcontinental telephone line. Bell was in New York, with Watson in California. Placing the first call across the new line, Bell repeated his famous quote, to which Watson replied, "It would take me a week to get there now."

In 1876, when he was still a congressman, James Garfield devised and published an original PROOF of the Pythagorean theorem. This might make him the NERDIEST man to ever become president.

AUTOMATED HANGING

Even the most strident supporters of the death penalty rarely want the honor of carrying out an execution themselves. And such was the case even back in the hanging heyday of the Old West. A Wyoming architect named James P. Julian had a solution to this paradox. In the 1890s he designed a Rube Goldberg-ian contraption known as "The Julian Gallows," which essentially forced the condemned individuals to hang themselves. When a doomed fellow stepped onto the gallows trapdoor, it pulled a plug from a bucket of water. The water would slowly empty out, triggering a counterweight that caused the beam under the trapdoor to break free, initiating the hanging. The Julian Gallows' most famous victim was hired gunman Tom Horn, who triggered his own hanging in 1903.

▇ WHO YOU CALLIN' FANCY?

During the 1920s, Italian immigrant Rodolfo Alfonso Raffaello Pierre Filibert Guglielmi di Valentina d'Antonguolla—or as he was more succinctly known to the moviegoing public, Rudolph Valentino—was one of the biggest stars of the silver screen. But only with the ladies. Women viewed Valentino as the zenith of romance. Men found his sultry good looks and exotic flair offensively effeminate.

In 1926, the *Chicago Tribune* published an anonymous article complaining about the feminization of American men, an imagined crisis that the reporter blamed in part on the popularity of Valentino. Sensitive about his public image, Valentino was enraged. So he did the manliest thing he could think of—he challenged the anonymous reporter to a boxing match.

When the reporter did not come forward, *New York Evening Journal* boxing writer Frank O'Neill happily volunteered, expecting to have the satisfaction of flooring a namby-pamby Hollywood actor. The fight took place on the roof of New York's Ambassador Hotel, and it only lasted two punches. O'Neill popped Valentino in the chin, then Valentino knocked O'Neill on his ass with a hard left. When O'Neill got to his feet he stopped the fight, later telling the press, "That boy has a punch like a mule's kick. I'd sure hate to have him sore at me."

Ironically, the anonymous reporter of the original *Tribune* piece had been a woman.

▇ THE SLOGAN MACHINE

Theodore Roosevelt was well known for his ability to turn a phrase. He called the White House a "bully pulpit." He called the radicals who occupy both ends of the political spectrum the "lunatic fringe." He introduced the metaphorical proverb, "Speak softly and carry a big stick," and the expression, "My hat is in the ring." And he unwittingly coined one of the best-known product slogans of the twentieth century.

In 1907, Roosevelt paid a visit to the Hermitage, the former Tennessee home of President Andrew Jackson. During his visit, Roosevelt was given a cup of coffee brewed by a local company. When asked what he thought of the taste, Roosevelt replied, "Good to the last drop." The coffee was Maxwell House, which was named after the Maxwell House Hotel in Nashville. And "Good to the Last Drop" would become Maxwell House's favored marketing slogan. In recent decades Maxwell House, now owned by Kraft Foods, has distanced itself from the Roosevelt connection, claiming it is only legend. Yet, in the 1930s, Maxwell House ran ads perpetuating the story and claimed it was true for years afterward.

AUNT JEMIMA DOCTRINE

In 1890, the R. T. Davis Milling Company hired a former slave named Nancy Green to portray Aunt Jemima, the spokesperson for their instant pancake mix. Many African Americans have charged that the Aunt Jemima character, a matronly black woman in an apron and kerchief, perpetuated the demeaning Mammy stereotype—that of a friendly black woman who obsequiously acts in the interests of whites. But to modern corporations Aunt Jemima is a hero and a trailblazer.

Back in the 1890s Aunt Jemima had become so popular that R. T. Davis signed Nancy Green to a lifetime contract and changed the name of his company to the Aunt Jemima Mills Company. Soon other companies began using the Jemima character. In 1915, Aunt Jemima Mills filed a suit against Rigney and Company, who had been using Jemima to advertise their pancake syrup. While this may seem like a no-brainer case now, back then there was no precedent. You couldn't rip off someone else's advertising if you were selling the same product, but syrup and pancake mix were two different things. The judge sided with Aunt Jemima Mills and ruled that consumers could be misled to think both products were made by the same company. The case put in place a new trademark legal model, often referred to as the Aunt Jemima Doctrine.

JUST A BUNCH OF CRIMINALS

Americans love poking fun at Australians over the fact that their country was initially founded as a penal colony for British convicts. Their national holiday, Australia Day, commemorates the arrival of the First Fleet at Sydney Cove in 1788—*carrying a boat full of prisoners!* It is hard to resist making jokes.

But Americans shouldn't be so quick to mock. That this occurred in 1788, during the American Revolution, is no coincidence. During the eighteenth century, America had been the Brits' preferred dumping ground for unwanted lowlifes and offenders. Thousands of criminals were chained and carried to our shores to be sold as servants and unskilled laborers, with most landing in Virginia and an unusually large number making up the population of Maryland at the time. (Insert your own joke about Baltimore's high crime rates here.) It was only after war broke out that Great Britain started poking around for a new continent to export their miscreants to.

 ## MORE THAN A PARTICIPATION TROPHY

The Heisman Trophy is given out each year to the most outstanding player in collegiate football. It is named after John Heisman, who coached football at numerous schools during an influential career that spanned from 1892 to 1927. Among Heisman's many contributions to the sport are the center snap, quarterbacks shouting "hike" or "hup" to start each play, the le-

galization of the forward pass, and dividing games into quarters instead of halves.

He also still holds the record for the most devastating ass-
kicking in college football history. In 1916, Heisman's Georgia
Tech beat the Cumberland College Bulldogs 222-0. Georgia
Tech already wildly outgunned the Bulldogs, but Heisman had
a chip on his shoulder from the previous season when Cumberland's semipro-stocked baseball team aggressively ran up the
score against Georgia Tech's team (also coached by Heisman).
Payback is a bitch.

HOUSTON, WE HAVE A PROBLEM

In April 1970 the ill-fated Apollo 13 mission held the
world captivated as its crew struggled for survival after an
explosion crippled the craft on its way to the moon. But
while concerned citizens huddled around their televisions,
praying for the safe return of Apollo's crew—Jim Lovell,
Jack Swigert, and Fred Haise—they probably should have
been praying for themselves too, because Apollo's Lunar
Excursion Module (LEM) had a plutonium power cell.

Called Systems for Nuclear Auxiliary Power (SNAP-
27), it contained 3.8 kilograms of plutonium, which is so
deadly that less than one millionth of a gram can cause
cancer. LEM was meant to be left behind on the moon,
but now Apollo was forced to carry it back to Earth. If
something went wrong on reentry, NASA had a potential
nuclear catastrophe on its hands. Fortunately, things went
as planned, and SNAP-27 was jettisoned into the South
Pacific Ocean. SNAP-27's radioactivity will last for over
two thousand years.

ALL ABOUT THE DEAD PRESIDENTS

Aside from earning your own monument in Washington,
D.C., getting your face on a coin or dollar bill has to be

chief among bragging rights for presidential ghosts. Not including the recent Presidential $1 Coin Program, which intends to release a special dollar coin for each of our presidents (making it the equivalent here of a participation trophy), here's a breakdown of who gets to brag:

Abraham Lincoln: one-cent piece, since 1909.

Thomas Jefferson: five-cent piece, since 1938.

Franklin D. Roosevelt: ten-cent piece, since 1946.

George Washington: twenty-five cent piece, since 1932.

John F. Kennedy: fifty-cent piece, since 1964.

Dwight D. Eisenhower: one-dollar coin, from 1971 until 1978.

George Washington: one-dollar bill, since 1869.

Thomas Jefferson: two-dollar bill, since 1869, then sporadically printed in 1928, 1953, 1963, 1976, and 1999.

Abraham Lincoln: five-dollar bill, since 1928. James Garfield, Ulysses S. Grant, and Benjamin Harrison all graced the five before him.

Andrew Jackson: twenty-dollar bill, since 1929. Washington, Garfield, and Grover Cleveland all graced the twenty before him.

Ulysses S. Grant: fifty-dollar bill, since 1913.

William McKinley: five-hundred-dollar bill, limited Federal Reserve Note.

Grover Cleveland: one-thousand-dollar bill, limited Federal Reserve Note.

James Madison: five-thousand-dollar bill, limited Federal Reserve Note.

Woodrow Wilson appeared on a 100,000-dollar bill, which was actually illegal for an individual to own and was meant solely for gold transactions between Federal Reserve banks.

Alexander Hamilton and Benjamin Franklin adorn the ten-dollar and one-hundred-dollar bills respectively, but neither served as president.

U-2

In 1960 the Soviet Union shot down a single-engine American U-2 jet along the Turkish-Russian border. After the Soviets got all braggy about their achievement, the US government revealed that the plane was part of a NASA program studying the upper atmosphere. The CIA thought they could get away with the explanation because they believed the U-2's pilot had died. He had not.

Capt. Francis Gary Powers had been on a surveillance spy mission, and though his craft flew at altitudes of 70,000 feet, he had miraculously survived the crash. The CIA would have been much happier if he had in fact died. After being forced by the Soviets to apologize for spying on them, Powers spent two years in a Russian cell before the CIA traded a captured Soviet spy for his freedom. When Powers returned to America he didn't exactly get a welcome-home parade. Rumors spread that he had defected and that he had intentionally landed his plane. Even those who believed he was an unfortunate victim thought he should have eaten the suicide pill the CIA had provided him in case of emergency.

Powers died at the age forty-seven in 1977, in a helicopter crash. It wasn't until June 15, 2012, that the Air Force stopped being jerks about the whole thing and presented Power's family with a Silver Star for his action during the U-2 spy plane incident.

A FAMILY ALSO DIVIDED

Mary Todd, the wife of Abraham Lincoln, was born in Kentucky to a slave-owning family. Like her husband, she was an abolitionist, yet many in the North—especially in the press—never stopped viewing her as a Southerner. Particularly, it did not escape the attention of the suspicious press that many members of Mary's family, including her siblings, were in the Confederate army.

When Mary's half-sister Emilie briefly came to live with the Lincolns after her husband died in the Battle of Chickamauga, the press declared that there were "rebels in the White House." When another half-sister, Martha, whose husband was still an active Confederate, came to Washington, Mary had to refuse to see her. But that didn't stop rumors from circling that Martha took medicine and other valuable items back to the South—with Mary Todd's help! The situation was so bad that the Lincolns could not publicly grieve the deaths of Mary's Confederate half-brother or brother-in-law when they were killed in action.

The Constitution of the Confederate States of AMERICA included this law: "The importation of NEGROES of the African race from any foreign country other than the SLAVEHOLDING States or Territories of the United States of America, is hereby FORBIDDEN."

BAD MIND FOR BUSINESS

Mark Twain is generally regarded as America's greatest wit. His literary talents earned him a sizable fortune, but by the time he died he had lost most of it in a series of poor investments.

Most devastating was his support of an automatic typesetting machine created by James Paige. The Paige Compositor was intended to revolutionize the typesetting field by being more efficient and less expensive than the standard human-run compositors. Twain sank much of his fortune into the machine (many millions in today's dollars), but with eighteen thousand separate parts, the Paige Compositor had an endless series of glitches that needed correcting, which prolonged its development phase (as well as Twain's monthly support). Before Paige could perfect his machine, Baltimore inventor Ottmar Mergenthaler introduced his Linotype, which would dominate the market for nearly a hundred years.

TEA TIME

The quick-history version of the Boston Tea Party generally goes as such: Great Britain passed the Tea Act, raising taxes on tea in the colonies, so the colonists protested by dressing as Indians and dumping crates of British tea into Boston Harbor. The truth is that no protest was actually necessary, because the Tea Act didn't raise taxes. It lowered them.

When the Townshend Revenue Act of 1767 raised taxes on tea, the colonists responded not by dressing up and committing vandalism, but as any normal consumer would— *they stopped buying British tea*. A black market for smuggled Dutch tea soon thrived, forcing Britain to pass the Tea Act of 1773, which lowered prices in order to allow the East India Company to sell their tea for *cheaper* than the black market. What tends to get overlooked in the rose-colored-glasses view of history is that many of the patriots who helped organize the protest of the Tea Act (which resulted in the Boston Tea Party) were tea smugglers who viewed the act as a threat to their black market enterprise.

THE MOST IMPORTANT MEAL OF THE DAY

The Black Panther Party was an African American militant organization that grew out of the racial strife of the 1960s. They believed it was imperative for black people to arm themselves. The FBI considered them a hate group and Panther members had several violent shootouts with the police. The Panthers also believed that children could not reach their full potential in school if they had empty stomachs. In 1969, the Black Panthers launched the Free Breakfast for School Children program at a church in inner city Oakland, California, where the Panthers cooked food for the underprivileged youth of the neighborhood. By the end of the year they had set up kitchens in cities across the nation and were feeding roughly ten thousand children every day before school started.

A NOT-SO-PLEASURABLE CRUISE

In 1893, the United States was in the midst of a financial crisis. Hundreds of banks across the country had failed and the national mood was grim. It was a time when America needed a strong president. Which is why the White House worried what might happen to the economy if the public learned that President Grover Cleveland needed emergency surgery to remove a tumor from the roof of his mouth. So a unique conspiracy was hatched.

The press was notified that Cleveland was taking a vacation aboard a private yacht. What they weren't told was that a makeshift surgical room had been created aboard the ship. During the course of Cleveland's pleasure cruise, most of his upper jaw was removed and replaced with a rubber appliance. Cleveland survived the surgery, and to cover the impairment left to his speech, the press was told he'd had two teeth removed (which was technically true). Amazingly, the truth about the secret surgery remained unknown until long after Cleveland's death in 1908.

 DOOM 'ROUND MIDNIGHT

In 1947, the Bulletin of the Atomic Scientists *premiered their famous Doomsday Clock. Featured on the magazine's cover, the clock face is an analogy for the threat of global nuclear war, with midnight representing disaster and the minute hand representing how close to disaster the world is. The first Dooms-day Clock had us at seven minutes to doom, or 11:53 p.m. The closest to midnight the clock has ever been set was 11:58 p.m. on the 1953 issue, after the Soviet Union successfully tested a nuclear bomb. The furthest away we've ever been was 11:43 p.m. in 1991, when the United States and the Soviets signed the Strategic Arms Reduction Treaty.*

THE RAIN WIZARD

In August 1891, an Australian named Frank Melbourne arrived in Cheyenne, Wyoming, while it was stuck in a terrible drought. Melbourne informed the desperate public that he could make it rain, for a fee. They accepted. And within a few days, rain came. So began Melbourne's briefly successful business as a rainmaker. Melbourne, who became known as the Rain King and the Rain Wizard, had a system that involved manufacturing gas or smoke on the ground, thus creating a fake cloud that would rise into the air, supposedly causing rainfall. He even claimed he could do it within three to five days. He traveled the Great Plains from 1892 to 1894 aboard a specially equipped railroad car, offering his services to any community in need of water. Eventually people caught on to the fact that Melbourne was arriving in towns where rain had already been forecast, then just sticking around until that rain finally came and taking credit.

JOHNNY JESUS-SEED

Most people know the folktale hero Johnny Appleseed from children's literature and cartoons, strutting around the country with bare feet and a pot for a hat, planting apple trees wherever he goes. But Johnny Appleseed was a real man. Born in Leominster, Massachusetts, in 1774, John Chapman became a legend in his own time for his dedication to the apple. He led a nomadic life, traveling the country starting apple nurseries and preaching to farmers about the glory of the fruit. He was also just as likely to preach the morals of The New Church (or Swedenborgian Church), a Christian sect based on the writings of Emanuel Swedenborg, who claimed to have witnessed Judgment Day in a vision in 1757. Fort Wayne, Indiana—where Chapman is believed to be buried—holds an annual Johnny Appleseed Festival in his honor.

COULD'VE ASKED HIM TO ROLL ON HIS SIDE

When John Wesley Hardin was finally captured by lawmen in 1878, he claimed to have killed forty-two men. This is surely an exaggerated number, but Hardin had a reputation as one of the meanest men of the West.

While staying at a hotel in Abilene, Kansas, Hardin became disturbed by the loud snoring coming from the room next to his. Not wanting to get out of bed, Hardin resolved to stop the snoring by firing his gun aimlessly into the wall. The man next door was hit by the bullets and killed. Presumably realizing that "snoring disturbance" was not covered under a self-defense plea, Hardin escaped from his window to avoid arrest.

ONE TOUGH SPEECH

Theodore Roosevelt is generally regarded as one of the most badass American presidents. He formed his own regiment to fight in the Spanish-American War, basically just for the sport of it. He hunted down horse thieves in the West and became friends with renowned Deadwood, South Dakota, lawman Seth Bullock. And he once killed a mountain lion with a hunting knife. Yet he was also one of the most articulate presidents. A rarity among modern presidents, Roosevelt wrote his own speeches, relishing in his distinctive verbiage.

In 1912, while Roosevelt was making a controversial return to the political world as a third party presidential candidate, running against the incumbent president and his former protégée, Howard Taft, those two prominent aspects of his personality crashed together in what is assuredly the defining moment in both Roosevelt's manliness and his public speaking career. On October 14, Roosevelt was readying for a speech when an assassin shot him point blank in the chest. Roosevelt would have died were it not for his eyeglasses case and the massive fifty-page speech he had folded up in his jacket's breast pocket. The combination of the thickly folded paper and the case slowed the bullet just enough that it did not pierce any vital organs. Never one to shy away from cultivating his image as a colossal badass, Roosevelt refused to go to the hospital until *after* he had delivered his speech—which he did with flair, leaving his jacket open so everyone could see the fresh blood on his shirt.

▰▰▰ HEIR UN-APPARENT

In 1897, con-woman Elizabeth Bigley upgraded from her typical low-level con of pretending to be a mystic. Under the name of Cassie Chadwick, she convinced a Cleveland lawyer that she was the illegitimate daughter of steel magnate Andrew Carnegie and that she stood to inherit millions when Carnegie died. Soon banks were offering her their services. Chadwick knew no one would dare ask Carnegie if he had a bastard daughter, so she was able to milk her con for years, racking up a series of loans from different banks. By the time a suspicious banker in Brookline, Massachusetts, finally called in one of her loans, it was 1904 and Chadwick had acquired nearly $5 million in debt to fuel her newly extravagant lifestyle. Andrew Carnegie even attended her trial, curious to see the sneaky woman who had fooled so many dupes. Chadwick died on her birthday in the Ohio State Penitentiary in 1907.

A HELL OF A QUOTE

When he observed the destruction from the attack on Pearl Harbor, Vice Admiral William Halsey Jr. muttered angrily, "Before we're through with them, the Japanese language will be spoken only in hell." When Japan finally surrendered at the end of WWII, they did so on the deck of Halsey's flagship, the USS Missouri, *which no doubt put warm fuzzies in the vengeance section of the vice admiral's heart.*

MONSTER DISTRICTS

In 1812, Elbridge Gerry, governor of Massachusetts, signed into law a bill that rather transparently rejiggered his state's districts in such a way that Republicans gained an important voting advantage over the Federalists. The Federalists complained that the bizarre and asymmetrical new districts looked more like salamanders wriggling all over the map. This inspired the *Boston Gazette* to publish a cartoon with one of the more absurdly shaped districts redrawn as a monster. They called their monster the Gerrymander. To this day the practice of redistricting to give one party an unfair advantage is known as gerrymandering.

 ## A FUZZY LEGACY

In November of 1902, President Theodore "Teddy" Roosevelt was invited on a hunting trip by the governor of Mississippi. On the trip, members of Roosevelt's entourage cornered an adult black bear, clubbing it into a daze and then tying it to a tree, thinking that the president would happily claim his prize. Roosevelt was an avid hunter, but somewhat paradoxically, he was also an ardent nature lover. Disgusted by the prospect of claiming the poor, beaten animal as a prize, Roosevelt refused, ordering his attendants to put the bear out of its misery themselves. The story became the subject of a popular series of political cartoons in the *Washington Post*, featuring a caricature of Roosevelt refusing to shoot what was generally portrayed as a cuddly bear cub. When New York candy shop owner Morris Michtom saw the cartoon, he was inspired to create a stuffed bear toy, which he named in honor of Roosevelt. And the teddy bear was born.

Though the public and press affectionately called Roosevelt "Teddy," he hated the nickname, finding it demeaning.

★ ★ ★ ★ ★ ★ ★ ★ ★ ★ ★ ★ ★ ★

President John Quincy ADAMS was elected a US representative from Massachusetts in 1830, making him the only person ever to serve in the House of REPRESENTATIVES after being president. Andrew Johnson is the only expresident to be elected to the US Senate.

★ ★ ★ ★ ★ ★ ★ ★ ★ ★ ★ ★ ★ ★

OUT OF SIGHT, OUT OF MIND

Americans debated the problem of slavery long before the Civil War. One of the key issues wasn't so much that racist Americans really wanted black slaves, but that racist Americans didn't want free black folks wandering around. Speaker of the House Henry Clay put things thusly: "Of all classes of our population, the most vicious is that of the free colored." So serious was this perceived problem that it was proposed that blacks be removed from the country altogether and sent back to Africa. This was a downright preposterous idea. So of course it actually happened. The exportation scheme seemed logical enough that President James Monroe was able to get $100,000 (that's over $1 billion today) to found the African colony of Liberia in 1822.

Thousands of free blacks went to the colony, and, fittingly, in 1847 the Republic of Liberia issued America its own Declaration of Independence. Its capital, Monrovia, was named after James Monroe.

FIRST IN MANY FIRST FLIGHTS

North Carolina uses the slogan "First In Flight" on its license plates because the Wright Brothers' first successful airplane flight occurred within its borders. But Ohioans should probably be the ones bragging. The Wrights were from Ohio. As was John Glen, the first American to orbit the Earth. As was Neil Armstrong, the first person to set foot upon the Moon. Impressively, Ohio has produced twenty-five astronauts, including Apollo 13's Jim Lovell.

A VERY EXPENSIVE PANTS SUIT

Roy L. Pearson Jr. was serving as an administrative law judge in Washington, D.C., in 2005 when he dropped off a pair of pants to be dry-cleaned at Custom Cleaners, run by the Chung family. When Pearson returned for his pants, he discovered that the Chungs had misplaced them. Several days later they said they had located the pants, but Pearson claimed they weren't his. He demanded $1,000, which he said was the price of the pants. The Chungs refused. So Pearson sued them…for $67 million.

In 2007, as the case ran on, Pearson reduced his demands to $54 million, which he broke down as such: $500,000 in attorney's fees, $2 million for discomfort, inconvenience, and mental distress, $15,000 for a rental car to drive to another dry cleaning service every weekend, with the remaining $51.5 million to be used to help other dissatisfied D.C. consumers sue evil businesses like Custom Cleaners.

The Chungs had a sign outside their store that stated "Satisfaction Guaranteed." And Pearson felt *very* unsatisfied.

Eventually the Chungs' community held a fundraiser to help pay their legal bills and fight Pearson. The District of Columbia Superior Court ruled in the favor of the dry cleaners. Pearson filed several appeals, but the case was dismissed each time, and eventually so was he. Pearson was not appointed to another term as a judge—his superiors felt his suit against the Chungs had demonstrated a lack of "judicial temperament." Pearson then filed suit against Washington, D.C., seeking $1 million and his job back. That case was also dismissed.

Algonquin Bible

Not too surprisingly, the first book published in America was a Bible. What might be surprising is that the book wasn't published in English. It was written in the language of the Massachusett Indians, who belonged to the larger Algonquian-language family. What is now generally referred to as the "Algonquin Bible" was the work of missionary John Eliot, who had made it his goal to convert the Native Americans of New England to Christianity. Eliot's Bible was no small task, considering that the Massachusett people had no written language, so first Eliot had to create one. The translation itself also proved tricky. Eliot consulted with the Indians to find the best translations, and in the many cases where there was no logical translation possible, Eliot included vocabulary from the King James Bible. The New Testament was completed in 1661, followed by the Old Testament in 1663.

Portable Hell

The phrase "hell on wheels" is generally used to label someone, or something, as being particularly tough or wild. But the phrase was originally used to describe something more literal—the itinerant vice districts that followed the construction of the American transcontinental railroad in the 1860s.

The First Transcontinental Railroad, which joined the western Central Pacific Railroad of California with the Union Pacific Railroad, was the most important development in American transportation and shipping commerce until President Dwight D. Eisenhower introduced the Interstate Highway System in the 1950s. The ambitious and grueling construction took place between 1863 and 1869, with Chinese immigrants making up the majority of Central Pacific's work force and Irish immigrants making up the majority of Union Pacific's crew. As the Union Pacific crawled across the West, connecting towns to the railroad line, the workmen had to move with it. This meant that towns along the way would suddenly find themselves with a major population influx. Peddlers of vice were quick to prey on the workers, who were left idle with money to burn come nightfall.

Tents and flimsy buildings were erected to serve as casinos, saloons, dance halls, and brothels. Violence and debauchery were routine and it was not uncommon for a murder to occur almost every night. Then the Union Pacific would move on, and the vice peddlers would pack up and follow, setting up shop at the next camp—hence, "hell on wheels." It is unknown who coined the phrase, but journalist Samuel Bowles was the first to use it in print. He also used the term "hangers-on" to refer to the peddlers and employees who worked in the itinerant sin cities.

 ## Look Out Below!

Ann Hodges of Sylacauga, Alabama, has the honor of being the first person in documented history to be hit by an extraterrestrial object. After farting around outer space for billions of years, the Sylacauga meteorite (commonly known as the Hodges meteorite) ended its wayward journey on November 30, 1954,

when the grapefruit-sized fragment crashed through Hodges's roof and struck her while she napped on the couch. She was seriously bruised, but not permanently injured. The meteorite now lives at the Alabama Museum of Natural History.

WE ALL GOTTA START SOMEWHERE

The Mississippi River is the fourth longest continuous river in the world, behind the Nile, the Amazon, and China's Yangtze River, and has been a vital part of North American commerce since long before Europeans snatched the continent. In the early 1800s several expeditions were sent to find the source of the mighty river, but the Mississippi runs up into Minnesota, which is known as the Land of 10,000 Lakes for a reason—it was extremely hard to pinpoint which of the state's gazillion lakes were the actual headwaters.

In 1832, geographer Henry Schoolcraft came up with the answer that stuck. He determined the source was the inconspicuously small Lake Itasca in southern Clearwater, Minnesota. At its birthplace, the Mississippi slips over the edge of Lake Itasca, only a few inches deep and half a dozen feet across. At its widest points in the lower half of the country the river is one mile across and 200 feet deep.

FILLMORE WAS BIG IN JAPAN

Vice President Millard Fillmore became President Millard Fillmore when Zachary Taylor died in 1850. After finishing out the remaining two and half years of Taylor's term, Fillmore never ran for reelection. This made him one of the more forgettable American presidents. But he did have a major impact on a different country.

By the mid-1800s, Japan had turned itself into an island in more than just a geographical sense; the Japanese had become hardcore isolationists and somewhat lost in time. Fillmore was interested in opening trade with Japan, and sent a fleet of ships to the Land of the Rising Sun hoping to establish friendly relations. This resulted in a major cultural upheaval in Japan, as the Japanese now became aware of just how far behind the times their country had slipped.

Japan westernized and ushered in a new era of economic productivity and military dominance. Sure, some pretty bad stuff came out of that military dominance for us and other countries down the road, but let's just focus on all the snazzy gizmos and electronic appliances we currently enjoy.

MONIKER CITY

A lot of cities have famous nicknames. Denver is The Mile-High City. New York City is The Big Apple. Chicago is The Windy City. Here are some lesser-known monikers:

Albertville, Alabama: The Fire Hydrant Capital of the World

Kenai, Alaska: The Village with a Past, the City with a Future

Dumas, Arkansas: Home of the Ding Dong Daddy

Azusa, California: A to Z, USA

Severance, Colorado: Where the Geese Fly and the Bulls Cry

Hamden, Connecticut: Land of the Sleeping Giant

Algona, Iowa: Home of the World's Largest Cheeto

Russell Springs, Kansas: Cow Chip Capital of Kansas

Northfield, Minnesota: Cows, Colleges, and Contentment

Peculiar, Missouri: Where the Odds Are with You

Cut Bank, Montana: Coldest Spot in the Nation

Cando, North Dakota: You Can Do Better in Cando

Glenpool, Oklahoma: The Town that Made Tulsa Famous

Eagle Pass, Texas: Where Yee-Ha Meets Olé

Aberdeen, Washington: Port of Missing Men

Lake Geneva, Wisconsin: Enjoyed for Over 100 Years by the Rich and Famous

Riverton, Wyoming: We've Got All the Civilization You Need

A Quote Within a Quote

What if you were being executed, and someone asked if you had any last words, and you then quoted *Braveheart*? It might strike you as unlikely that hundreds of years from now people would study your geeky reference in history books. But that is exactly what happened to Nathan Hale, who was hanged as a spy by the British during the Revolutionary War. His famous last words, "I only regret that I have but one life to give for my country," have become part of the Revolutionary Era fabric. But Hale was paraphrasing—or possibly just poorly quoting—*Cato, a Tragedy,* a play written by Joseph Addison in 1712. Specifically the line, "What a pity it is/That we can die but once to serve our country."

Addison's play is about Marcus Porcius Cato Uticensis (95–46 BC), who opposed the tyranny of Julius Caesar. Its themes of republicanism and liberty made it particularly popular among the Founding Fathers, who often quoted and referenced the play in correspondence. Patrick Henry's famous line, "Give me liberty or give me death!" is quite likely a reference to *Cato* too, specifically the line, "It is not now time to talk of aught/But chains or conquest, liberty or death."

Lazy Naming

When animator Matt Groening needed a name for the fictitious setting of his television series *The Simpsons*, he selected Springfield because it was the most generic city name he could think of. And he was very close.

Springfield is the fourth most common city name in America, with twenty-eight uses. Greenville is the most common name, clocking in with a whopping forty-nine uses. The top ten breaks down thusly: Greenville (49), Franklin (30), Clinton (29), Springfield (28), Salem (25),

Fairview (24), Madison (23), Washington (24), George-
town (22), and Arlington (21).

If you strung all the days together,
motorcycle daredevil EVEL KNIEVEL
spent three years of his life in a hospital
bed.

His Accidency

In 1841, when President William Henry Harrison died
unexpectedly from illness, John Tyler became the first vice
president to replace a president. The Constitution stated
that in the death of a president, the duties of office shall
"devolve on the vice president." Now that it had actually
happened, many wondered what exactly "devolved" meant.
Did Tyler simply have the duties of the president, or was
he now president himself?

The answer may seem obvious today, but it threw
Washington into a tizzy at the time. When Tyler claimed
the full power and title of the office, some were outraged.
His detractors mocked him as "His Accidency," and when
Tyler vetoed a bill meant to establish a national bank, most
of his cabinet resigned. Tyler then had the honor of being
the first commander in chief to incur impeachment proceedings. The impeachment never went to trial, but before
his term ended Tyler was gifted one final crappy statistic
when he became the first president to have a veto overrid-
den by Congress.

One might also credit Tyler as the first ex-president to
commit treason, as, when out of office, he encouraged his
native Virginia to join the Confederacy in rebellion against
the Union and was elected to the Confederate Congress.

Frozen Dead Guy

In 1989, a Norwegian citizen named Trygve Bauge preserved the corpse of his recently departed grandfather, Bredo Morstøl, on dry ice and transported him to a cryonics facility in California. Then in 1993, Trygve moved Bredo to Nederland, Colorado, where he and his mother, Aud, planned to create their own cryonics facility. But after the body was moved, Trygve was deported for overstaying his visa, leaving Aud to keep Bredo's body cryogenically frozen in a shack behind her unfinished house. In 1995, Aud was threatened with eviction because her unfinished home violated public ordinances. Panicked, Aud told a reporter about Bredo's preserved body, which she knew would thaw out if she were evicted. The word quickly spread around about Nederland's iceman. A Denver radio station helped Aud build a new shed to store Bredo in, and a local environmental company has kindly supplied the dry ice necessary to preserve her father since 1995.

Starting in 2002, the town of Nederland has celebrated Frozen Dead Guy Days on the first weekend in March. Activities include coffin races, a slow-motion parade, icy lake swims, a dance called Grandpa's Blue Ball, local art shows, and a specialty ice cream flavor. Tours of the shed where Bredo "lives" were suspended by Trygve and Aud in 2005. But they resumed in 2010 as the popularity of the festival grew.

City of the Dead

As the twentieth century was getting underway, San Francisco found itself hungry for real estate. City officials determined that cemeteries were eating up too much prime space, so they passed an ordinance evicting almost all the existing cemeteries from city limits and outlawing the construction of new ones. But this didn't stop San Franciscans from continuing to die. Something needed to be done.

In 1924, the town of Colma, California, was founded as a necropolis (though it was originally named Lawndale). Today the town has a population of around 1,800 persons living above ground and 1.5 million residents living six feet under. It has several famous dead residents, like newspaper tycoon William Randolph Hearst, lawman Wyatt Earp, baseball legend Joe DiMaggio, and even historical oddity Phineas Gage.

Thomas JEFFERSON introduced the presidential custom of SHAKING guests' hands. Both of his predecessors, George Washington and John Adams, had BOWED to greet their guests in office, as was considered more stately.

WHERE'S THE SPECIAL EXTENDED COLLECTOR'S EDITION?

If only one descriptor is applied to Thomas Jefferson, it is usually "author of the Declaration of Independence." While this isn't untrue, it leaves out a considerable amount of information on the subject. The document was not something Jefferson dreamed up, composing in solitude and then triumphantly presenting to America as a whole and perfect text.

In 1776, after the Continental Congress had put into motion the decision to declare total independence from Great Britain, a special five-member committee was appointed to draft an official declaration statement. The committee consisted of John Adams of Massachusetts, Benjamin Franklin of Pennsylvania, Thomas Jefferson of Virginia, Robert R. Livingston of New York, and Roger

Sherman of Connecticut. The committee wanted Adams to write the document, but Adams felt that Jefferson's way with words would be better suited. Jefferson tried to refuse what he deemed an unenviable task, but after some further prodding Adams was able to convince him (Jefferson was not immune to flattery).

Jefferson's hesitancy to invest himself in the document was quickly proven valid when he turned in his first draft and saw it torn to shreds. Congress deliberated at length on Jefferson's wording and subject choices, both broad and negligible. A total of eighty-six revisions were made, trimming the document by over four hundred words. One particular sticking point had been Jefferson's inclusion of slavery, which he framed as a curse placed on America by Britain; in the end all references to slavery or slaves were removed. Decades later, Jefferson's political opponents put forward that the Declaration of Independence could not be considered the work of one man when so many cooks had been in the kitchen. Even John Adams became ornery and jealous that Jefferson received so much credit and praise for simply putting into words what had been the collective ideas of Congress. But Jefferson's supporters and the slow wash of time eventually won out on Jefferson's side.

SOME THINGS NEVER CHANGE

Abraham Lincoln's Gettysburg Address is one of the most unfading speeches ever delivered by a president. It begins with easily the most famous six words from any speech in American history: "Four score and seven years ago..." But when Lincoln delivered it on November 19, 1863, at the dedication of the Soldiers' National Cemetery in Gettysburg, Pennsylvania, the response was typical of partisan politics. Lincoln was a Republican. A Republican-leaning newspaper from Springfield, Massachusetts, hailed the speech as a "perfect gem…deep in feeling, compact in thought and expression, and tasteful and elegant in every word and comma." Whereas a Democratic-leaning newspaper from Chicago scathingly remarked that, "the cheek of every American must tingle with shame as he reads the silly, flat and dishwatery utterances of the man who has to be pointed out to intelligent foreigners as the President of the United States."

 ## Some Choice Downtown Real Estate

The Ann W. Richards Congress Avenue Bridge crosses Lady Bird Lake right in the heart of downtown Austin, Texas. Which makes it an unlikely home for the world's largest urban bat colony. Every summer 1.5 million Mexican free-tailed bats journey from their winter retreat south of the border to roost under the bridge, which means that Austin's bat population is double that of its human population. At dusk, tourists and local spectators can gather on the Congress Ave Bridge to watch the awe-inspiring daily spectacle of the bats leaving their roost in search for food.

The Convention Convention Is Born

Nominating conventions are an ingrained part of the presidential election system, held by almost all political parties for the purpose of officially selecting the party's nominee. But they haven't always been a part of the process. And neither Democrats nor Republicans can take credit for starting the tradition.

In 1826, an irate Freemason named William Morgan threatened to write a book exposing the secrets of the Masonic brotherhood. Leveraging their considerable influence, the Masons had Morgan arrested on a minor charge, then spirited Morgan away from his jail cell in the night—never to be seen again. The scandal lit the fuse on a powder keg of preexisting anti-Freemason sentiment in the country and became the catalyst for the formation of the Anti-Mason Party. The Anti-Masons gathered in Baltimore to select a candidate for the 1832 presidential election, selecting former Mason William Wirt. Wirt won only one state in the election, Vermont, ultimately losing to former Masonic grand master Andrew Jackson. But in subsequent elections, the Democrats and Republicans began holding their own nominating conventions.

A KILLER SPEECH

"When we land against the enemy, don't forget to hit him and hit him hard. When we meet the enemy we will kill him. We will show him no mercy. He has killed thousands of your comrades and he must die. If your company officers in leading your men against the enemy find him shooting at you and when you get within two hundred yards of him he wishes to surrender—oh no! That bastard will die! You will kill him. Stick him between the third and fourth ribs. You will tell your men that. They must have the killer instinct. Tell them to stick him. Stick him in the liver. We will get the name of killers and killers are immortal. When word reaches him that he is being faced by a killer battalion he will fight less. We must build up that name as killers."

—*General George S. Patton to his troops before the invasion of Sicily, 1943*

THE PETTICOAT AFFAIR

Margaret "Peggy" O'Neale's father owned the Franklin House, a Washington, D.C., boarding house that served as the social center for many politicians in the early 1800s. Peggy was an attractive coquette with many suitors, and in

1816, seventeen-year-old Peggy married thirty-nine-year-old John Timberlake, a purser in the United States Navy. Rumors had it that she also began a lengthy affair with twenty-eight-year-old Senator John Eaton. When Timberlake died at sea in 1928, the rumors were confirmed for many when Peggy married Eaton without enduring a mourning period that high society deemed proper. The society women of Washington refused to embrace Peggy, an alleged former mistress, and ostracized the Eatons. This angered the easily angered President Andrew Jackson, who was sympathetic to Eaton's plight, believing that similar societal nastiness contributed to the early death of his late wife Rachel. So Jackson appointed Eaton his secretary of war, thinking this would put a stop to things. But it only made it worse, and what became known as the Petticoat Affair (referring to the popular women's undergarment) commenced. Jackson was put at odds with his cabinet, stocked full of men whose wives were tied up in the anti-Peggy movement.

Since Floride Calhoun, wife of Vice President John Calhoun, was the leader of the anti-Peggy coalition, Jackson dropped Calhoun from his reelection campaign, replacing him with Martin Van Buren (the only unmarried member of Jackson's cabinet). Eventually all but one of Jackson's cabinet was replaced or resigned because of the scandal, including Eaton.

 # A BASTARD'S BEQUEATH

The Smithsonian Institution in Washington, D.C., is the largest museum complex in the world, with over 137 million items in its collection. It is named after its founding donor, James Smithson, a British chemist and mineralogist, and the illegitimate son of the 1st Duke of Northumberland. When the childless Smithson died in 1829, his will stipulated that his fortune should to go his nephew Henry James Hungerford, but should Hungerford die childless, the fortune would be trans-

ferred to the United States to create a grand educational insti-
tution. Hungerford died in 1835, unmarried and without an
heir. So Smithson's fortune of roughly $500,000 (that's around
$10 billion today) went to America. Such grand bequeathals to
the arts and sciences are not uncommon among the exceedingly
rich. What makes Smithson's gesture particularly interesting
and unusual is that he had never actually been to America.

UNABOMBER

At the age of sixteen, Theodore John Kaczynski won a
scholarship to study mathematics at Harvard University.
Celebrated as a brilliant mathematician, he became an assistant professor at the University of California, Berkeley,
at the age of twenty-five, but resigned just two years later
due to chronic social and emotional problems. In 1971
he completely withdrew from society, settling in a cabin
without electricity or running water in Lincoln, Montana.
Starting in 1978, after two universities rejected a paper he
wrote, Kaczynski sent sixteen bombs to targets around the
country, including universities and airlines, killing three
people and injuring twenty-three more over the course
of two decades. The FBI referred to the unknown terrorist as the Unabomber, taken from an acronym they used
to label the case files, UNABOM (UNiversity and Air-
line BOMber). When Kaczynski began sending letters to
newspapers, his older brother David recognized the writing style and notified the FBI. In April of 1996, Kaczynski
was arrested.

In 2012, the Harvard Alumni Association celebrated
the fiftieth anniversary of the class of 1962, Kaczynski's
year. In the Red Book (a giant volume of updates on former students published every five years) given to alumni,
Kaczynski lists his occupation as "prisoner." For his accomplishments, he lists, "eight life sentences." He gives his
address as the federal prison in Florence, Colorado.

HOARDER HUGHES

When Howard Hughes died in 1976 he was one of the richest men in the world. Yet malnutrition contributed to his death.

At age nineteen, Hughes inherited his father's company, Hughes Tool Company, and spun it into a fortune reaching the billions. In 1966 Hughes went to Las Vegas and got a room at the Desert Inn. And he didn't leave. When the owners of the hotel started getting antsy, Hughes simply bought the whole place. He even bought the Silver Slipper casino just so he could move the hotel's trademark neon silver slipper, which he disliked being able to see from his bedroom window at night.

But lest you think this is a story about Hughes being a money-droppin' baller and living it up in Sin City, it is important to note that Hughes almost never left the hotel. He turned the Desert Inn's eighth floor into his business headquarters and permanently moved into the ninth-floor penthouse. The warning signs of Hughes's mental quirks had been visible for a while. In 1957 he went into a private Los Angeles screening room to watch some movies and stayed there for four months, hoarding Kleenex boxes and never bathing, grooming, or cutting his hair or nails.

But this time his hermitage took permanent hold. He completely withdrew from public life. In 1972 Hughes bought the Xanadu Beach Resort and Marina in the Bahamas and set up a new residence on its thirteenth floor. Hughes lived in shocking squalor and displayed textbook hoarding behavior as well as mysophobia (fear of germs). He reportedly wore Kleenex boxes on his feet and collected his urine in jars. When Hughes died on April 5, 1976, fingerprints were required to confirm his identity, for his 6 foot 4 inch body now weighed only 90 pounds. An autopsy X-ray revealed five broken-off hypodermic needles in the flesh of his arms. Malnutrition and painkiller use had destroyed his kidneys, which caused his death.

Otto Rohwedder was a successful Missouri JEWELER who eventually sold all his jewelry shops to focus on his dream creation: presliced bread.

In 1917 a fire destroyed his prototype machine, forcing Americans to SLICE their own bread like suckers until Rohwedder gained enough funding to complete his innovation in 1928. For decades afterward, any new technological innovation in consumer goods was generally referred to as "the greatest thing since sliced BREAD."

LADIES LIKE WHISKERS

In October of 1860, just a few weeks before Abraham Lincoln was elected president, an eleven-year-old girl named Grace Bedell sent Lincoln a letter. The content of the letter? Reporting to Lincoln that she had seen a picture of his clean-shaven face and was urging him to grow a beard. "All the ladies like whiskers and they would tease their husbands to vote for you and then you would be President." Lincoln even wrote back to Grace, "…as to the whiskers, have never worn any, do you not think people would call it a silly [affectation] if I were to begin it now?" But shortly thereafter, for the first time in his life, Lincoln grew out the excellently distinctive beard that would help immortalize his image.

So who suggested he wear top hats?

CIA PROSTITUTES

The patron of a brothel may often worry that he is walking into a setup with police officers ready to jump out the moment he presents his cash. But he probably feels secure in the assumption that the brothel isn't a covert CIA test site, and that the prostitutes aren't secretly dosing him with LSD while agents study his reactions from behind one-way glass. But that is exactly what happened during the 1950s to gentlemen who visited a brothel on San Francisco's Telegraph Hill.

The operation—known by the soft-core porno–sounding name of Operation Midnight Climax—was part of a CIA project known as MKUltra that sought to uncover new approaches to interrogation and behavior modification using chemicals and other unorthodox techniques. In particular they thought LSD might be used as a truth serum or potential mind-eraser that could prime subjects for brainwashing. Most tests where done using volunteers, but others were not.

Because of their experimentation with LSD and purported experiments trying to unlock mind control, MKUltra has long been a favorite topic of conspiracy theorists. Some believe that the project's title is an acronym for Manufacturing Killers Utilizing Lethal Tradecraft Requiring Assassinations. But the name was a cryptonym (or code name), with MK signifying that it was part of the CIA Technical Services Division and "Ultra" having no literal significance.

DRAWING A LINE

When talking about life in the North or the South, the Mason-Dixon Line is often conjured as the symbolic boundary separating the two cultural and political halves of America. But what exactly is the Mason-Dixon Line?

The story starts with some fudged geography. King Charles I of England granted Cecilius Calvert, 2nd Baron Baltimore, a charter to create the Province of Maryland in the 1630s. Then, in the 1680s, King Charles II granted a land tract to William Penn to create the Province of Pennsylvania. Both provinces were to share a border along the fortieth parallel. The problem was that Pennsylvania and Maryland didn't agree on where exactly the fortieth parallel crossed, with both claiming an overlap of land. Charles II tried to implement a compromise, but it didn't stick, and by the early 1730s violence was erupting between settlers along the blurred border. Soon Pennsylvania and Maryland were deploying military forces, and all-out war was prevented only by the intervention of King George II.

Clearly something needed to be done, so the Crown put its foot down and established definitive boundaries. Once this boundary was accepted by Pennsylvania and Maryland, a team was commissioned to survey the newly established border. For this task, two surveyors and astronomers were selected—Charles Mason and Jeremiah Dixon.

The Mason-Dixon Line became official in 1767. But it wasn't until Pennsylvania abolished slavery in 1781 that the Line took on the symbolic characteristic that eventually made it a reference point. During the 1800s, long after the country expanded westward from the East Coast, the Mason-Dixon Line became shorthand for describing the stark division between Northern and Southern ideology. Even in the twenty-first century you may still hear someone say "south of the Mason-Dixon" to refer to Arkansas or Mississippi, even though the Mason-Dixon Line only extends to the western border of Pennsylvania.

YOU GOT SERVED BY BILLIE JEAN

Nobody denied that Billie Jean King was a champion women's tennis player. But many people (i.e., many men) denied that *she was as good as the best male players. One man was particularly vocal in this sentiment: Bobby Riggs, a former men's champion who had taken to mocking all women's sports in the press. So inferior were female athletes, claimed Riggs, that even at fifty-five years old he could defeat the top female players. King initially refused Riggs's challenge, but when promoters added $100,000 to the pot, King accepted. The two played each other in a winner-takes-all match at the Houston Astrodome on September 20, 1973. Forty million TV viewers watched King trounce Riggs in three straight sets.*

The Minneapolis SKYWAY System is the largest continuous network of skyways in the world, spanning 8 miles and CONNECTING sixty-nine blocks in downtown Minneapolis, Minnesota, like a massive system of hamster TUBES to protect residents from the freezing winters.

AND YOU THOUGHT GOLF WAS A BORING SPECTATOR SPORT

Long-distance walking, officially known as pedestrianism, was a popular sport in post–Civil War America. Wobbles, as races were called, drew crowds and fierce gambling. A popular style of wobble was for competitors to attempt to walk 100 miles in less than twenty-four hours. One of pedestrianism's greatest American champions was Edward Payson Weston, who was accused by English pedestrianism fans of using performance-enhancing drugs to achieve his impressive strolls. His drug of choice? He had a fondness for chewing coca leaves for energy.

Weston's most impressive accomplishment came in 1913, when he walked 1,546 miles from New York to Minneapolis in fifty-one days—at the age of seventy-four. Weston dedicated much of his time to advocating walking as exercise. He saw the automobile as a curse to American health. And he was more right than he knew. Weston was struck by a taxicab in 1927, rendering him unable to walk for the remainder of his life.

THE HANGING JUDGE

"I have ever had the single aim of justice
in view... 'Do equal and exact justice,'
is my motto, and I have often said to the
grand jury, 'Permit no innocent man to be punished, but
let no guilty man escape.'"
—*Judge Isaac C. Parker, 1896*

Judge Isaac C. Parker held the bench of the US Court for the Western District of Arkansas for twenty-one years during the height of the Wild West, meaning that, while the average district judge mostly heard civil cases, Parker was deluged with thousands of criminal cases. He took his position in 1875, coming on the heels of a corrupt predecessor. Knowing that his district was in bad need of a makeover, Parker began with a splash, ordering six men doomed to execution to be hanged simultaneously, lined in a row, as a symbol that the court wasn't joking around anymore. He sentenced 160 people (four of them women) to death, seventy-nine of whom were hanged. This earned Parker the nickname The Hanging Judge, and cozy place in Wild West lore.

Author Charles Portis featured Parker in his novel, *True Grit*, which has been adapted into a film twice.

Bad Fitting Genes

In 1928, author Ernest Hemingway received the tragic news that his father Clarence had committed suicide, to which Hemingway morosely responded, "I'll probably go the same way." This proved a prescient comment when he died in 1961, at the age of sixty-one, from a self-inflicted shotgun wound. To many, Hemingway's death seemed to fit his persona as a surly, hard-drinking, and passionate artist prone to mood swings.

But his mental decline can most likely be attributed to a far less romantic culprit: lousy genes. Shortly before his death, Hemingway was diagnosed with hemochromatosis, an inability to metabolize iron that generally leads to mental and physical deterioration later in life. Since hemochromatosis is a genetic disorder, and because the symptoms of Ernest's and Clarence's mental decline were so eerily similar, it is quite likely that Hemingway's father had also succumbed to hemochromatosis.

What Dreams May Come

According to Ward Hill Lamon, a close friend and self-appointed bodyguard of Abraham Lincoln, the president once related to Lamon a troubling dream he'd had the night before. In the dream, Lincoln said that he walked through the White House, disturbed by the sound of people crying. Investigating the sound, he came into a room where a group of mourners surrounded a body draped in funeral vestments. When Lincoln asked one of the mourners who had died, they replied, "The president. He was killed by an assassin."

Three days after sharing his dream with Lamon, Lincoln was assassinated by John Wilkes Booth. Normally Lamon would have accompanied Lincoln to Ford's Theatre the night he died, but Lincoln had sent him on an out-of-town assignment.

FILIBUSTED

These days when we say "filibuster" we're presumably referring to the action of a senator or a series of senators extending debate in the US Senate for the purpose of blocking legislation. But a filibuster, or freebooter, once referred to someone who engaged in the unsanctioned military support of insurrection in a foreign country for personal gain. The best known filibuster was William Walker, an adventurer who traveled to Nicaragua in 1855 with fifty-seven men he dubbed the Immortals and managed not only to take over a group of rebels waging a civil war against their government, but to successfully overthrow that government too—and then make himself president! But the neighboring Central American countries quickly rallied to oust Walker, who was forced to flee back to the United States. In 1860 Walker returned to Central America with a new plan for seizing power, but was captured by the British Royal Navy, who turned him over to the government of Honduras, who expeditiously executed him.

GIVE ME YOUR TIRED, YOUR POOR, JUST NOT YOUR ASIANS

New York City's Ellis Island—the first stop for immigrants journeying across the Atlantic from 1892 until 1954—was an iconic part of the early American immigrant experience. Lesser remembered is San Francisco's Angel Island, often referred to as the Ellis Island of the West, which served as an immigration station from 1910 to 1940. It also served as a holding tank and quasi-prison for Chinese immigrants. The Chinese Exclusion Act of 1882 had essentially banned all immigration from China, until the Immigration Act of 1924 allowed for a bit of wiggle room. But Chinese immigrants were treated as hostiles the moment they arrived, with family members split apart and placed in cells that most described as "cages." They were then subjected to repeated and baffling interrogations, often kept on the island for weeks or months, and in few rare cases, over a year, before either being allowed into the country or sent back to China. The immigration station was closed in 1940 after an electrical fire destroyed the administration building.

President William Howard TAFT had the Oval Office constructed in the White House's West Wing in 1909. Because of Taft's SIZABLE girth, many Washington insiders joked that the office's unique shape was a necessity to accommodate his ROTUND body.

THE SHY PRESIDENT

Thomas Jefferson was a devil with a fountain pen and is generally considered one of the best writers that American politics has ever had—if not *the* best. But unlike Theodore Roosevelt, who excitedly crafted long monologues to also show off his oratory skills, Jefferson was somewhat shy.

Jefferson did not like public speaking, feeling that he could better express himself on paper. So much so that while he was president he communicated with Congress in written letters, even though his predecessors, George Washington and John Adams, had addressed Congress in person. Jefferson's approach apparently appealed to the presidents that followed too. Poor Congress. It was not until Woodrow Wilson that a president addressed them in person again—which Wilson wound up doing more than any other president, likely making many in Congress wish the tradition of silence had persisted longer.

BAD MOJO

Robert Todd Lincoln was the only one of Abraham Lincoln's four children to survive into adulthood, so you could consider him lucky. You could also consider him incredibly unlucky, at least for American presidents. After his father was shot at Ford's Theatre, Robert was at his father's side when he died. Years later, in 1881, Robert was at the Sixth Street Train Station in Washington, D.C., when President James Garfield was shot. Garfield died with Robert at his side. Then in 1901, Robert just happened to be in Buffalo, New York, when President William McKinley was shot. Upon hearing the news, Robert once again rushed to the president's side, only to see McKinley die. In the years after McKinley's death, Robert refused all invitations to attend presidential functions, once remarking, "…there is a certain fatality about presidential functions when I am present."

 ## EGGS-TRAVAGANZA

In the 1870s it became a common practice every Easter for families to use the Capitol grounds in Washington, D.C., as a park, gathering for picnics and Easter egg shenanigans. Congress became irked with the mess and destruction the citizens were leaving behind, so in 1876 they passed the Turf Protection Act, forbidding the tradition. When a group of children made a personal plea to President Rutherford B. Hayes, the president offered up the South Lawn of the White House for children to congregate. The White House Egg Roll has remained an annual tradition ever since.

BELL'S METAL DETECTOR

In 1881, when famous inventor Alexander Graham Bell learned that an assassin had shot President Garfield and that doctors had been unable to locate the bullet lodged in Garfield's torso, Bell was struck by inspiration. Using principles similar to the ones he used creating the telephone, Bell built an early version of the metal detector. It worked flawlessly in his tests, but when he tried it on Garfield, something seemed wrong. Bell then realized that the president was lying on a bed with a metal frame.

He tried to have Garfield moved, but the physicians, who had already been skeptical of Bell's weirdo device, would not allow it. The bullet was never located and Garfield died, and the modern metal detector would not be put into use for another forty years.

A TERRIBLE CASE OF INDIGESTION

On the Fourth of July, 1850, President Zachary Taylor attended a celebration at the still-under-construction Washington Monument. It was a particularly hot day, so Taylor retired to the White House where, by his own admission, he proceeded to drink copious amounts of ice water and cold milk, and then gorged himself on green apples and cherries. If his mother had been present, she no doubt would have told him that carrying on in such a fashion would give him a bellyache. And sure enough, the next day Taylor developed crippling stomach cramps and diarrhea. Doctors were baffled and unable to help him, and he died on July 9 from what was most likely gastroenteritis.

In the twentieth century the theory that Taylor may have been poisoned was tossed into the historical community, and the theory gained enough traction that in 1991 Kentucky's chief medical examiner authorized the exhumation of Taylor's corpse. But tests revealed no evidence of poisoning. It looks as though Taylor did indeed die of a bad bellyache.

JERSEY SHORE SHARK ATTACK

On July 1, 1916, twenty-five-year-old Charles Epting Vansant went for a swim in the Atlantic at Beach Haven, New Jersey. When he began screaming and flailing in the water, a lifeguard went to his rescue. As Vansant was pulled ashore, the lifeguard realized that Vansant's thigh was completely stripped of flesh. The injury was grave, and Vansant bled to death before he could be taken to a hospital. He had been attacked by a shark.

Shark attacks were incredibly rare at the time and, as odd as it sounds now, many believed that sharks *wouldn't* attack humans. Then on July 6, 45 miles north of Beach Haven, twenty-seven-year-old Charles Bruder was attacked and killed by a shark too. Now panic started to set in along the Jersey Shore. But the swimmers of Matawan Creek, near Matawan, New Jersey, likely still felt safe. Sharks don't go up rivers, after all. Which is exactly what Thomas Cottrell was told on July 12 when he informed his Matawan neighbors that he had just seen a shark swimming up the river. But in just a matter of hours no one would think Cottrell was crazy. Eleven-year-old Lester Stillwell and his friends were swimming in the river when they spotted the dorsal fin of a shark. The boys swam for the shore, but Stillwell was pulled under the water before reaching safety. The other boys returned with help, including Watson Stanley Fisher who dove into the water to look for Stillwell's body. Like a scene from a horror movie, the other townspeople then witnessed Fisher attacked by the sinister fish (Fisher bled to death at the hospital). And the shark wasn't through yet.

A half-mile up the river, the shark grabbed hold of fourteen-year-old Joseph Dunn's leg. Dunn's brother and a friend jumped into the fray and a ghastly game of tug-of-war ensued. But ultimately the boys won. Dunn was injured but he survived.

Was this all the work of one hungry shark? Or several coincidental incidents? No definitive evidence ever arose, and the species of the shark was never conclusively determined either. Though on July 14, a New York taxidermist name Michael Schleisser caught a young 7.5-foot great white, which he claimed had what resembled human flesh in its stomach when he cut it open. No other attacks occurred after Schleisser's catch, but that could be purely coincidental, as people stopped going in the water when the media feeding frenzy set in.

The Jersey Shore attacks would later inspire author Peter Benchley to write *Jaws*, about a giant great white shark that plagues a Long Island resort town.

The last time American "GREEN CARDS" were actually green was 1964.

THE UNPATRIOT ACT

John Adams was the first president to serve only one term. This had everything to do with the wildly unpopular Alien and Sedition Acts, which were kind of like the grandfather of today's Patriot Act. The Alien and Sedition Acts were four bills passed in 1798 under the pretense of protecting American interests against foreign interference in the wake of the French Revolution. French Americans and French-sympathizing immigrants were outraged that Adams was not supporting the new French Republic and had entered the country into an undeclared naval war with France (the so-named Quasi-War). Now unrest was spreading across the United States. John Adams and his fellow Federalists became a little paranoid.

The Alien and Sedition Acts put forth several controversial laws, such as extending the duration of residence required for immigrants (or "aliens") to become citizens of the United States, from five years to fourteen years. They also gave the president the power to deport any alien considered "dangerous to the peace and safety of the United States" and the power to apprehend and deport aliens if their home countries were at war with the U.S. Most controversial of all, the acts cut into First Amendment rights, curtailing what could be published or even spoken about (or against) the president. Thomas Jefferson and his fellow Democratic-Republicans were outraged, calling the Alien and Sedition Acts outright unconstitutional. Adams's popularity further nosedived with each new report of an Alien and Sedition Acts abuse.

The most notorious abuse may have been the 1798 case of Luther Baldwin, the lowly pilot of a garbage scow, who was arrested in a Newark, New Jersey, tavern for making "treasonous" statements against the president. Adams and his wife had stopped in Newark and were greeted by a celebration, including a salute of cannon fire. When Baldwin, several pints into a sozzled day, was asked about Adams's cannon salute, he replied loudly that he "did not care if they fired through his arse." For this harmless quip, Baldwin was arrested, fined, and tossed in jail for two months.

In the 1800 election, Federalists at almost every level of government lost to Democratic-Republicans. When Thomas Jefferson assumed the presidency, he pardoned everyone still serving sentences under the Sedition Act. But, rather hypocritically, he also used the statutes to prosecute several of his most vocal critics before the acts expired.

▰ MORMON PORN

A 2006–2008 study on pornography consumption in America found that states that implement the most conservative social legislation also have the highest consumption of porn. And Utah has the highest of them all. Looking at porn subscription rates per thousand home broadband users, Utah clocks in at 5.47. For comparison, neighbor states Idaho and Montana have rates of 1.98 and 1.92 respectively. For many states with high online porn consumption, income and median age play an important factor, as younger people and people with higher incomes are more likely to subscribe to a porn site. But even when income, age, education, and marital status are taken into account, Utah residents still consume disproportionately more porn than people in other states. A likely factor may be related to the scarcity of adult entertainment outside the home in the predominately Mormon state.

★★★★★★★★★★★★★★★★★★★

Eight presidents were born British subjects: George Washington, John ADAMS, Thomas Jefferson, James MADISON, James Monroe, John Quincy Adams, Andrew JACKSON, and William Henry Harrison.

★★★★★★★★★★★★★★★★★★★

THE LAND THAT TIME ALMOST FORGOT

In the summer of 1705, in Claverack, New York, a Dutch tenant farmer discovered a gigantic five-pound tooth the size of his fist. So he did what any of us would—he traded it to a politician for some rum. The politician gifted the tooth to Lord Cornbury, the royal governor of New York, who in turn sent the tooth to London, labeled "tooth of a Giant." British scientists dubbed whatever creature this massive tooth came from *incognitum*, the unknown species. Similar teeth were later discovered in South Carolina and African slaves noted that the fossils looked an awful lot like an elephant's tooth. When the wooly mammoth was discovered in Siberia, Americans realized the New World must have had similar beasts. As it turned out, we had two—mammoths and mastodons.

By the end of the century more and more mammoth and mastodon bones were being uncovered. Thomas Jefferson ardently believed that the giant mammals might still survive in the mysterious interior of North America. When Jefferson sent Lewis and Clark on their historic mission to the Pacific coast, he had high hopes they would encounter mammoths, among other giant prehistoric monsters. They didn't find any. Though they did discover the adorable prairie dog.

PRESIDENTIAL SLAVERY

Thomas Jefferson wrote these words into the Declaration of Independence: "We hold these truths to be self-evident, that all men are created equal, that they are endowed by their Creator with certain unalienable Rights, that among these are Life, Liberty and the pursuit of Happiness." Those with an interest in objective history are quick to point out that Jefferson owned slaves. This is true. But it is also a little misleading to single out Jefferson just because he authored the Declaration.

Of the first eighteen presidents, twelve owned slaves at some point in their lives, and eight owned slaves *while* they were serving as president. Some of the presidents owned hundreds of slaves. Of the first five presidents, only John Adams managed to get by without slaves. Along with Jefferson, George Washington, James Madison, James Monroe, Andrew Jackson, Martin Van Buren, William Henry Harrison, John Tyler, James Polk, Zachary Taylor, Andrew Johnson, and Ulysses S. Grant all purchased or inherited slaves—though Taylor was the last to own slaves while in the White House.

Abraham Lincoln, the president credited with ending slavery, never owned slaves and abhorred the idea. But he also came from a poor family that could not have dreamed of affording even a single slave at a time when inheriting slaves was how most people came into the practice in the first place. So he started off on the right foot.

No Clemency

"I can only say that, by immeasurably increasing the chances of atomic war, the Rosenbergs may have condemned to death millions of innocent people all over the world.

The execution of two human beings is a grave matter. But even graver is the thought of the millions of dead whose deaths may be directly attributable to what these spies have done."

—*President Eisenhower,*
stating why he was declining the plea for clemency in the
death sentences of Julius and Ethel Rosenberg, who had been
convicted of passing atomic secrets
to the Soviet Union

Best Seller and War Starter

Harriet Beecher Stowe was born to a family of ministers and abolitionists who worked as part of the Underground Railroad. Stowe's staunch abolitionism inspired her to expose the reality of slavery by writing the novel *Uncle Tom's Cabin*. Published in 1852, the book became a sensation, galvanizing the antislavery movement and earning scathing critiques from angry Southerners who were quick to point out that Stowe had never actually been to the South. It sold 300,000 copies within its first year (for comparison, *The Hunger Games* sold about that much in two years, and the US population is thirteen times larger than it was then). War between the North and South was inevitable, but *Uncle Tom's Cabin* heightened the tensions that had long been festering in the nation. In 1862, during the Civil War, Stowe met President Abraham Lincoln. Allegedly, his first words were, "So, you are the little lady who started this great big war." Not too many novels can claim to have helped incite a civil war.

AMERICA'S BIRTH CERTIFICATE

Americans aren't usually taught about the German cartographer Martin Waldseemüller in school, but he played a uniquely critical role in American history. He's the reason we even call it "American" history.

After Christopher Columbus landed in the New World, he believed he had reached some part of Asia. Since people back in Europe had no choice but to believe him, North America was thusly labeled "Indies" on many maps from the era. On more skeptical maps it was labeled "Terra Incognita" (unknown land). Waldseemüller changed all this in 1507 when he produced *Cosmographiae Introductio*, a book on mapmaking that included the first appearance of the word "America" to describe the New World. He named the mysterious new landmass after Italian explorer Amerigo Vespucci. Today scholars debate the exact accomplishments of Vespucci, who made several voyages across the Atlantic after Columbus, but the relevant thing here is what Waldseemüller believed. And he believed that Vespucci discovered South America. He feminized Vespucci's first name, because Europa and Asia both derived their names from women. The name stuck and spawned North America too, once everyone conclusively realized the upper continent was most definitely not part of Asia.

The Lincoln MEMORIAL was initially conceived as a massive PYRAMID with a statue of Lincoln perched on the top, like a figurine on an enormous wedding CAKE.

ELLIS ISLAND NURSING HOME

In 1954, Ellis Island's immigration station was closed down and no one was quite sure what to do with the prime New York Harbor real estate. So the government opened the floor to private business proposals. Numerous pitches came across the table, including a clinic for alcoholics and drug addicts, an innovative "college of the future," condos, a nursing home for the elderly, a shelter for juvenile delinquents, and even a lavish resort. But no one offered the government quite enough money to snag the property.

In 1965, President Johnson signed a proclamation that made Ellis Island part of the Statue of Liberty National Monument. Today it is one of the most visited tourist destinations in the National Park Service. Though that "college of the future" sounded neat.

 ## THE CORNERSTONE FOUNDING FATHER

Benjamin Franklin was the only Founding Father to sign all four of the documents most responsible for the creation of the United States—the Declaration of Independence (1776), which announced America's independence; the Treaty of Alliance, Amity, and Commerce with France (1778), which secured France's financial and military support during the Revolutionary War;

the Treaty of Paris (1783), which ended the war with Great Britain; and the Constitution (1787), which formalized the laws and political governances of the United States.

UNCLE SAM WANTS YOU

Uncle Sam is well known as the mascot (or personification) of the American government. According to US lore, the name comes from a meat packer named Sam Wilson who supplied provisions for the soldiers during the War of 1812. His packages were labeled "E.A. – US." The E. A. stood for Elbert Anderson, the name of the distributor. When someone asked what the US stood for, someone else apparently replied, "Uncle Sam," referring to Wilson. Or so the story goes. The US of course actually stood for "United States."

Whatever the true origin, the nickname did not gain full traction until 1917, when it was combined with the now famous image created by illustrator James Montgomery Flagg. Flagg had been hired to create an Army recruitment poster for World War I. Inspired by a British WWI recruitment poster—which featured the real-life Lord Kitchener pointing outward, with the text "Britons: Lord Kitchener Wants You"—Flagg drew his Uncle Sam character as a white-bearded, stern-faced man in a blue coat and a white top hat. And Uncle Sam was born.

THE GREAT ESCAPE

There have been numerous WWII films made about American prisoners of war held captive on Nazi-controlled soil. But America took prisoners too.

Though cinema hasn't etched it into our collective memory, some 400,000 German POWs were brought to the United States during the war. And like the characters in such iconic films as *The Great Escape*, the Germans staged plenty of daring jailbreaks too. The biggest occurred on December 23, 1944, in Compound 1A at Papago Park near Phoenix, Arizona. Twenty-five prisoners, comprised of U-boat commanders and their crews, escaped from the camp via a 178-foot tunnel they had laboriously dug throughout the year. The escape triggered the largest manhunt in Arizona history, lasting over a month and utilizing local law enforcement, the FBI, and even Papago Indian scouts. While many of the POWs were caught, many also turned themselves in, having underestimated the hardships of the Arizona desert. U-boat commander Jürgen Wattenberg was the last man standing, and was captured in Phoenix only after his accent raised the suspicions of a man Watternberg stopped for directions.

SOME CLOSE CALLS

When the *Titanic* sank in 1912, it claimed several famous Americans, including millionaires John Jacob Astor IV and Benjamin Guggenheim, as well as Isidor Straus, the owner of Macy's department store, and mystery novelist Jacques Futrelle. But far more impressive is the list of Americans who *almost* died on the *Titanic*, but for one reason or another, never got on the ship.

Looking to save some money, novelist Theodore Dreiser (*An American Tragedy*) opted to take a cheaper ship across the Atlantic. Milton Snavely Hershey, creator of the Hershey chocolate bar, had made a down payment on a stateroom aboard the *Titanic*, but pressing business in America forced him to take an earlier voyage. J. P. Morgan, the "Napoleon of Wall Street," had a personal suite with his own private promenade deck, but decided to remain on his vacation in France a while longer. Alfred Gwynne Vanderbilt, heir to the Vanderbilt railroad empire, canceled his passage on the *Titanic* so late that many early reports listed him among the causalities. It seems, however, that the ocean had it in for Vanderbilt—he died three years later, in another famous ship disaster, when the *Lusitania* was torpedoed by a German U-boat.

 # WIN ONE FOR THE FAKE GIPPER

President Ronald Reagan's nickname was The Gipper, a moniker he had carried since 1940, when he starred in the movie Knute Rockne, All American. *In the film Reagan played real-life Notre Dame footballer George "The Gipper" Gipp, who died tragically during his senior season from a throat infection. On his deathbed Gipp supposedly asked Notre Dame coach Knute Rockne to "win just one for the Gipper." Whether this actually happened is unknown, but Rockne told the story to rally his team to a 12-6 underdog victory over the undefeated West Point Army team in 1928. Reagan even repurposed Rockne's rallying appeal at the 1988 Republican National Convention when he told Vice President George H. W. Bush, "George, go out there and win one for the Gipper."*

THE AX MURDERS OF IOWA

Shortly after midnight on June 10, 1912, in the small town of Villisca, someone entered the home of Joe Moore and his family. Creeping into Joe's bedroom, the stranger hoisted an ax and brought it down on Joe's head. Before Joe's wife, Sarah, had even woken, she met the same fate. The killer then moved to the other bedrooms, where the Moore's four children—Herman, eleven; Katherine, ten; Boyd, seven; and Paul, five—all calmly slumbered. He murdered all four children in the same fashion as their parents. So swift and powerful were the killer's swings that none of the victims appeared to have woken before it was their turn. Not even Katherine's two friends, Lena and Ina Stillinger, who were sleeping down stairs. They too were killed as they lay sleeping.

After dispatching all eight victims, the killer returned to them one-by-one and used the ax to reduce their heads to pulp, striking Joe's skull around thirty times. The killer then covered their faces in articles of clothing. The killer also covered all the mirrors in the house, and wrapped a 2-pound slab of bacon in a towel, then left it on the floor. Why? No one ever learned. Theories on who committed the murders took all forms, from a local hit paid for by one of Joe Moore's enemies, to the senseless act of a crazy drifter. But the maniac was never caught.

★ ★ ★ ★ ★ ★ ★ ★ ★ ★ ★ ★ ★ ★ ★

Like FDR and JFK, President Lyndon B. Johnson is sometimes referred to simply as LBJ. But in his household that wasn't very descriptive. LBJ were also the initials of his wife, Lady Bird Johnson, his two daughters Lynda BIRD Johnson and Luci Baines Johnson, and even his dog, Little BEAGLE Johnson.

★ ★ ★ ★ ★ ★ ★ ★ ★ ★ ★ ★ ★ ★ ★

A GENERAL SOFT SPOT

General Robert E. Lee, commander of the Confederate army of North Virginia, known for his battlefield prowess, apparently had a soft spot for animals. During the Civil War he acquired a chicken, which he named Nellie. He kept Nellie with him whilst kicking the Union army's ass, letting her sleep in his tent, and refusing to move on to a new location until she had been located and safely placed on a wagon. During the Siege of Petersburg, Virginia, while under heavy fire, Lee's soldiers observed him stop to rescue a baby bird that had fallen from its nest before he mounted his horse and retreated. On another occasion, during the Battle of the Wilderness, Lee scolded an incoming courier for riding his horse too fast. The courier noted that Lee fed the horse a biscuit before returning his attention to the battle at hand.

It should also be noted that General Ulysses S. Grant of the Union army once took time out of his equally busy schedule to punish a teamster he found whipping a horse on the side of the road. Grant had his soldiers tie the man to a tree for several hours.

 ## It Was Worth a Shot

In 1735, well over one hundred years before the Civil War, the colony of Georgia passed a law that prohibited the importation and use of black slaves. The motivation had little to do with morals or liberty, and everything to do with Great Britain's desire to farm out white indentured servants to the New World. By 1750, due to pressure from plantation owners who preferred African slaves, the trustees of Georgia had repealed the prohibition on slavery and things were back to business as usual.

The first state to permanently abolish slavery was Vermont, in 1777.

 ## A Real Foul Ball

It was the top of the fifth inning, August 16, 1920, when shortstop Ray Chapman took to the plate for the Cleveland Indians in a game against the New York Yankees. On the pitcher's mound was Carl Mays. Mays was a notorious spitball pitcher, meaning he purposefully dirtied up the baseball to make it fly irregularly and harder to hit. Spitballing was still allowed at the time, but that was about to change. Mays lobbed a fast pitch to Chapman, beaning him in the head. Chapman died in the hospital twelve hours later, making him the only person in Major League Baseball history to die from an injury sustained at bat.

In the aftermath of Chapman's death the league created a new rule that required umpires to replace the ball whenever it became dirty or otherwise altered. Oddly, batting helmets were not introduced for another three decades.

A Sleepy Defense

Albert Tirrell was the son of a respectable family in Weymouth, Massachusetts, who became notably unrespectable in 1845 when he left his wife and two children to take up with a Boston prostitute he'd fallen in love with. His new soul mate was named Maria Bickford and it supposedly bothered Tirrell that, even after he left his wife, Bickford continued hooking. This may explain why later in the year Tirrell nearly decapitated Bickford with a razor and then tried to burn down her brothel before fleeing the state. Since numerous people witnessed Tirrell entering and exiting the brothel, he was tracked down and arrested.

Tirrell's wealthy parents hired Boston attorney Rufus Choate, who had a reputation for inventive defense strategies. And he came up with a doozy for this one. Choate argued that on the night of the murder Tirrell had been gripped by the madness of…sleepwalking. Remarkably, the jury bought it and Tirrell was acquitted. This was the first time that sleepwalking had ever been successfully used as a defense for murder.

Rollin', Rollin'

The phrase "keep the ball rolling" sprang from the 1840 presidential campaign of William Henry Harrison. Harrison's campaign also gave us one of the best remembered political slogans in US history: "Tippecanoe and Tyler Too," a reference to Harrison's 1811 victory over the Shawnee Indians at the Battle of Tippecanoe and his running mate John Tyler. Harrison's campaign also utilized a bizarre novelty stunt known as a "victory ball," which was a massive ten-foot sphere made of tin and leather, plastered in Harrison's slogans. Supporters were invited to "keep the ball rolling," literally pushing the ball from one town to the next. And the saying kept on rolling too.

According to hospital records, around 5,600 workers DIED from diseases and accidents during the United States' construction of the PANAMA CANAL. Upward of twenty-two thousand may have died during the prior French construction period.

PLANNING AHEAD

Benjamin Franklin loved to write humorous and satirical verses. In 1728, at the age of twenty-two, he composed his own mock epitaph, which read:

> *The Body of*
> *B. Franklin*
> *Printer;*
> *Like the Cover of an old Book,*
> *Its Contents torn out,*
> *And stript of its Lettering and Gilding,*
> *Lies here, Food for Worms.*
> *But the Work shall not be whlly lost:*
> *For it will, as he believ'd, appear once more,*
> *In a new & more elegant Edition,*
> *Corrected and Amended*
> *By the Author.*
> *He was born on January 6, 1706.*

When he died in 1790 at the age of eighty-four, his true epitaph simply read:

Benjamin and Deborah Franklin: 1790

ARCHAIC NASCAR

The first automobile race in the United States revved into the history books on Thanksgiving Day in 1895. It was sponsored by the *Chicago Times-Herald* and ran from Chicago to nearby Evanston, Illinois, and back. Humorously, the race's initial date had been postponed after several of the drivers were unable to bring their vehicles into the city. At the time it was illegal to use an automobile on city streets, and the owners were ironically instructed that they would have to tow their horseless carriages behind actual horses. But with some finagling the Times-Herald was able to get special permission for the vehicles.

Only six automobiles participated in the race—three of the cars were creations of Karl Benz, the man later behind Mercedes-Benz. But it was Charles Duryea's Motorized Wagon that ultimately won the race, completing it with a time of seven hours and fifty-three minutes, a dazzling average speed of 7 miles per hour!

 ## LABOR DAY

In the summer of 1894, the workers of the Pullman Palace Car Company in Chicago went on strike after their wages were cut by 25 percent (the cut was a response to the economic panic of 1893). When the strike persisted, shutting down rail traffic, President Grover Cleveland sent in the army to break things up, using the excuse that the strikers were obstructing the US mail and thus affecting public safety. Things did not go well, and several strikers died. Mere days later, looking to appease laborers, the Cleveland administration pushed legislation through Congress making the first Monday of every September a national holiday—Labor Day.

NOTABLE NOBELS

Barack Obama received the Nobel Peace Prize in 2009 for "extraordinary efforts to strengthen international diplomacy and cooperation between peoples," making him only the third acting president to become a Nobel laureate. The first was Theodore Roosevelt, who won in 1905 for helping end the Russo-Japanese War. Woodrow Wilson was the second, winning in 1919 for his sponsorship of the League of Nations. Jimmy Cater won in 2002, while out of office, for his humanitarian efforts.

Al Gore is the only vice president with a Nobel Prize, winning in 2007 for his efforts to reduce global warming and his promotion of stricter environmental standards. Despite a common misconception, Al Gore did not win an Academy Award for the 2006 documentary *An Inconvenient Truth* (in which he starred). The film's director, Davis Guggenheim, received the award.

HAVE NICE DAY

The smiley face is one of the paragons of twentieth-century graphic design. The utter simplicity of the image makes it hard to pinpoint its first usage, but the birth of the classic smiley as we know it—with the yellow background—occurred in the lethargic span of ten minutes in 1963, when a commercial artist named Harvey Ball was paid $45 to design something to boost the morale of the evidently glum State Mutual Life Assurance employees in Worcester, Massachusetts. Ball surely had no idea that his slapdash design would become one of the most recognizable images in the Western world.

Over the next decade the image was repurposed for a variety uses, until two industrious brothers from Philadelphia named Bernard and Murray Spain saw the true potential of ol' smiley—novelty products! T-shirts, bumper stickers, coffee mugs, etc. It was here that smiley was paired with his most recurrent partner, the catchphrase "Have a Nice Day." Soon millions of smiley buttons were flooding the market. And soon smiley would become an ironic symbol of the decaying American dream in the post-Nixon era. But smiley survived the '70s and '80s and lives on, smiling away.

RICH MAN'S WAR, POOR MAN'S FIGHT

When the Civil War kicked off, the Union and the Confederacy had little trouble stocking their armies. The venomous hostility that had built up in the years preceding the war had left everyone full of piss and vinegar. Men were practically chomping at the bit to assist the war effort. But as the battles raged on, both armies ran into a quandary: the men who wanted to serve were already doing so, and those who had been reluctant or had outright refused to serve weren't exactly changing their minds once the shocking casualty reports started coming in. Plus, many of the original volunteers were now dead, had deserted, or simply declined to reenlist.

In March of 1863, the United States Congress passed The Enrollment Act, also known as the Civil War Military Draft Act. Drafts are never popular, but it was a specific proviso in the Enrollment Act that ruffled the most feathers. Any man who was drafted was given two options for opting out of service: 1) he could pay $300 (around $5,000 now), or 2) he could provide a suitable substitute to take his place, which generally required a sizable amount of cash too. Working-class citizens felt that these were clearly loopholes created to protect the wealthy, and a wave of public resentment swept the Union. Similar practices already existed for the Confederate army—protestors in both the North and the South used the slogan, "rich man's war, poor man's fight"—but the Union's lower class weren't as willing to take things in stride.

On July 13, discontent members of the working class took to the streets of New York City to protest the draft. But things quickly got out of hand and turned into a full-scale, three-day riot. The New York City police force was not large enough to contain the chaos, forcing President Lincoln to divert several regiments of militia away from the war to quash a civil rebellion happening inside Union borders. Further deepening the sad irony here, rioters attacked dozens of African Americans, burnt the homes of white abolitionists, and even destroyed an asylum for black orphans, all out of displaced anger or sympathies for the Confederate cause. Not counting the Civil War itself, the New York City draft riots remain the largest civil insurrection in United States history. No exact figures were ever tallied, but the riot death toll has been placed at anywhere between one hundred and two thousand fatalities.

Future president Grover Cleveland paid a substitute $150 to take his place in the war, something his opponents tried and failed to use against him in the 1884 election.

Lincoln Chooses Swords

Abraham Lincoln wasn't known for being a quarrelsome man, but he did participate in one duel. In 1842, the *Sangamo Journal* of Springfield, Illinois, began publishing a series of anonymous letters satirizing and otherwise besmirching state auditor James Shields. Though several individuals were likely responsible for the letters, Lincoln wound up receiving all the blame. So Shields challenged Lincoln to a duel.

Dueling was illegal in Illinois, but as the challenge had become publicly known, Lincoln decided he should accept. But Lincoln had no intention of trying to kill Shields, and certainly had no intention of risking Shields killing him. And since it was Lincoln's privilege as the challenged party

to select the means of dueling, Lincoln got playful. He chose cavalry broad swords. Armed with pistols, Lincoln had no advantage. But at 6 feet 4 inches and of gangly proportions, Lincoln knew that his reach almost comically exceeded that of Shields. This became quite apparent to Shields as well when the two men faced off on September 22 along the Mississippi River. After witnessing the towering Lincoln cut a rather high branch from a tree while loosening up, Shields called for peace before a single blow had been struck. Lincoln happily welcomed a truce.

 ## BULLETPROOF PADRE

On October 28, 1893, a Chicago priest named Casimir Zeglen learned that his mayor, Carter Harrison, had just been shot and killed. Zeglen then became consumed with the idea of creating an article of clothing sturdy enough to withstand a bullet. He constructed a vest made of thin steel plating pressed between tightly woven silk. He first tested his vest on a corpse. Then on a dog. Then—in front of a terrified crowd—on himself. It worked every time. Father Zeglen had created the first practical bulletproof vest. Zeglen left the church to found Zeglen Bullet Proof Cloth Company and set out to save the human targets of the world. Supposedly Zeglen, in an attempt to promote his vest, offered one to President William McKinley. The White House professed interest, but said the matter would have to wait until the president had returned from the Pan-American Exposition in Buffalo, New York. McKinley was shot in the chest and killed by an assassin at the exposition.

 ## A CHANGE OF WIND

The windmill was a valuable farming machine in Europe, generally used for grinding grain into meal and flour. Typically designed with four huge blades, they were large, expensive to build, and required skilled maintenance. So they weren't really an option for most American farmers venturing out into the western frontier in the nineteenth century. That is, until Daniel Halladay changed things up in 1854 when he introduced an innovative new design. Halladay's wind turbine was small, forgoing the classic four long blades in favor of a tight wheel of numerous thin wooden blades that could pivot in order to regulate wheel speed. Halladay's design was also self-governing, automatically turning to face changing wind directions. Halladay used his design to create the windpump, which could draw water from a ground well to be stored in a nearby tankhouse.

When he opened his factory in Batavia, Illinois, business exploded as every farmer and rancher on the prairie snatched one up. By the twentieth century the windpump, with its multi-bladed wind turbine perched atop a lattice tower, had become a familiar fixture of the landscape throughout rural America.

A TWAIN BY ANY OTHER NAME

Samuel Clemens is better known by his pen name, Mark Twain. Previously, Clemens had signed some of his humorous writings as "Josh" or "Thomas Jefferson Snodgrass" before finally settling on his favored nom de plume. In typical Twain fashion, the name itself is a pun taken from the vocabulary of Mississippi riverboatmen. "Twain" is an archaic term for "two," and "mark" referred to a step on the measuring line. So riverboatmen would shout "mark twain" as shorthand to indicate that the river's depth was two fathoms (or 12 feet), a safe depth for boat passage. But as Mark Twain told the story, he was not the man who came up with the jokey pen name. In his memoir, *Life on the Mississippi*, he related the origin of the name as such:

> *"Captain Isaiah Sellers was not of literary turn or capacity, but he used to jot down brief paragraphs of plain practical information about the river, and sign*

them 'MARK TWAIN,' and give them to the New
Orleans Picayune. They related to the stage and condition
of the river, and were accurate and valuable....At the
time that the telegraph brought the news of his death, I
was on the Pacific coast. I was a fresh new journalist,
and needed a nom de guerre; so I confiscated the ancient
mariner's discarded one, and have done my best to make
it remain what it was in his hands—a sign and symbol
and warrant that whatever is found in its company may
be gambled on as being the petrified truth; how I have
succeeded, it would not be modest in me to say."

Harry S. Truman's middle INITIAL does
not stand for anything. His mother chose
"S" to HONOR Harry's two grandfathers,
Shipp Truman and Solomon Young,
without playing favorites.

MALAISE FOREVER!

Jimmy Carter is widely regarded as one of the most active
and engaged ex-presidents, having won a Nobel Prize for
his post-presidency humanitarian efforts. But his presidency was plagued by the perception that he was a lame
duck. Carter's advisers convinced him that he needed to
display decisive leadership and start acting "tougher" in
the lead-up to the 1980 presidential election. So when the
Soviet Union invaded Afghanistan in December of 1979,
Carter decided to make a stand.

On January 20, 1980, Carter delivered an ultimatum—if
Soviet forces didn't withdraw from Afghanistan, the United
States would boycott the 1980 Moscow Olympic Games.

It was a bold move that drew support from foreign governments and most of the US population. The only problem was it didn't gain the support of the people it most needed to—the athletes. While Carter was able to influence the US Olympic Committee, he was dismayed to see that the Olympic Committees of our allies were not falling in line. As independent organizations, many foreign committees refused to participate in the boycott, even if their government supported the idea. Carter's boycott failed to ruin the Moscow games, and came to be viewed as a petty diplomatic tactic. Carter lost the 1980 election to Ronald Reagan.

ON A SHOOTING STAR

Author Mark Twain was born in 1835, the same year that Halley's Comet passed through the sky. One of the more enduring tidbits from Twain's indelible persona was that he proclaimed he would leave this world when Halley's Comet returned in 1910, not unlike Babe Ruth pointing to which section of the stands he planned to hit his homerun. Twain's claim has endured because he was proven right, dying of a heart attack on April 21, 1910, one day after the comet's closest approach to Earth.

What is generally left out of this fun story is that Twain didn't make his bold claim early in life. He made it in 1909, when he already knew he was dying of heart disease. His full quote on the matter is maybe less impressively prescient, but it gives a more interesting perspective into Twain's mind:

> "I came in with Halley's Comet in 1835. It is coming again next year and I expect to go out with it. It will be the greatest disappointment of my life if I don't go out with Halley's Comet. The Almighty has said, no doubt: 'Now here are these two unaccountable freaks they came in together they must go out together.' Oh I am looking forward to that. I've got some kind of a heart disease and

Quintard [Twain's doctor] won't tell me whether it is the kind that carries a man off in an instant or keeps him lingering along and suffering for twenty years or so. I was in hopes that Quintard would tell me that I was likely to drop dead any minute but he didn't. He only told me that my blood pressure was too strong. He didn't give me any schedule but I expect to go with Halley's Comet."

THE ZIMMERMANN NOTE

During World War I, British authorities intercepted a coded telegram from Arthur Zimmermann, the German foreign secretary, to Count Johann von Bernstorff, the German ambassador to Mexico, stating that in the event of war with the United States, Mexico should ally itself with Germany. In return, Germany would restore Mexico's lost territories of Texas, New Mexico, and Arizona.

President Woodrow Wilson allowed the US State Department to publish the note in the press, which helped turn public opinion against Germany. On April 2, President Wilson, who had previously fought to keep America *out* of WWI, asked Congress to declare war on Germany. Four days later, Congress did.

SEMANTICS WAR

The United States has only declared war five times in its history, though this is a rather misleading statistic, since the nation has certainly fought in significantly more than five wars. This discrepancy exists because, when drafting the Constitution, the Founding Fathers chose to replace the phrase "make war" with "declare war," which would theoretically allow the president to use the military for special needs, such as a sudden attack (a plausible fear at that time), while still limiting the president's ability to wage full-on war without the explicit approval of Congress. Only Congress has the ability to make a formal Declaration of

War, which they did with the War of 1812, the Mexican-American War (1846), the Spanish-American War (1898), World War I (1917), and World War II (1941).

Through this wording loophole, the president can ask Congress to authorize military combat, even if it takes on the form of a war, which Congress did in the First and Second Barbary Wars. When the UN was formed after WWII, international laws changed the warfare world. Though what was meant to decrease combat really just changed the phrasing the government used. Since then America has not *declared* war. Formal wars have been replaced by "extended military engagements," either authorized by Congress or authorized by United Nations Security Council Resolutions and funded by appropriations from Congress. That is why some sticklers refer to the "Vietnam Conflict" and not the "Vietnam War."

Semantics aside, the United States' most extended military conflict never received any kind of classification whatsoever. The US Army waged a nearly ceaseless war against the Native American populations throughout the 1800s as the country expanded westward.

PRESIDENTIAL POLE POSITION

John F. Kennedy once said, "No one has a right to grade a President—even poor James Buchanan—who has not sat in his chair, examined the mail and information that came across his desk, and learned why he made his decisions." But that hasn't stopped anyone from doing so. In 1948, Harvard University historian Arthur M. Schlesinger Sr. conducted a famous survey of his fellow historians to see how all the presidents shook out. And that was just the beginning. Since then, from TV news networks, to newspapers, to magazines, to online polls, to Rasmussen Reports polls, to Gallup polls, ranking presidents has become a fun game to play (for those who find such things fun).

The grading of recent presidents is usually too subjective to be enlightening—as someone like Ronald Reagan may appear at the very top of one person's list, and at the very bottom of another's—but spread out over the entire history of the United States it is interesting to see which presidents Americans collectively revere or jeer. George Washington, Abraham Lincoln, Thomas Jefferson, Franklin D. Roosevelt, Theodore Roosevelt, Harry Truman, Woodrow Wilson, and Dwight D. Eisenhower consistently rank near the top as our greatest presidents, while Warren Harding, James Buchanan, Richard Nixon, Herbert Hoover, Andrew Johnson, Franklin Pierce, Ulysses S. Grant, and John Tyler routinely pad out the bottom of the barrel.

Despite his feelings on the matter, Kennedy would be pleased to know that he generally fares above average.

▤ PRESIDENT JOSEPH SMITH

Joseph Smith was not only the first Mormon (having founded the Church of Jesus Christ of Latter-Day Saints in 1830), but he was also the first Mormon to run for president of the United States. At the time, Mormons faced fierce persecution from other Christians. After a mob killed eighteen Mormons in Caldwell County, Missouri, in 1838, and were never prosecuted, Smith and his followers settled in Illinois. Smith bought the town of Commerce, renaming it Nauvoo, and serving as mayor. The town became one of the largest cities in Illinois, and Smith's militia matched the official state armed forces in size. Emboldened by his rising influence, Smith decided to run for president as a third-party candidate in the 1844 election. He sent a group of missionaries—including future Latter-Day Saints notable Brigham Young—to campaign in every state.

Smith's platform was liberal, calling for the abolition of slavery, the creation of a national bank, prison reform, and a pay cut for congressional members. Smith and the Mormons had already been unpopular in the communities in which they lived, but Smith's candidacy spread awareness of the religion around the country, which in turn spread the hate.

Former members of his community were also turning against him, viewing his run for the White House as megalomania. When the *Nauvoo Expositor* published a series of exposés impugning Smith, Smith sent several hundred men to destroy the newspaper's office. A warrant was issued for Smith's arrest, which prompted him to declare martial law in Nauvoo and call in his five thousand–strong militia. Now Smith was charged with treason. On June 25, Smith surrendered to Illinois authorities. Two days later a mob of two hundred men broke into the jail and shot Smith to death. Only five men where charged in the assassination, but none were found guilty.

▤ THE BUSINESS PLOT

In 1934, during the midst of the Great Depression and a year after Franklin D. Roosevelt had taken office, a retired Marine Corps general named Smedley Butler claimed that the representative of a cabal had covertly approached him. The cabal wanted Butler, a respected and popular military hero, to lead an army of five thousand veterans in a march on the White House.

The goal was to overthrow President Roosevelt and replace him with a secretary of general welfare. Butler claimed that he was told J. P. Morgan and other powerful Wall Street moneymen were financing the coup because they believed Roosevelt's New Deal was an attack on the American capitalistic spirit. The press lambasted Butler as the perpetrator of an outlandish hoax, but the House Un-American Activities Committee felt they had enough to go on to hold several closed-door hearings. While no indictments were ever issued against those implicated in the plot, the committee's final report ultimately supported and vindicated Butler's claims.

Fred Baur was an organic chemist and food storage technician who helped develop FREEZE-DRIED ice cream. But his crowning achievement was patenting the tubular PRINGLES container and the method for safely stacking the delectable chips within it. When Baur died in May 2008, his CREMATED ashes were buried inside a Pringles can, as per his wishes.

Which Day to Give Thanks

Days set aside for giving thanks had been sporadically celebrated by various presidents since George Washington. Sometimes the Thanksgiving Day was celebrated in September, October, or even December. James Madison held two Thanksgivings in 1815, neither in autumn. Thanksgiving Day didn't become an official national holiday until 1863, when Abraham Lincoln was looking for something to raise spirits during the Civil War. Lincoln positioned the new holiday on the last Thursday of November, where it remained until 1939.

November 1939 had five Thursdays (as opposed to the more common four), with the final day of the month falling on Thursday. American retailers, still fighting off the Great Depression, were upset that this calendar fluke was cutting short their much-needed annual Christmas shopping season, which typically stretches from the day after Thanksgiving to Christmas Eve. In August 1939, retailers appealed to President Franklin D. Roosevelt, and he agreed to move Thanksgiving up one week, to November 23. Retailers were happy, but calendar makers were aghast, as now all the calendars they sold the previous years were inaccurate. Football coaches, owners, and organizers were upset as well, as their big Thanksgiving Day games now came *after* Thanksgiving. Republicans called it an affront to Lincoln (Roosevelt was a Democrat), and began referring to November 30 as the Republican Thanksgiving and November 23 as Franksgiving. Twenty-three states celebrated Franksgiving, while twenty-two did not (wily Texas took both days off as holidays).

Even when November went back to having four Thursdays in 1940 and 1941, Roosevelt again implemented his next-to-last policy. Congress had apparently had enough tomfoolery on the matter, and passed a joint resolution fixing Thanksgiving Day to its traditional last-Thursday date. Though they also passed an amendment stating that in the case of rare five-Thursday Novembers, Thanksgiving would fall on the fourth Thursday.

 ## A MODEL PRESIDENT

If you asked people who was the handsomest American president, most would likely say John F. Kennedy or Barack Obama, or possibly young Ronald Reagan. Few, if any, would name Gerald Ford. Yet Ford was quite dashing as a young man, earning money as a male model and once appearing on the April 1942 cover of Cosmopolitan. Ford had gotten into the business while dating New York model Phyllis Brown, who initially talked her handsome boyfriend into joining her for a spread in Look *magazine. Ford even became a silent partner in the Conover Modeling Agency, founded and run by a modeling friend named Harry Conover. But Ford and Brown eventually broke up and Ford went into politics, leaving his glamorous (and handsome) days behind him.*

🇺🇸 A LUCKY LENGTH OF ROPE

One fateful day, as a ferocious storm pummeled the *May-flower* on its perilous trip to the New World, passenger John Howland was knocked from the ship into the turbulent sea. By the most implausible luck, Howland managed to grab a length of rope that was trailing behind the ship. As he clung for dear life, he was pulled safely, if a bit sickly, back onto the ship. Howland survived the incident, going on to marry fellow passenger Elizabeth Tilley and fathering ten children. Had he died, his eighty-two grandchildren never would have been born. Neither would any of his descendants, including Presidents Franklin D. Roosevelt, George H. W. Bush, and George W. Bush.

Famously liberal actor Alec Baldwin would likely prefer that neither of the Bushes had been born, though he shouldn't be too quick to curse that lucky length of rope—he too is a descendant of Howland.

MUST BE SOMETHING IN THE WATER

Of all the countries that can lay claim to the top ten human beings ever verifiably recorded, only the United States can claim more than one. Not only that, the top three are all American. In total, five of the top ten tallest people to place in the record books are American. Robert Wadlow (1918–1940) from Illinois is the tallest person in recorded history, once standing at 8 feet 11 inches. Second place goes to John Rogan (1868–1905) who stood at 8 feet 9 inches. Third place goes to John F. Carroll (1932–1969), who stood at 8 feet 7 inches. Conversely, America only claims one spot on the list of the top ten shortest people in recorded history, with 2 foot 3 inch Bridgette Jordan (born 1989) as the lone American.

Predictably, America claims nine out of ten on the list of history's heaviest humans.

A CRAPPY BELL

The Liberty Bell, with its large and prominent crack, is one of the most celebrated symbols of American independence. Which is an unlikely legacy for what is technically a shitty bell that played no significant role during the Revolution. The bell was commissioned in 1752 to hang in the Pennsylvania State House (now known as Independence Hall). It was made in London by the respected Whitechapel Bell Foundry, a company that still exists, but apparently they were off their game when forging ol' Liberty. During its first sound check in America, the bell cracked. Philadelphia authorities tried to return it to Whitechapel, but the ship that had carried the bell from London was unable to retake it on board. So Philadelphia recast the bell themselves. They fixed the crack, but the sound the bell produced was awful. So they had it recast yet again. The sound was slightly better this time, but the crack eventually reappeared (the earliest written record of the new crack is from 1846).

The Liberty Bell was not held with any notable esteem until 1847, when it was utilized in a story written by George Lippard for *Saturday Review* magazine. The story, "Fourth of July, 1776," featured an old bellman waiting to learn if the Continental Congress would declare independence. When the man's grandson arrives with the good news, the old man lets the bell ring. Lippard's story proved extremely popular, and through the telephone game of time the fiction was eventually taught as a true story. But no bells were rung in the State House on July 4 of 1776. Philadelphia did hold a special ceremony to celebrate the Declaration of Independence on July 8, at which time numerous bells were rung.

THE GREEN RIVER KILLER

When people think of the most horrific serial killers in American history, the names of Jeffrey Dahmer or Ted Bundy or John Wayne Gacy tend to come up. Nicknames like Son of Sam or The Zodiac Killer or The Boston Strangler come to mind as well. Rarely does the name Gary Ridgway ring any bells, which is probably a good thing—America's "most prolific serial killer" isn't exactly something that deserves to be in public school textbooks.

Gary Ridgway, who worked in a factory painting trucks, was arrested in 2001 and charged with killing over ninety women between 1982 and 1993 after DNA analysis finally gave authorities the evidence they needed to apprehend him. Ridgway almost exclusively killed prostitutes and runaways, soliciting them, then strangling them and dumping the bodies in the wooded areas around the Green River in Washington State—which earned him the nickname The Green River Killer in the press. Ridgway said he eventually lost count of how many victims he claimed, confessing to seventy-one. He was convicted of killing forty-eight. He was paid to paint trucks, but Ridgway felt that murdering young women was his "career."

Ridgway was spared the death penalty in exchange for cooperation in locating the remains of victims. He is currently incarcerated at Washington State Penitentiary in Walla Walla.

▰ OUR SURLIEST PRESIDENT

Seventh president of the United States, and face of the twenty-dollar bill, Andrew Jackson earned the nickname "Old Hickory" for being tough as old hickory wood on the battlefield. And he was just as tough off the battlefield. In 1806, when fellow plantation owner Charles Dickinson published an article in the paper calling Jackson a "worthless scoundrel," Jackson challenged Dickinson to a duel without delay. Dickinson shot Jackson in the ribs, and then Jackson calmly killed Dickinson. The bullet in Jackson's ribs was too close to his heart to ever be removed. In fact, Jackson sustained so many injuries from his frequent duels and altercations that it was said he "rattled like a bag of marbles."

Jackson's abrasive and quarrelsome nature extended into his presidency too, and earned him two very fitting statistics—Jackson is both the first president to ever be physically attacked while in office (by Robert B. Randolph, whom Jackson had dismissed from the navy for embezzlement) and the first president that anyone tried to assassinate. On January 30, 1835 Richard Lawrence, an unemployed housepainter, pulled out a pistol and fired it at Jackson while the president was leaving the United States Capitol. The gun misfired, so Lawrence pulled out a backup pistol. It also misfired. Legend says Jackson then attacked Lawrence with his cane, savaging the man.

On his last day in office, Jackson was asked if he had any regrets from his presidency. Jackson replied that he had two: that he had been unable to shoot Henry Clay or to hang John Calhoun. Clay had been instrumental in Jackson's loss of the 1824 presidential election, which made John Quincy Adams president. Calhoun had been vice president during Jackson's first term.

★★★★★★★★★★★★★★★★

Richard Nixon is the only president to ever RESIGN the office. He is also the only person to have been ELECTED twice as both vice president and president.

★★★★★★★★★★★★★★★★

WHEN ANIMALS ATTACK

Statistically speaking, the only wild animal that Americans should be at all fearful of is the bee. Roughly fifty people die every year because of bee sting allergies, which is twice as many as all other venomous animal fatalities combined. The reality is that wild animals pose almost no dangers to Americans. Just as you're far more likely to be murdered by someone you know than by a stranger, you're far more likely to be kicked by a horse or bitten by a dog than you are to be attacked by a mountain lion or a shark. Out of the over three hundred million people living in the United States, probably only one person will be attacked by a mountain lion in a given year. And they probably won't die. Of course, that's because most people aren't strolling through mountain lion territory as part of their daily routine. When you increase the proximity between humans and dangerous animals, the attacks and the fatalities become more frequent. Such as in Florida…

Florida has a population of nineteen million humans. It also has a population of one million alligators. In the twentieth century, alligator attacks were incredibly rare, because the alligator had been hunted to near extinction. But a concerted effort on the part of conservationists during the 1970s and 1980s saw the species bounce back with an unexpected verve, and in 1987 the American alligator was removed from the endangered species list.

As the human and alligator populations in Florida continued to grow healthily and the alligator's habitat was rapidly being depleted, attacks on humans started becoming more frequent. Between 1970 and 2000 there were only nine fatal alligator attacks. Since 2001 there have been twelve. In May 2006, alligators killed three different people…*in one week!* While alligator attacks can still be considered statistically rare compared to drunk driving fatalities or muggings, the modern Floridian can be excused if they think twice about approaching the edge of a river.

He Ain't Heavy, He's My Idiot Brother

When Georgia's Jimmy Carter won the 1976 presidential election, he became the first candidate from the Deep South to take the office since Louisiana's Zachary Taylor won in 1848. Carter's Southern image was not helped much by his beer-swilling brother Billy, who proudly flaunted his drunken good ol' boy shenanigans for all to see.

In 1977, Billy endorsed an infamously terrible brand of beer named in his honor: Billy Beer. And he once urinated on an airport tarmac as press and important politicos looked on. But a far more embarrassing incident for Jimmy came in 1978 when Billy took several trips to Libya and supposedly received a loan worth over $200,000 from the Libyan government. Dubbed "Billygate" by the press, a Senate subcommittee was formed in 1980 to investigate whether the Carter administration had any connection to Billy's activities. Nothing was uncovered. And Billy kept on being Billy.

During his presidency, Ulysses S. Grant was issued a $20 SPEEDING ticket in Washington, D.C.,…for riding his HORSE too fast.

Lo and Behold!

In school, children are often taught historic first messages. We're taught that Samuel Morse's first message over the telegraph was, "What hath God wrought?" That Alexander Graham Bell's first words over the telephone were, "Mr. Watson, come here, I want to see you." That Neil Armstrong's first words to Mission Control from the Moon were, "The *Eagle* has landed." But what about the Internet? The Internet is one the most history-changing innovations, if not *the* most history-changing innovation in modern history. So what was the first message on the 'Net, and who sent it?

What we now call the Internet began in the 1960s as ARPANET (Advanced Research Projects Agency Network), a rudimentary computer network commissioned by the US Department of Defense. ARPANET's first connection was between UCLA's SDS Sigma 7, installed by Professor Leonard Kleinrock, and the Stanford Research Institute's SDS 940. The first message across ARPANET occurred on October 29, 1969. Kleinrock was supervising his student/programmer Charley Kline as Kline prepared to send a message from the SDS Sigma 7 to Bill Duvall at the SDS 940. Kline attempted to send the word "login," and managed to get the "l" and "o" out before the system crashed. The timing of the failure amused Kleinrock, as he took "lo" to be symbolic of "lo and behold!" They tried again later and successfully sent "login."

"Lo" may be an unexciting first message, but three decades later, when the World Wide Web changed the way Americans communicated, learned, and lived, Kleinrock's imagined declaration of "lo and behold" seems rather apt.

CULTURE SHOCK

John Parker was a veteran of the American Revolution and a Texas Ranger known for his experience negotiating with Native Americans. Which is exactly why he was recruited to establish a fortified settlement in Texas to curb the Comanche raids that had been impeding the safe colonization of the territory for years. But Parker was not prepared for the ferocity of the Comanche. In May 1836, a force of Comanche warriors attacked Fort Parker, quickly overpowering the defenders. Some settlers were able to escape, but many were captured, including Parker and his nine-year-old granddaughter, Cynthia Ann Parker. Cynthia watched as John Parker was castrated and his genitals were stuffed into his mouth before he was scalped and finally killed. Cynthia was then spirited away by the Comanche.

Cynthia's father Silas Parker would spend the next twenty-four years searching for his lost child. In December 1860, a group of Texas Rangers finally found her. But she was no longer Cynthia Parker. She had been adopted by a Comanche couple and later married chieftain Peta Nocona, bearing his three children. She now spoke only broken English, but enough to confirm that she indeed used to be Cynthia Ann Parker. The Rangers executed the man they believed to be Nocona (though there is debate on whether they had the right guy), and took Cynthia back to the white man's world with her two-year-old daughter. Cynthia's return was a media sensation, which only compounded her feelings of alienation. She may have looked white, but she never grew at ease in white society. Unable to see her two sons, when her daughter died of influenza in 1864, Cynthia gave up on the world, later starving herself to death.

Her son, Quanah Parker, would be the last free Comanche chief, and became something of a celebrity himself after the Comanche moved onto a reservation in 1875. Quanah grew to be rather wealthy, counted President Theodore Roosevelt as a friend, and was the father of twenty-five children with his multiple wives.

★★★★★★★★★★★★★★★★★★

Little Women author Louisa May Alcott served as a nurse during the CIVIL WAR.

★★★★★★★★★★★★★★★★★★

OPERATION PANDORA'S BOX

Samuel Byck, an unemployed former tire salesman, first came to the Secret Service's attention in 1972 after he was arrested for protesting outside the White House without a permit and for making threatening comments regarding President Richard Nixon. Byck believed that the Nixon administration was conspiring to oppress the poor, like him. But upon questioning Byck, the Secret Service determined that he was harmless. They were quite mistaken.

In 1974, after his life had failed to turn around, which he continued to believe was due to the policies of Richard Nixon, Byck put into motion a high-concept assassination scheme he called Operation Pandora's Box. He planned to assassinate Nixon by hijacking an airliner and crashing it into the White House. Byck stole a revolver from a friend, and on February 22 he drove to the Baltimore/Washington, D.C., International Airport. He shot and killed an Aviation Administration police officer in the process of storming Delta Airlines Flight 523 as it was preparing to taxi for takeoff. When the pilot and copilot refused Byke's orders to proceed with takeoff, he shot them both, then ordered a random passenger to try to fly the plane. Needless to say, this plan didn't get him very far. Local police soon surrounded the plane, and Byck was wounded in the subsequent shootout. When police boarded the plane, Byck shot himself in the head.

While planning Operation Pandora's Box, Byck made several recordings detailing his plot and his reasoning for plotting. In one of the tapes he said, "It's very unfortunate that a good, wholesome guy like me has to kill himself or get killed to make a point.…One man's terrorist is another man's patriot.…It all depends on which side of the fence you happen to be on at the time."

The Dude Would Approve

President Richard Nixon was an avid bowler. In 1969, he had a bowling lane installed in the White House basement where he would unwind in solitude at night. His average score was 152, and his highest ever score was 232.

Code of the Secret Service

In 1939, when Jerry Parr was nine years old, he saw a movie called *Code of the Secret Service*. So taken with the film was Parr that he begged his father to take him again. Then again. Then again. Parr decided right then and there that he wanted to grow up to be a Secret Service agent, bravely protecting the president. In 1962 he joined the service, working his way up through the ranks. He protected foreign dignitaries, then heads of state, then the vice president, and then in 1979 he found himself protecting President Jimmy Carter.

In 1981, Parr finally had his movie moment, when John Hinckley Jr. opened fire on newly elected President Ronald Reagan. Parr did his duty, braving the bullets and pushing Reagan into the president's limousine. It was Parr who noticed that Reagan had been hit and ordered the limousine to go to the hospital, saving the president's life, just like his hero Brass Bancroft from *Code of the Secret Service* would have done. The actor who played Brass Bancroft? A popular leading man of the time named Ronald Reagan.

 ## Talk About Getting Singled Out

Georgia's Andersonville prison was used as a Confederate prisoner-of-war camp during the Civil War and was the site of one of the most controversial horrors of the conflict. Of the forty-five thousand Union prisoners held at

Andersonville, around twelve thousand died from starvation, malnutrition, disease, diarrhea, and alleged abuse at the hands of the guards.

Understaffed and under-stocked with provisions, the camp descended into hell during the summer of 1864. The water supply became polluted by its proximity to so many men and the prisoners began turning on each other in their desperation. A group calling themselves the Andersonville Raiders stole food and clothing from their fellow inmates, often killing their victims. So another group calling themselves the Regulators rose up to stop and punish the Raiders. And all the while the soldiers were withering down to mere skeletons. Ironically, the problems were partially caused by Union blockades that cut off Confederate supplies.

Out of options, Captain Henry Wirz, commander of Andersonville, temporarily paroled five Union soldiers to deliver a petition to Union forces asking that the Union reinstate prisoner exchanges. But the request was denied. This did nothing to improve Wirz's image with his prisoners though. Wirz was a strict disciplinarian and was said to brandish his pistol, threatening new prisoners as they arrived. Some former captives later claimed that Wirz killed several prisoners personally (though this is disputed). One might say that Wirz was just doing his job, but the Union didn't see it that way. When the war ended Wirz was arrested and put on trial for war crimes. On November 10, 1865, he was executed by hanging. This may not seem so noteworthy, but Wirz was the only Confederate service member executed for war crimes. The only one.

A man named Champ Ferguson was also tried and executed for his actions during the war, but Ferguson wasn't a soldier. Ferguson willingly admitted to killing over one hundred Union soldiers and pro-Union civilians as part of his guerrilla activities.

An Eye for Boxing

President Theodore Roosevelt had been an avid boxer in his youth. When he became president he decided to take it up again to stay in shape, but it proved a short-lived exercise routine. He later explained to the press: "When I was president I used to box with one of my aids, a young captain in the artillery. One day he cross-countered me and broke a blood vessel in my left eye. I don't know whether this is known, but I never have been able to see out of that eye since. I thought, as only one good eye was left me, I would not box any longer."

 ## Great Uncle Emperor

Charles Joseph Bonaparte was born in Maryland in 1851. He became a lawyer and political activist and was appointed secretary of the navy by President Theodore Roosevelt. After becoming attorney general in 1906, Bonaparte created the Bureau of Investigation, which later became the FBI. He was also the great-nephew of Emperor Napoleon Bonaparte—Charles's grandfather was Jérôme Bonaparte, Napoleon's youngest brother.

Anti-Masturbation Crackers

Reverend Sylvester Graham was a Presbyterian minister and a dietary advocate who developed a zealous group of followers that adhered to his Graham Diet. Graham preached vegetarianism, believing that an unhealthy diet caused excessive sexual desire, which in turn irritated the body and spread disease. Alcohol was a no-no, as were spicy foods; dairy was lightly permitted and butter was to be used only sparingly. Bland foods—the blander the better—were the cornerstone of good health and helped curb harmful sexual desires. Graham thought that masturbation was particularly dangerous, confident that it could lead to blindness. To help combat the cruel ravages of jerking off among young males, Graham set out to create the perfect boner-killing food.

In 1829, Graham introduced his wonderfully insipid creation: the graham cracker. The graham cracker as we know it today is generally sweetened with sugar, honey, or cinnamon to make it, well, to make it something anyone would actually want to eat. It is a popular snack for children and makes appearances at campfires around the country (being a key ingredient in s'mores). But this would have sent Reverend Graham into a tizzy. Graham's original cracker was a dream of sheer blandness. Graham failed to kill adolescent masturbation with his cracker, but he did inspire another dietary advocate, Dr. John Harvey Kellogg, who would later create his own addition to the popular bland food market: corn flakes cereal.

I CANNOT TELL A LIE

In 1800, the year after George Washington's death, a preacher and bookseller named Parson Weems published *A History of the Life and Death, Virtues and Exploits of General George Washington*. In the book Weems relates a story supposedly told to him by an elderly cousin of Washington, in which a six-year-old George chops down his father's cherry tree with a hatchet. When asked about the tree, George confesses, saying, "I can't tell a lie." Though the story was wholly untrue, America's love of George Washington was at a fever pitch following his death and the tale fit perfectly into the lionization already underway—as did Weems's fictional account of Washington saying a prayer at Valley Forge.

Weems's book was more fable than biography, but it provided a morally instructive story for America's children, turning George Washington into something more than a mere military commander or president. Children are still told the tale of the cherry tree, making it distinctly possible that this bit of fiction is the most widely known detail from Washington's life.

When Albert EINSTEIN died April 18, 1955, in Princeton, New Jersey, his final words died with him. Why? Because despite being an American citizen, the father of modern PHYSICS uttered his last words in his native GERMAN tongue—which his nurse could not speak or understand.

57 VARIETIES

Henry J. Heinz, founder of H. J. Heinz Company, was riding an elevated train through New York City in 1896 when he saw an ad for a women's shoe store boasting "21 styles." Heinz was taken with the gimmick, and decided to apply it to his own company. Presumably that shoe store actually had twenty-one different styles of shoe, but Heinz was only concerned with the symbolic quality of the boast, not its accuracy. His company made over sixty products, but five was Heinz's lucky number, so he knew that his boast should be somewhere in the fifties. He selected seven because of its powerful psychological status as a lucky number. Thusly, the Heinz Company's famous "57 Varieties" slogan was born. The upside to the number's utter randomness? It hasn't had to change in over a hundred years, regardless of how many varieties of products Heinz makes.

The first product that Heinz slapped with the 57 Varieties label wasn't ketchup, but horseradish.

THE CAMEL CORPS

After the Mexican-American War (1846–1848), newly appointed secretary of war, and future president of the Confederacy, Jefferson Davis became convinced that horses were not the optimal animals to use in the arid desert regions of the Southwest. He had a better idea: *camels*! Congress backed his scheme, and in 1856 a couple dozen camels were procured from Turkey and shipped to Camp Verde, Texas. At first the Camel Corps were proving the success that Davis had envisioned. The animals were strong and able to move briskly across terrain that horses found arduous. And best of all, they could go incredibly long periods of time without water. But they also had their drawbacks. Camels can be aggressively stubborn, and Camp Verde's horses and mules never got used to being around them. When the Civil War broke out, the Camel Corps was dissolved. Some of the camels were sold off, while a good number of them escaped or were allowed to escape. Sightings of feral camels roaming the Texan desert were reported up to the turn of the twentieth century.

 # HOLLYWOOD SUICIDE

Sadly, suicide is not uncommon among the fragile egos, volatile personalities, and cutthroat politics of the entertainment industry. From Kurt Cobain to Sylvia Plath to Margaux Hemingway to Alan Ladd, suicide is a familiar yet dark aspect of the creative pursuit. But the most symbolically dramatic suicide in arts and entertainment history surely belongs to Peg Entwistle.

Entwistle was born in 1908 and found modest success acting on the stage. Like so many before and after her, she was lured to Los Angeles by Hollywood dreams. She made her first and only film in 1932, in David O. Selznick's Thirteen Women *starring Myrna Loy and Irene Dunne. But before the film was released, Entwistle lapsed into a serious depression caused by financial and personal woes. On September 16,*

she wrote a suicide note, tucked it into her purse, then told her uncle she was going to the drugstore. Instead she hiked up to the Hollywoodland sign (the "land" was removed in 1949), climbed to the top of the H, and jumped to her death.

One of the contributing factors to Entwistle's depression had been the outcome of her marriage to actor Robert Keith. She had been granted a divorce from Keith in 1929 on the grounds of cruelty and deception. Keith had a six-year-old son named Brian from a former marriage, two details that Entwistle had been unaware of when they wed. That secret son was Brian Keith, who would grow up to have a successful acting career, starring as the lead in the popular 1960s TV series Family Affair *and Disney's classic film* The Parent Trap. *In 1997, at the age of seventy-five, Keith took his own life too.*

How Awkward

World War I was the first large-scale war between industrialized countries, and its modernized carnage had a profound impact on the generation that survived its horrors. There was a sense that something had broken in the world, that a line had been crossed, that war—as bad as it always was—had just become unacceptably worse. This earned WWI the nickname "the war to end all wars," which proved laughably inaccurate.

But at the time, the international community felt like something needed to be done to prevent such a conflict from ever arising again. Even while the war was still blasting away, a number of world leaders began scheming on solutions. President Woodrow Wilson and his adviser Colonel Edward M. House were into the idea of an association of world powers that would collectively act as a peacekeeping mechanism. The idea was the centerpiece of Wilson's 1918 "Fourteen Points" speech, and he campaigned tirelessly to drum up support for the idea. For his efforts he was awarded the Nobel Peace Prize. In 1919, the Treaty of Versailles established the League of Nations, with forty-one nations joining the global covenant. America was not one of them. Despite all his effort, Wilson, a Democrat, was unable to win the support he needed from Republicans in the Senate.

The League of Nations was dissolved after World War II and replaced by the United Nations.

Martin VAN BUREN was the first president born a CITIZEN of the United States of America.

Murder Castle

Herman Webster Mudgett, better known by his alias Dr. H. H. Holmes, is often referred to as America's first serial killer. That is debatable, but he was certainly America's most inventive serial killer. In 1886, Holmes took a job at a drugstore in the Chicago suburb of Englewood. Holmes charmed the widow who owned the store into selling him her business, and then promptly killed her, telling people she had moved to California. In 1889, using funds from the drugstore, Holmes bought up property across the street and built a hotel meant to service the influx of tourists and new residents drawn by the upcoming Chicago World's Fair in 1893.

The three-story building, which Holmes designed himself, took up an entire city block, earning it the nickname "the Castle." The ground floor contained Holmes's relocated drugstore, as well as other commercial space. The upper two floors contained his personal office and a curious a maze of windowless rooms, with doorways opening to brick walls, stairs leading nowhere, and doors openable only from the outside. Holmes changed builders several times during the construction of the Castle, so in the end only he knew all its secrets.

After the Castle's completion, Holmes began an expert murder streak. His victims were females, selected from employees, lovers, and unfortunate hotel guests. His employees were required to take out life insurance policies, for which Holmes kindly paid the premiums and less kindly made himself the sole beneficiary. He locked some of his victims in soundproof rooms fitted with gas lines that allowed him to asphyxiate them at his leisure, while others were locked in a large vault and left to suffocate. Those were the lucky ones. Most were tortured before being killed. Once dead, Holmes sent the corpses into the basement of the Castle by means of a secret chute. Here they were stripped of their flesh and turned into skeleton models, which Holmes would then sell to medical schools. The rest of the bodies were either burnt in the Castle's giant furnace or dissolved in specially constructed pits of acid.

Holmes eventually left Chicago, continuing his crime spree, until the law finally caught up with him in 1894. Police estimated that Holmes possibly killed as many as one hundred victims in the Murder Castle, but were only able to verify twenty-seven. Holmes was hanged in Philadelphia in 1896.

NEW KIDS ON THE BLOCK

Fifty stars on the American flag for fifty states in the Union. It is such a perfectly round number that it creates an air of predestination for the United States. The idea of adding one more star, of ruining that wonderfully perfect number, seems almost sacrilegious. For the younger generations, fifty stars has always been the way of the world. It is easy to forget how very recently there were only forty-eight states. Alaska and Hawaii did not officially join the Union until 1959. And Arizona and New Mexico didn't join until 1912. Many readers of this book quite likely have a grandparent who was born in Arizona or New Mexico Territory, when they were still vestiges of the Wild West.

Delaware was the first state to ratify the Constitution, making it the first state to join the Union on December 7, 1787, and earning it the nickname The First State.

 ## PARATROOPER PADRE

Father Francis L. Sampson was ordained as a Catholic priest in 1941. In 1942 he got permission from his church to enlist in the army. Despite modestly saying after the war, "Please remember that no pair of knees ever shook more than my own in times of danger," Sampson threw himself headlong into dangerous situations behind enemy lines. Twice captured by the Germans, he once narrowly escaped execution only when a German soldier—who just happened to be a devout Catholic—realized that Sampson was a priest. But Sampson's lasting legacy came when he learned of the tragic and near simultaneous death of the three brothers: Bob, Preston, and Edward Niland (though it later turned out that Edward had been captured). When Sampson discovered that a fourth Niland, Fritz, was still alive, he personally tracked Fritz down and saw to it that the young man was sent home. The incident would later inspire the movie Saving Private Ryan.

 ## ONCE YOU GO BLACK...

Following the Civil War, Hiram Rhodes Revels became the first African American and the first nonwhite person to serve in the United States Senate, representing the state of Mississippi during the period of Reconstruction. It surely must have given Revels some satisfaction knowing that the previous person to hold his position was Albert G. Brown, the former Governor of Mississippi. Brown was a vocal proponent not just for the right to own slaves, but also for the purposeful expansion of the slaver way of life. He once said: "I want a foothold in Central America...because I want to plant slavery there....I want Cuba,...Tamaulipas, Potosi, and one or two other Mexican States; and I want them all for the same reason—for the planting or spreading of slavery."

¡Yo Quiero Liberty Bell!

On April 1, 1996, the fast food chain Taco Bell took out a full-page ad in seven major-market newspapers announcing that the company had purchased the historic Liberty Bell to help reduce the national debt. They had also renamed it the "Taco Liberty Bell." Within hours gullible Americans across the country were thrown into a rage. Protests were being put into motion. Then at noon Taco Bell revealed the obvious—the ads were an April Fool's Day prank.

The ads cost a total of $300,000. Taco Bell estimated that they received a roughly $25 million equivalent in free publicity, with a major spike in business on April 1 and 2.

The Roman Empire set the standard for driving on the LEFT side of the road, but in the 1800s Emperor Napoleon Bonaparte decreed that his subjects should use the RIGHT. French colonial influence resulted in the American adoption of the practice.

President Aaron Burr?

Aaron Burr became forever infamous when he killed Alexander Hamilton in a duel—while Burr was serving as vice

president, no less! Yet he was just one vote away from being the third president of the United States. Because of an
oddity in the Electoral College at the time, even though
Thomas Jefferson had beaten John Adams in the 1800 presidential election, Jefferson wound up tied with his own running mate, Aaron Burr. The Federalists who had supported
Adams immediately saw a chance for vengeance, and threw
their support behind Burr. This new sub-election was to
be decided in the House by the respective states; each got
a single vote. They went through thirty-two ballots, each
bringing Burr and Jefferson to a tie.

Finally, John Bayard, a Federalist who had supported
Burr and who controlled Delaware's vote, abstained just
so everyone could go home and the government could get
back to business. Thomas Jefferson went on to be one of
the most successful and respected presidents in US history. Burr, in the years after killing Hamilton, went on to
be accused of plotting to overthrow the government and
charged with treason.

THE FAIRER TEA PARTY

In 1774, in response to the Boston Tea Party (which itself
was a response to the Tea Act of 1773), the British Parliament passed a series of domineering new laws known as the
Intolerable Acts. The acts mostly affected Massachusetts,
as Parliament hoped the punitive measures would reverse
the trend of colonial resistance to British authority. But it
only led to more outrage and protests. One of the most notable protests occurred in Edenton, North Carolina, when
fifty-one people gathered to sign a statement vowing to
boycott British tea and other products. They then sent a
copy of the statement to the British press. In England the
reaction was…*laughter*. Why? Because all fifty-one signers
of this declaration were women.

Though the Edenton Tea Party is barely remembered
today, it was nonetheless a landmark moment, represent-

ing one of the first instances of political action by women in America. The protest was organized by Penelope Barker, who reasonably presumed that a boycott on tea and other household goods would mean a lot more coming from women (i.e., the ones generally in charge of acquiring these items). Barker underestimated the amount of dismissive sexism it would receive in Great Britain, but her declaration was praised in America and it inspired many other colonial women to take up their own boycotts.

THE GREATEST PITCHER WHO NEVER WAS

The April 1985 issue of *Sports Illustrated* featured an article by reporter George Plimpton about an amazing new athlete named Sidd Finch who could pitch a baseball at 168 miles per hour with robotic accuracy (the record speed was 103 miles per hour). Astonishingly, Finch had never played a game of baseball in his life. He had gained his prowess in the mountains of Tibet, studying the yogic mastery of mind-body from monks. Then one day he showed up at the New York Mets' training camp in Florida. He pitched wearing a hiking boot on one foot, leaving the other foot bare. His pitches were so fast and accurate that the catcher said it was as if the ball just appeared in his glove. The players said that Finch's pitches were humanly impossible to hit. The Mets immediately offered him a place on the team, but Finch had to think about it. He was also interested in pursuing a career as a French horn player.

Sports Illustrated received thousands of letters in response to the article. On April 15 they admitted that Plimpton's story was a hoax. And Plimpton himself noted that he'd left a coded message in the subheading of the article notifying readers of the truth. The subheading read: "He's a pitcher, part yogi and part recluse. Impressively liberated from our opulent life-style, Sidd's deciding about yoga—and his future in baseball." If you take the first letter from every word in the first two lines of the sub-heading, they spell out, "Happy April Fool's Day."

WE'RE GONNA NEED A BIGGER FLAG

The American flag originally had thirteen stars and thirteen stripes to represent the thirteen states in the Union. When Vermont and Kentucky were accepted into the Union, the flag was adjusted to have fifteen stars and fifteen stripes. When Tennessee, Ohio, Louisiana, Indiana, and Mississippi joined the Union it became clear that we needed a different approach, lest the flag become incredibly detailed or incredibly large. In 1818 Congress decided that they would go back to thirteen stripes, and only add stars for new states. The new act also specified that new flag designs would become official only on the first July 4 following the admission of a new state.

RED JOURNALISM

The *New-York Tribune* was established in 1841 by Horace Greeley and became the leading voice for the short-lived Whig Party and then later the Republicans. Greeley used the newspaper's influence to champion his many causes, such as the Homestead Act of 1862, which encouraged expansion of the country west of the Mississippi River. It was in a Homestead Act–related editorial that Greeley used the phrase for which he is best remembered: "Go west, young man." But looking back on the history of the *Tribune*, the role it played in Whig and Republican politics seems far less interesting than the tangential role it played in communism.

From 1852 to 1861, Karl Marx and Frederick Engels, fathers of the Marxist theory and authors of *The Communist Manifesto*, served as European correspondents for the *Tribune*, both writing under the same byline (though Marx penned the vast majority of the articles). Marx viewed the newspaper as a "filthy rag," but, hey, a man's gotta pay the bills.

 ## CRISIS OF FAITH

Franklin Pierce is the only elected president not to have been sworn in using a Bible. Right before he took office as the four-teenth president, Pierce and his family were in a train wreck. The wreck killed his eleven-year-old son, which didn't really leave Pierce in a religious mood. So at his inauguration he put his hand on a law book. And he refused to swear *to his presidential oath, instead* affirming *it. He was also the first president to recite the oath from memory.*

 ## FRESHLY BREWED IDEA

Up through the mid-nineteenth century, coffee beans were sold green, which required the purchaser to roast the beans at home. Only after a successful roast could the beans be ground and brewed. If the roasting process was done im-properly, the entire batch was ruined. This was presumably annoying for anyone who wanted to brew a cup of coffee at home, but it was more trouble than it was worth for cow-boys and settlers living out in the Wild West, where coffee beans were roasted in a skillet over a campfire. Worst yet, even if you successfully roasted your beans in the skillet, it was rarely of a consistent quality or flavor.

Fortunately John Arbuckle came to the rescue. In the early 1860s, while working at his family's grocery company in Pittsburgh, Pennsylvania, Arbuckle began experiment-ing with ways to seal in the aroma and flavor of already roasted coffee beans. He discovered that by adding an egg and sugar glaze to the beans after roasting, he could retain their freshness if he packed them snuggly into an airtight container. And thusly Arbuckle Ariosa Coffee was born (the "A" was for Arbuckle, "rio" for Rio de Janeiro, and "sa" for Santos, which were both important Brazilian coffee ports). Arbuckle's coffee immediately became a must-have for anyone living on the frontier and within just a few shorts years Arbuckle became the biggest coffee importer in the United States. Though, after Arbuckle's death in 1912 the company faded away.

Nearly HALF of the Native American population were not considered US citizens until the INDIAN Citizenship Act of 1924.

To Tax or Not to Tax?

Unpopular taxes were one of the catalysts of the Revolutionary War, as American colonists grew increasingly tired of footing the bill for Great Britain's expensive empire. So the Founding Fathers definitely had taxes on the brain when writing the Constitution. But as the Unites States grew, so did our own bills. Abraham Lincoln introduced the first federal income tax to help finance the Civil War—the Revenue Act of 1861 put a flat tax of 3 percent on annual income above $800 (about $20,000 today). The following year it was upped to 3 to 5 percent on income above $600. But the tax disappeared when the war was over.

Then the Wilson–Gorman Tariff Act of 1894 attempted to create an ongoing federal income tax of 2 percent, but the Supreme Court got involved. In the landmark *Pollock v. Farmers' Loan & Trust Co.* case, the Supreme Court proclaimed that a direct income tax was unconstitutional. This left the government with only one logical option: change the Constitution!

The 16th Amendment was ratified in 1913, allowing the government to implement a federal income tax. This also changed how taxes were collected. The Internal Revenue Service no longer acted as tax collectors. Taxpayers now filled out a tax form, leaving the IRS to validate its accuracy, and giving Americans an important new thing to procrastinate on every year.

A NOBLE FAILURE

The 18th Amendment and the Volstead Act, more commonly known collectively as Prohibition, banned the sale, manufacture, and transportation of alcohol from 1920 until the 21st Amendment put things back in place in 1933. Prohibition is also sometimes referred to as the "Noble Experiment," putting a rather positive spin on what was a complete and embarrassing failure. Even looking past the undeniable fact that booze is great and should be legal, Prohibition ended up causing significantly more problems than it sought to solve. Just at face value it was a procedural fiasco—in 1927 there were an estimated thirty thousand illegal liquor establishments (or speakeasies) operating across the country. That is twice the number of *legal* establishments prior to Prohibition.

The reason some may consider Prohibition noble was that its aim was a moral one, to eliminate the kind of social rot and delinquency associated with the "demon alcohol." But organized crime got a phenomenal boost from Prohibition. Prior to the 1920s, organized crime was something that existed only in the underbelly, with gangsters earning modest cash through gambling, prostitution, and petty theft. The amount of money to be made through the alcohol black market was staggering. It completely changed the image of the modern gangster to something worthy of cinematic glamour, and it turned many cities into battle-grounds of warring mafia factions.

But far more deadly than a gangster's bullet was the bootleg alcohol itself. Homemade moonshine and so-called bathtub gin—often distilled by people who barely knew what the hell they were doing or by shysters cutting their booze with industrial methanol—could be outright poisonous. By 1926, it is estimated that roughly 750 people in New York City had died from poisons found in bad booze, and thousands more had suffered injuries ranging from blindness to paralysis. On New Year's Day 1927, forty-one revelers died at New York's Bellevue Hospital from alcohol-related poisonings.

 ## Teddy Saves Football

American football is an extremely dangerous sport, with an ever-growing dossier of disturbing studies detailing the long-term impact it has on players. But it used to be even more dangerous. In 1905, eighteen players died from injuries sustained during games, and this was back when the league had substantially fewer players. This alarmed President Theodore Roosevelt, who feared that the sport would be abolished if something didn't change. So Teddy invited representatives from the Big Three schools, Harvard, Yale, and Princeton, to a meeting at the White House. He convinced the representatives that the sport needed to become safer. As a result both the American Football Rules Committee and the National Collegiate Athletic Association (NCAA) were formed. And the sport became safer—at least in a short-term sense.

Messy Language

The Simplified Spelling Board was established in 1906. Funded by steel tycoon Andrew Carnegie, the organization sought to reform the spelling of the unwieldy English language, simplifying it and making it easier to learn.

The board began by publishing a list of three hundred new spellings. The list proposed changing the ending *ed* to simply *t*, so "wished" would be "wisht." It also suggested replacing *ough* with *o*, so "although" would be "altho."

President Theodore Roosevelt believed in the cause, and in August of 1906 he ordered the Government Printing Office to start using the SSB's changes immediately. In December of 1906 Congress voted to reinstate the old spellings. Carnegie died in 1919, and the SSB was forced to disband the following year, unable to find a new benefactor.

HAS ANYONE SEEN THIS CHILD?

The first child born to English settlers in America was named Virginia Dare. Virginia came into the world on August 18, 1587, in the Roanoke Colony of what is now North Carolina. Three short years later, Virginia also became colonial America's first missing toddler.

Roanoke was England's first attempt to create a permanent settlement in the New World. It was organized by Sir Walter Raleigh, who selected his friend John White to serve as the colony's governor. White in turn brought his daughter Eleanor and her husband Ananias Dare (Virginia's parents). Shortly after the birth of his granddaughter, John White returned to London to acquire fresh supplies. When he arrived home he discovered that England was at war with Spain. It was three years before White was allowed to return to Roanoke, which he finally did on August 18, 1590, his granddaughter's third birthday. As distressing as returning to London to find his country at war had been, it undoubtedly paled in comparison to what he found at Roanoke—*absolutely nothing*. The entire colony, over one hundred people, had up and vanished.

The only clue the colonists left behind to explain their absence was the word "Croatoan" carved into a post.

White took this to mean that everyone had moved to the nearby Croatoan Island, likely seeking the aid of local Native Americans, but a coming storm forced White and his crew to leave before being able to conduct a search. And the Lost Colony mystery was born. The mystery of Roanoke has been a favorite topic for historical theorists, with theories ranging from the plausible (the colonists were assimilated into an Indian community) to the sensational (Indian cannibals ate the colonists). Virginia Dare became a popular figure in fiction writing starting in the 1800s and continues to appear in literature, film, television, and comic books today.

BILLS, BILLS, BILLS

As president, Thomas Jefferson reduced the national debt, but he was less adept with his personal finances. In fact, he was notoriously awful at managing his money. Shortly before he died in 1826 he came to the worrisome realization that his astronomical debts would prevent him from leaving anything to his children and grandchildren. So, in characteristic Jeffersonian fashion, he came up with a wild idea for reducing his cash woes—he would hold a lottery, with pieces of his property at Monticello as the prizes.

Lotteries were illegal, so Jefferson used his considerably persuasive talents as a writer to petition the Virginia legislature to cut him some slack. And they did. The plan was for 11,477 tickets to be sold at $10 a pop (a high price for the time), but when word got out that the man who wrote the Declaration of Independence was in such dire straits, committees around the country were set up to raise aid for Jefferson. The lottery was quietly set aside. Unfortunately, even though $16,500 (around $313,800 today) was raised in Jefferson's honor, it hardly made a dent in what he owed. When Jefferson died in July of that year, his oldest daughter Martha was left penniless, and his estate was auctioned off to cover his outstanding debts.

▬ LEAVING A BIG MARK

John Hancock may have the strangest legacy of any of the Founding Fathers—that of the guy with the largest signature on the Declaration of Independence. It is an act he became so monumentally famous for that the name John Hancock is now a synonym for signature. His name is more widely known in the United States than most of the presidents, yet most Americans couldn't even begin to tell you just *why* his signature was so big. A common folktale paints Hancock as something of a merry prankster, brazenly being the first to sign the Declaration while others hesitated, then hogging a bunch of space with his flamboyant autograph, proclaiming that he wanted King George III to be able to read his name without spectacles. But this is not even partially true.

The true story is maybe less sensational, but no less flattering for Hancock. Despite popular mythology, when the Declaration of Independence was formally adopted, the Founding Fathers did not gather around to triumphantly sign it—not even its author, Thomas Jefferson. And the document wasn't addressed or sent to King George III either. The purpose of the Declaration was to explain to American colonists why the Continental Congress felt it was necessary to break from Britain's rule. Hancock was president of Congress, and thus it was his duty to authenticate and sign the finalized Declaration on July 4, 1776, so that it could be printed and distributed throughout the colonies. The original Declaration had only two signatures on it: Hancock's and that of Charles Thomson, secretary of the Continental Congress. This meant that Hancock was the only delegate whose name appeared on the treasonous document, which put him at a great risk should the Declaration fail to gain support.

The celebrated official parchment Declaration of Independence preserved in the National Archives was not produced until later in the summer, and was signed piece-meal between August and November 1776. The size and placement of Hancock's signature on *this* Declaration was simply a formal representation of his position as president in the Continental Congress. The backstory of the original Declaration likely faded from memory because the fantasy of all the Founding Fathers signing the important document together, as Thomas Jefferson's ink was still drying, is just more rousing.

THE HARRISON DYNASTY

John Scott Harrison was a member of the House of Representatives from Ohio. He never became president of the United States, but he was closely related to two presidents—his dad was William Henry Harrison and his son was Benjamin Harrison. John Scott is the only man in history to be able to boast of such a connection. He did not live to see his son elected to the White House, but one of his sons regrettably wound up witnessing something quite unexpected after John Scott died in 1878...

At the time it was a grotesque yet not uncommon practice for grave robbers to dig up the recently deceased and sell the corpses to universities to be used in medical education. John Scott's children wanted to make sure their father didn't meet such an undignified end, so they took special precautions with their father's grave, mixing heavy stones in with the dirt placed over the grave. On the day of John Scott's funeral, it was discovered that the body of Augustus Devin, a relative who had died the previous week, was missing from his grave. Benjamin Harrison needed to return to Indianapolis to resume work, but his younger brother John stayed behind to discover who had spirited away their cousin Augustus. The day after his father's funeral, John joined authorities as they searched Ohio Medical College. They didn't locate Augustus, but they found someone else—John Scott Harrison, freshly dug up and dangling from a rope. The discovery caused a sensation and exposed a trail of grave robberies (including Augustus's corpse, found soaking in a vat of brine). John Scott was reinterred in a safer location and Ohio passed a law stiffening the punishment for grave robbery.

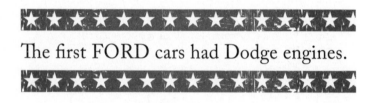

The first FORD cars had Dodge engines.

ROOSEVELT RIVER

Theodore Roosevelt can lay claim to many achievements. As president he set aside more federal land for national parks and nature preserves than all of his predecessors combined. He was the first president to invite an African American (Booker T. Washington) into the White House as a guest. His book *The Naval War of 1812* remains one of the most esteemed studies of naval warfare. But his most unique and unparalleled achievement may be mapping an uncharted river, an adventure he undertook when he was nearly sixty years old.

In 1913, looking to reenergize himself after a failed presidential campaign the previous year, Roosevelt—along with his son Kermit and a host of Brazilian officers and other explorers—set out to map the appropriately named River of Doubt in South America. The "doubt" was that no one knew where the river went or how long it was. The journey was an arduous and heinous one. Roosevelt contracted malaria and nearly died, losing 50 pounds along what ended up being a 625-mile river voyage.

Upon returning to America he said the trip had probably shaved ten years off his life, and sadly he was correct. The remaining few years of his life saw several flare-ups of his malaria until finally, on January 6, 1919, Roosevelt's famed strength gave way in his sleep. His son Archie telegraphed the rest of the family, saying, "The old lion is dead." The River of Doubt was renamed Rio Roosevelt in his honor.

I SIEG HEIL, TO THE FLAG

The Pledge of Allegiance made its first appearance in 1892 in the pages of the popular children's magazine *The Youth's Companion*. It was penned by a Baptist minister and socialist named Francis Bellamy in support of a nationwide public school celebration of the four hundredth anniversary of Christopher Columbus "discovering" America. Bellamy's original pledge read: "I pledge allegiance to my flag and the republic for which it stands, one nation indivisible, with liberty and justice for all."

Bellamy had planned to use the words "equality" and "fraternity" instead of "liberty" and "justice," but determined this would render the pledge too controversial for a nation still mired in gender and racial inequality. Interestingly, even though Bellamy was a minister, someone else added the "under God" portion, well after Bellamy's death in 1931. Bellamy did, however, live to see "to my flag" changed to "the Flag of the United States of America." The National Flag Conference instituted the alteration in 1923, so as not to confuse immigrants about which nation they were swearing allegiance to, but Bellamy felt it ruined the "rhythmic balance of the original composition."

Bellamy took his short pledge seriously. He even designed the salute to be performed while delivering the pledge. The "Bellamy salute" began with the right hand stretched out at full length toward the flag, with the palm facing down, and at the end of the pledge the palm was raised up. But in the 1930s, when Hitler took power in Germany, people started to notice that the Bellamy salute looked uncomfortably similar to the Nazi salute. So in 1942, Congress amended the Flag Code, instating the still-used hand-over-heart salute.

At 345 feet, Britton Hill is the HIGHEST natural point in Florida, which makes Florida the shortest state (elevation-wise) in the country. California has trees TALLER than that.

Balloons Away!

On May 5, 1945 six people were killed by a Japanese attack in Bly, Oregon, making them the first and only mainland American combat casualties of World War II and bursting the perception bubble that the contiguous forty-eight states were safe from enemy attacks. Sure, Pearl Harbor had happened, but the United States had been caught unprepared, and besides, Hawaii is over 2,000 miles from the West Coast. No one thought that the Japanese stood any chance of successfully reaching the mainland. As it turns out, the Japanese didn't think so either, which necessitated some outside-the-box thinking on their part.

Between November 1944 and April 1945, the Japanese Navy launched over nine thousand hydrogen balloons loaded with antipersonnel bombs and incendiary devices toward North America. Known as fire balloons, the weapons were carried by the recently discovered Pacific jet stream and were meant to start forest fires and cause other indiscriminant damage. Around 340 of the balloons reached America, some drifting as far inland as Nebraska. Though they did cause minor damage here and there, the fire balloons were largely ineffective as weapons. The only reason the Bly balloon claimed its six victims—a teacher and five of her students—was because one of the students tampered with the fallen device, unaware of what it was.

GUT PUNCHED

Erik Weisz, better known by his stage name Harry Houdini, was a magician famous for his sensational escape acts. He first gained fame as "The Handcuff King," touring Europe and challenging local police to lock him in their shackles and toss him in their jails—and then escaping every time. By the early 1900s, Houdini had become even more sensational, hanging himself upside-down in a straightjacket, dangling from the tops of buildings or a tall crane. He dazzled and terrified crowds by being restrained and submerged into a tank of water, as well as performing increasingly more dangerous variations on his "Buried Alive" stunt. Yet Houdini died from being punched in the gut.

Well, that's only half true. In October of 1926, Houdini was in Montreal to perform, as well as to give a lecture about debunking mediums and spiritualists (a favorite hobby of his) at McGill University. At the lecture, he befriended a McGill student and invited the lad to visit him backstage at the Princess Theater. The student, along with two friends, including one J. Gordon Whitehead, took Houdini up on his offer. Though there is dispute about the exact details of what followed, the undisputed facts are that the McGill students ventured back to Houdini's dressing room, where Whitehead decided to test a famous claim of Houdini's—his ability to withstand a punch to the gut by expertly flexing his abdomen muscles. Some claim that Houdini had been boasting his strength and invited Whitehead to punch him, while others claim that Whitehead delivered his blows without permission.

Houdini was notoriously proud of his physical prowess, so it is entirely possible he challenged Whitehead, because that same pride is ultimately what killed him. Houdini had already been suffering from stomach pains, but had refused any medical treatment (he had also broken his ankle the week before but refused to cancel any performances). And despite the agonizing pain that followed his encounter with Whitehead, Houdini was still determined to soldier on. After collapsing on stage during a show at the Garrick Theater in Detroit, Houdini was taken to the hospital where surgeons discovered that his appendix had ruptured and he was suffering from peritonitis (inflammation of the inner wall of the abdomen). It is extremely unlikely that Whitehead's blows caused the rupture, but they surely exacerbated or caused the peritonitis. Houdini managed to cling to life for several days, but finally passed away on Halloween at the age of fifty-two.

SUPREME COURT PRESIDENT

Before he became president, William Howard Taft served on the Ohio Superior Court. He always maintained that his true dream was not to sit in the White House, but to sit on the Supreme Court. Supposedly it was his wife, Helen Herron Taft, who saw the potential for her husband and pushed him to attain the higher office.

In 1903, President Theodore Roosevelt offered Taft his dream job, to replace the retiring Justice George Shiras Jr. Taft declined due to his obligations as governor-general of the Philippines. But according to White House lore, it was Mrs. Taft, not wanting to see her husband locked into a life-long commitment so soon, who pleaded with Roosevelt to offer William Taft a different position, one that would allow him to stay involved with the Philippines and also allow the potential for upward mobility. So in 1904, William Taft became Roosevelt's Secretary of War. Whatever the truth, in the end, both Taft and his wife got what they wanted. Upon leaving the White House in 1913, Taft returned to his first love: law. Then in 1921, following the death of Chief Justice Edward Douglass White, President

Warren Harding nominated Taft for the position. The Senate approved Taft with near-unanimous support.

The chief justice of the United States is the head judge of the Supreme Court, with the other eight judges referred to as associate justices. Among the chief justice's many duties, one is swearing in new presidents. Taft held the office until he died in 1930, giving him the unique perspective in presidential history of swearing in two other presidents, Calvin Coolidge and Herbert Hoover. Taft is the only person to have ever served as both president and a Supreme Court judge.

DEFENDING THE ENEMY

In 1770, during a public disturbance on Boston Green, British soldiers fired into a crowd, killing five colonists. Angry Americans called it the Boston Massacre. The Brits still refer to it by the far more innocuous "Incident on King Street." But the "incident" further heightened the anti-British enmity in the colonies and eight British soldiers were arrested and charged with murder. With public outrage in full swing, few wanted to take on the thankless task of defending the men. So in stepped an outspoken patriot lawyer and future president named John Adams, who, despite his feelings regarding the British government, wanted to see the soldiers get a fair trial. Arguing that the soldiers had felt justifiably threatened by the surly crowd, Adams got six of the soldiers acquitted, and the remaining two convicted of manslaughter instead of murder.

ACTING POLITICIANS

Many actors become involved in politics, but only a few make the bold decision to cross the line from activist to actual politician. Ronald Reagan became governor of California and then president of the United States. Clint Eastwood became mayor of Carmel, California. Shirley Temple became ambassador to Ghana and Czechoslovakia. Comedian Al Franken became a US senator from Minnesota. But no Hollywood political transition story is more unlikely than that of the cast of the 1987 action-sci-fi film *Predator*. Audiences watching Ronald Reagan pal around with a chimpanzee in 1951's *Bedtime for Bonzo* surely would have found it odd to know they were looking at a future president. But with *Predator*, in which a collection of beefy tough guys engage in jungle warfare with a ten-foot-tall alien, the chances of getting not one, not two, but three future political hopefuls seems too funny to even be true. But in this case, biceps translated to votes.

In 1998, former pro-wrestler Jesse "The Body" Ventura stunned the political world when he was elected governor of Minnesota, after a groundbreaking campaign as a third-party candidate. Ventura even capitalized on his role in *Predator*, using his popular line from the film—"I ain't got time to bleed"—as a metaphorical mantra about his commitment.

Then, in 2003, inspired by Ventura's success, Arnold Schwarzenegger entered a California recall election to replace then-Governor Gray Davis and won. That same year, also inspired by the *Predator* alumni success, Sonny Landham ran for governor of Kentucky, but failed to get the Republican nomination. Landham then ran for the US Senate as a Libertarian in 2008, but was dropped by the party after making offensive remarks about Arabs on a radio show.

THE KING AND TRICKY DICK

In December of 1970, Elvis Presley had a fight with his wife and father over his spending habits and erratic behavior, so Elvis took off. In no way placating his family's concerns about erratic behavior, Elvis immediately flew to Washington, D.C., then immediately to Los Angeles, then back to Washington, D.C., the next day. While on the airplane Elvis composed a rambling letter, several pages long, addressed to President Richard Nixon asking the president

to appoint him a "Federal Agent at Large" to help combat communism and illegal drugs (ironic considering Elvis was a habitual drug user who would die from an overdose later in the decade, and was presumably out of his mind on drugs at that exact moment). When Elvis landed in D.C. he had his limousine take him straight to the White House. Elvis presented his letter to security and, somewhat surprisingly, was granted a meeting with Nixon—they didn't call Elvis "The King" for nothing, it would seem.

Wearing tight purple velvet pants, a matching cape, and carrying a gun that no one knew about, Elvis strolled into the Oval Office on December 21. He had been given five minutes of the president's time, but Elvis drew things out considerably longer. Elvis showed Nixon pictures of his baby and of his wife. They talked about growing up poor, about the burdens of fame. Elvis related his theories that The Beatles' lyrics contained anti-American sentiments and professed his supposed concerns about drugs. They posed for pictures, and Elvis gave Nixon a bear hug. Nixon agreed to give Elvis a gold badge that would make him a Federal Agent at Large for the Bureau of Narcotics and Dangerous Drugs. And Elvis then pissed off the Secret Service when he suddenly pulled out that gun—a commemorative World War II–era Colt .45 pistol, which he presented to Nixon as a gift.

The commemorative pistol is on display in the Nixon Library in Yorba Linda, California. The gold badge still hangs in Graceland, Elvis's mansion in Memphis, Tennessee.

▭ THE CAVALRY RIDES AGAIN

In 2001, when Army Special Forces personnel slid into Afghanistan shortly after the September 11 terrorist attacks, they found themselves dealing with something few of them were prepared for: *horses.* The horse-mounted United States Cavalry had once been a pivotal branch of the military, but the flesh and blood of horses eventually gave way to the metal and oil of tanks and other mechanized vehicles. The US Army's last horse-mounted cavalry charge occurred in the Philippines on January 16, 1942, when the 26th Cavalry Regiment charged Japanese forces on the Bataan Peninsula. After WWII ended, the Cavalry branch was absorbed into the Armor branch. Then the Vietnam War saw the introduction of helicopters as "Air Cavalry." Horses were now relics of the past, and not something a soldier is faced with during boot camp.

Since a full-scale military offensive was not yet underway in Afghanistan, Green Berets were forced to rely on the technology and assistance of Afghan warlords who were also trying to overthrow the Taliban regime. That meant horses, which, aside from being all the Afghans really had, were also necessary to navigate the narrow mountainous paths of the region that no Jeep could hope to traverse. But, even as skilled and highly trained as they were, most of the Green Berets had no experience riding a horse. Even the few soldiers familiar with horses had to deal with the much smaller Afghan breeds and awkward wooden slabs covered with goatskin that the locals used as saddles. It was on horseback that Special Forces and their Afghan allies took the city of Mazar-i-Sharif.

The horse soldiers retired their saddles once regular army and marine units arrived in the country.

 ## IKE V. THORPE

Long before he became the thirty-fourth president of the United States, Dwight "Ike" Eisenhower was a varsity starting running back for the army football team at West Point. By all accounts, Ike was an excellent player, but any football aspirations he may have had were cut short by an injury. But for the rest of his life he at least had the satisfaction of knowing that he was sidelined by one of the greatest men to ever play the game, Jim Thorpe.

Thorpe, of mixed Native American ancestry and later voted the "Greatest Athlete of the Twentieth Century" in a poll con-

ducted by ABC Sports, was then a student at Carlisle Indian Industrial School. The fateful game occurred on November 9, 1912, at West Point. Ike was determined to take the already famous Thorpe out of the game, and even managed to tackle him once. But Thorpe was simply too good, and eventually pulled a clever juke that caused Ike to collide with one of his own teammates, injuring his knee. Eisenhower never finished another game. He closed out his football career as a cheerleader. But hey, he did become president. So he had that going for him.

▦ LADY LINDY CONSPIRACIES

Amelia Earhart was the first woman to fly solo across the Atlantic Ocean and remains one of the most famous names in aviation. Despite all her accomplishments, her enduring fame has a lot to do with the mysterious nature of her death. In 1937, Earhart and navigator Fred Noonan disappeared over the Pacific Ocean while attempting to circumnavigate the globe along the equator. Their plane and bodies were never found. The prevailing theory is that Earhart and Noonan just ran out of fuel, then crashed and sank into the ocean. But that is depressingly unsatisfying for a beloved pioneer like Earhart. So other theories and conspiracies are plentiful.

Some believe Earhart landed safely on Gardner Island, part of the Phoenix Islands, and eventually died there when rescue never came. This theory has gained some traction due to the recent discovery of a freckle cream container on the island that matches the brand Earhart used. Moving in sillier directions, others believe Earhart was captured and executed by the Japanese. Why? Because her flight was actually a secret spy mission! Supposedly US forces later found her plane on a Japanese military base, but had it destroyed as part of a cover-up. Another riff on this motif has Earhart taken prisoner by the Japanese and forced to deliver Japanese propaganda over the radio as one of many women collectively referred to as "Tokyo Rose." One soldier claimed to have seen Earhart working as a nurse during WWII at Guadalcanal.

In 1970, author Joe Klaas published *Amelia Earhart Lives*, which presented the theory that after being held captive by the Japanese, Earhart was rescued and given a new identity in America as New Jersey banker Irene Bolam. Irene Bolam wasn't exactly pleased with her sudden media attention and sued Klaas.

CIVIL WAR IN VERMONT

The Civil War was fought mostly in the South and lower portions of the Union. But the northernmost incident took place in St. Albans, Vermont, just 15 miles from the Canadian border. In October of 1864, a Confederate officer named Bennett Young and twenty other men snuck into the town posing as vacationers. They then staged three simultaneous bank robberies, netting $208,000 (over $4 million now) before fleeing into Canada. Since Canada was neutral in the Civil War, Young and his soldiers could not be extradited. After the war, Young was eventually permitted to return to the country.

THE FIRST FEMALE PRESIDENT

Woodrow Wilson's wife, First Lady Edith Wilson, was a staunch opponent of the suffrage movement. She viewed the notion of women gaining the right to vote as "disgusting," and in 1917, when her husband had the suffragists demonstrating in front of the White House arrested, she referred to them as "those devils in the workhouse." While it is unfair to paint First Lady Wilson too unfavorably given the era in which she lived (men weren't the only ones who thought women belonged in the home), her views on the decision-making aptitude of females becomes keenly more interesting considering that she wound up running the country for a while.

When Woodrow Wilson suffered a debilitating stroke in 1919 that left him completely incapacitated, Edith conspired with the president's physician to hide the extent of her husband's impairment—not just from the American public, but from the entirety of the American government, including the vice president, Congress, and Wilson's own cabinet. With no one allowed to see the president, Edith acted as go-between, bringing him important documents to read and sign and relaying the president's wishes. But the president was nearly comatose at times, which surely forced Edith to act as proxy to keep up the subterfuge.

Wilson recovered enough to return to cabinet meetings, but mostly as a figurehead. He retired from public life when he left office in 1921, and died two years later. Edith's actions following her husband's stroke were cited heavily in the argument for the 25th Amendment, which articulates the line of succession to the presidency and establishes procedures for responding to presidential disabilities.

Several presidents have had HALF-SIBLINGS, but no president has ever been an only child.

LONG LIVE THE AIRDROME

Founded in 1921, White Castle was the original fast food restaurant. But McDonald's would eventually eclipse it to an extent almost undreamed of for a burger joint, becoming a global empire and one of the most recognized brands in the world by the end of the twentieth century. For better or worse (and let's be honest, mostly worse), no other company, aside from Coca-Cola, is more directly connected with being American than McDonald's. Yet the chain began its life called The Airdrome.

In 1937, Patrick McDonald opened The Airdrome near the airport in Monrovia, California, serving hamburgers and all-you-can-drink orange juice. In 1940, his two sons, Maurice and Richard, took over the business and moved it to San Bernardino, California, where they renamed it McDonald's Famous Barbeque. Maurice and Richard served over forty barbequed items, but eventually they realized that most of their business was coming from burger sales. So in 1948 they simplified their menu and simplified their name to just McDonald's. Their new system clicked and they quickly franchised. They also introduced their mascot, Speedee, a man with a burger-shaped head wearing a top hat. In 1955, a businessman named Ray Kroc opened the ninth McDonald's franchise, in Des Plaines, Illinois. Kroc soon bought the whole company from the McDonald brothers and began aggressively transforming the business. He wanted McDonald's to be the number-one restaurant chain in the country. The golden arches were introduced, as was the Big Mac, and Speedee was junked and replaced with Ronald McDonald. The company became listed on the public stock market and it began its worldwide expansion. It now has locations in over one hundred countries.

In 2010, however, Subway surpassed McDonald's as the world's largest restaurant chain.

GOOD ENOUGH FOR GOVERNMENT WORK

In 1999, as part of a series highlighting American landmarks, the US Postal Service introduced a new 60-cent stamp commemorating the Grand Canyon. One hundred million stamps were printed. It was only after the stamps had been completed that someone with a basic grasp of geography happened to take a look at them and realized that the stamps said, "Grand Canyon, Colorado." The Grand Canyon is in Arizona. The entire stash was destroyed and another hundred million stamps were reprinted with the error corrected, at taxpayer expense.

But when a ranger at the Grand Canyon National Park got a look at the new stamps, he quickly called the post office to inform them of a new mistake—the image of the canyon was reversed, like a mirrored reflection. The Postal Service decided they could live with that, hoping that the average person does not have as intimate a knowledge of the canyon as the ranger did.

THE TROUBLE WITH GOATS

Lawman Pat Garrett is best known for killing the outlaw Billy the Kid, an act that secured Billy the Kid's place in Old West history. But Garrett himself met a rather unglamorous end. In 1908, suffering from financial woes incurred from excessive gambling, Garrett was forced to rent out his New Mexico ranch to a man named W. W. Cox—the brother-in-law of a man Garrett once arrested. Cox allowed his business partner Jesse Wayne Brazel to use Garrett's ranch as a grazing pasture for goats. Garrett had assumed it would be used for cattle. Goats, apparently, Garrett found unacceptable. When he confronted Brazel about the goats, the two men argued, and Garrett wound up dead, shot in the gut and head. Brazel reported the killing to the local sheriff and was eventually acquitted on self-defense. W. W. Cox threw a barbeque in celebration of the jury's verdict.

AN "A" MOMENT FOR A B-MOVIE

On June 17, 1972, five men were arrested for breaking and entering into the Democratic National Committee headquarters at the Watergate office complex in Washington, D.C. When it was discovered that the burglars had been hired by the reelection campaign for President

Richard Nixon, and that the Nixon administration had tried to cover the whole thing up, a scandal broke out that was so intense that to this day political scandals both big and small generally get a nickname with the word "gate" slapped at the end. But the scandal may have never happened if it weren't for the movie *Attack of the Puppet People*.

B-movie kings at American International Pictures released the film in 1958, directed by Bert I. Gordon, who also directed *The Amazing Colossal Man, The Food of the Gods,* and *Earth vs. the Spider*. The film tells the tale of a deranged doll-maker who creates a machine that can shrink humans down to only a few inches tall. But back to business…

On the night of the Watergate break-in, a man named Alfred C. Baldwin III was stationed in a room across the street at the Howard Johnson's Motor Lodge. He was acting as a spotter for the burglars, on the lookout for police cars. He was also watching *Attack of the Puppet People* on TV. What Baldwin had not anticipated was that the squad car that normally patrolled the Watergate area was not available to investigate the suspicious activity taking place that evening. Instead, when the call came in, the closest available officers were all dressed as hippies, riding in an undercover police vehicle. Distracted by *Puppet People*, Baldwin took little notice when the undercover car pulled up outside the Watergate. It wasn't until it was too late and the officers were already inside that he happened to look over and see three hippies carrying handguns. By the time he jumped on the walkie-talkie, the burglars did not have enough time to escape.

▀▀▀ A POOR HOMECOMING

The 1936 Summer Olympics were held in Berlin, hosted by Adolph Hitler. It would be another three years before Germany would invade Poland and kick off WWII, but things were already tense in Europe. Hitler was an extremely controversial character and, leading up to the games, the Nazi Party propaganda machine had only exacerbated the controversy by proclaiming that the games would demonstrate Aryan racial superiority for the entire world to see. As one might expect, the entire world was dying to see them eat their words during the games. When African American Jesse Owens took home four gold medals in track and field (a record that went unbroken for fifty years), it was a poetic response to Hitler. Here this member of a supposedly inferior race had bested Aryan perfection! It was a coup for the melting pot of America, with an ending right out of a Hollywood movie when a furious Hitler refused to congratulate Owens.

But Hitler didn't congratulate any foreign winners. And he never made any negative comments about Owens in public. Owens himself later said, "Hitler didn't snub me. It was FDR who snubbed me. The president didn't even send me a telegram." In Berlin, Owens was allowed to travel and stay with his white teammates. When Owens returned to the United States a hero, he received a ticker-tape parade of Fifth Avenue in New York City. Yet he was forced to ride the freight elevator at the Waldorf-Astoria to reach his own reception party.

At the Olympics, Owens became the first African American athlete to receive a sponsorship deal. While in Berlin, Owens was visited by Adi Dassler, founder of the Adidas shoe company. Owens won his gold medals wearing Dassler's shoes.

The First Mistress

In 1914, Lucy Mercer was hired by Franklin D. Roosevelt's wife, Eleanor, as a personal secretary, and sometime soon after Mercer and Franklin reportedly began an affair. The evidence is circumstantial, deriving largely from a memoir published by a former Roosevelt aide, but the rumor mill posits that the affair continued for decades after Mercer's employment with the family ended. Mercer visited the White House six times between 1944 and 1945, when Eleanor was conveniently gone. She was also with Franklin on April 12, 1945, the day he suffered the cerebral hemorrhage that caused his death.

Hundreds of years before the "more advanced" Europeans settled in America, the south FLORIDA Native Americans built a 20-foot-deep, 2.5-mile-long canal to facilitate TRADE between Naples Bay and the Gulf of Mexico. Archeologists still aren't entirely sure how the CANAL was built.

It's All a Popularity Contest

The town of New Madbury, New Hampshire, was founded in the 1770s. Unlike New York or New Jersey, which were named after places in England, the Madbury that this town was the "new" version of was also located in New Hampshire—and still is. So in 1780 the residents renamed the town Adams in honor of newly elected President John Adams. But Adams proved an unpopular president, and by the time the town was incorporated in 1829, people were ready for a change. So they renamed it yet again, to Jackson, in honor of the current president, Andrew Jackson. This time the name stuck.

☰ The Forgotten Pandemic

Mention the Spanish flu to most people today and they may think you're making a joke about diarrhea or stomach cramps caused by drinking bad water in Mexico. Yet the Spanish flu was one of the most devastating pandemics in history, killing—even at its lowest estimates—3 percent of the world's population.

In January 1918, reports of a serious flu began emerging in Kansas. Then a cook at Fort Riley reported sick the morning of March 4, and by noon that same day, nearly one hundred soldiers were in the hospital. By March 11, people were falling ill in Queens, New York. Then it hopped the Atlantic to France, while Europe was still embroiled in WWI. It was an outbreak of influenza. It got nicknamed the Spanish flu because it wasn't until the virus spread from France to Spain, and away from war-imposed media blackouts, that the press finally caught wind of the pandemic. No one knows exactly where the Spanish flu originated, but the prevailing theory is that the virus came from Asia, then mutated in the United States before spreading to Europe.

With the close quarters and disease that already existed in European military camps, the Spanish flu tore through WWI soldiers just as devastatingly as mortar fire. Here the flu mutated yet again and became even deadlier. By the end of summer, the virus swung back to America with a vengeance. Around 200,000 people died in the month of October, with over four thousand dying in Philadelphia in a single week. One out of four Americans became infected—President Woodrow Wilson was still suffering from the Spanish flu while negotiating the Treaty of Versailles to end WWI. People were dying so quickly and in such large numbers that there was a troubling shortage of coffins and morticians to handle all the dead. Funerals were even given time limits. And then, just as fast as it came, the pandemic ended. An estimated 675,000 Americans died from the Spanish flu—ten times as many as died in the war.

THE POWER OF FICTION

"Listen my children and you shall hear
Of the midnight ride of Paul Revere,
On the eighteenth of April, in Seventy-five;
Hardly a man is now alive
Who remembers that famous day and year."

Despite how that stanza ends, Henry Wadsworth Longfellow's poem "Paul Revere's Ride" forever etched the celebrity of Paul Revere into the collective American mind. But not very accurately. Revere was an important member of the patriot movement and did indeed play a role in spreading the news of the British army's arrival that preceded the Battle of Lexington. But the image of Revere galloping on horseback across the countryside screaming, "The British are coming," is pretty far off base. Not only did he never utter that famous line, but he spent the majority of that evening captured by British soldiers. On top of that, let's just say he wasn't exactly a paragon of secrecy with his captors, who eventually let Revere go after talking with him so they could go *warn their own comrades* that the colonists knew of their presence.

We should probably be singing the song of old-timey postman Israel Bissell, who rode some 350 miles on horseback over the course of four days (that's fast) shouting, "To arms, to arms, the war has begun!" Bissell was the subject of his own epic poem, "Ride, Israel, Ride," by Marie Rockwood. But presumably "Bissell" doesn't rhyme as nicely with other words as "Revere," for Rockwood's poem has not stood the test of time.

 # CRASHING INTO LEGEND

"The Ballad of Casey Jones" is a popular folk song dating back to the early 1900s, inspired by real-life railroad engineer John Luther "Casey" Jones. In the wee hours on April 30, 1900, Jones pulled his train into the station in Memphis, Tennessee,

ready for a layover before taking on another shift. But he was asked if he could take another train on to Canton, Mississippi, because the scheduled engineer had called in sick. Jones agreed. Since the train was already behind schedule, Jones and his fireman Sim Webb set out to make up for lost time.

They got the train up to 75 miles per hour and things were going according to plan, until they neared Vaughan, Mississippi. That's when Webb spotted the red lights on the caboose of a stalled train. With no time for talk, Jones ordered Webb to jump from the engine, taking on the impossible task of slowing the train himself. Miraculously he slowed his metal monster down from 75 to 35 miles per hour before colliding with the other train. The decrease in speed saved the lives of Jones's passengers. There was only one fatality from the crash—Casey Jones.

THE NAUGHTIEST PRESIDENT

From President Bill Clinton's "improper relationship" with White House employee Monica Lewinsky to the popular rumor that John F. Kennedy was sleeping with actress Marylyn Monroe, adultery has long been a common theme in political gossip and scandals. But likely no other president had more "women scrapes"—as his attorney general Harry M. Daugherty gently put it—than the twenty-ninth president, Warren Harding. Shortly after marrying his wife, Florence, Harding began an affair with her closest friend from childhood, Susie Hodder. After that, he purportedly entered into a fifteen-year secret relationship with Florence's closest friend from adulthood, Carrie Fulton Phillips. Apparently unhappy with this basic level of philandering, during his lengthy affair with Phillips, Harding also took on another mistress, his Senate aide Grace Cross.

While Harding had to deal with the typical ramifications of his horny behavior—angry discoveries by his wife, blackmail, cover-ups—he had been able to successfully keep it all out of the press and from encumbering his political career. He wasn't so lucky with his fourth and final mistress, a twenty-two-year-old campaign volunteer named Nan Britton. Britton maintained that Harding had fathered her daughter Elizabeth and that their affair had continued into the White House (quite literally). In 1928, after Harding's death, she made presidential mistress history when she wrote a book, *The President's Daughter*, documenting her romance with Harding.

On August 2, 1923, Harding died suddenly while still in office. He had heart problems, and his doctors confidently declared that congestive heart failure was the culprit. But because Harding had collapsed alone in a room with his wife Florence, and because Florence declined an autopsy to determine the exact cause of her husband's death, naturally, given the circumstances, this fueled rumors that Florence had poisoned the president.

BLAME THE COW

On October 8, 1871, the city of Chicago caught on fire. By the time the flames were snuffed out two days later, between two hundred and three hundred people had died and 3.3 square miles of the city were destroyed, leaving 90,000 of the city's 300,000 residents homeless. And it all started with a cow. Or so the legend goes. The famous story of the Great Chicago Fire was made all the more famous by the almost comical way it began—a cow belonging to one Catherine O'Leary kicked over a lantern while being milked, setting the barn on fire.

In 1893, Michael Ahern, the reporter who first wrote about O'Leary's sinister bovine, admitted to fabricating that detail to make his story more colorful. Irish immigrants were unpopular in Chicago at the time, so Ahern's admission did little to erase the myth. It was simply too good a story for anyone to care about trivial things, like whether it was true or false. For contrast, fire also broke out in Peshtigo, Wisconsin, *on the exact same day* the Chicago fire started. The Peshtigo Fire is the deadliest fire in

US history, having killed around 1,500 people. But no arsonist cows or Irish Catholics were purportedly involved, so it faded from memory in short order.

The Chicago Fire Academy now stands where Mrs. O'Leary's barn once did.

How Do You Say "Die Juden sind unser Ungluck" in American?

The storybook version of the Civil War tends to paint the conflict as a battle of good versus evil, with the North valiantly fighting for the rights of equality against the dastardly racists in the South. But the North was not quite the land of enlightened and open-minded heroes that we now like to imagine it was. Nothing makes that clearer than General Order No. 11.

The Civil War posed an ironic problem for both the North and South. The North was dependent on Southern cotton. And the Southern cotton producers were dependent on Northern buyers. So despite the fact that both sides were trying to kill each other, some trade was still allowed under special license from the US Army. The situation was ripe for corruption, and a cotton black market immediately sprung up. Union Major-General Ulysses S. Grant was confident that he knew the culprits: Jews. So in December 1862 he issued General Order No. 11, which called for the expulsion of all Jews in his district (areas of Tennessee, Mississippi, and Kentucky). The order read like something from Nazi Germany:

> *The Jews, as a class violating every regulation of trade established by the Treasury Department and also department orders, are hereby expelled from the department within twenty-four hours from the receipt of this order.*

> *Post commanders will see to it that all of this class of people be furnished passes and required to leave, and any one returning after such notification will be arrested and held in confinement until an opportunity occurs of sending them out as prisoners, unless furnished with permit from headquarters. No passes will be given these people to visit headquarters for the purpose of making personal application of trade permits.*

The outcry from the Jewish community and the Democrats in Congress was such that President Abraham Lincoln revoked the order within just a few weeks. Grant later made amends with Jews. While in the White House, Grant became the first president to attend a synagogue service.

In 1953, CALIFORNIA made the grizzly bear the state's official animal. But by then the California GRIZZLY had gone extinct. The last wild grizzly in California was shot and killed in 1922.

KARMIC EARTHQUAKES

Lilburn and Isham Lewis were both nephews of Thomas Jefferson, though they both seemed to lack any of their uncle's humanitarian spirit. One December night, during a drunken rage, the two men became incensed with George, one of the slaves on their Kentucky farm, after he dropped a pitcher of water. Responding as any sane people would, Lilburn and Isham tied George to the floor, called in their other seven slaves, locked the door, and made the slaves watch as they murdered George with an ax. The brothers then ordered the other slaves to dismember George's corpse and burn the pieces in the fireplace. But a massive earthquake shook the ground and destroyed the fireplace before they could continue.

The following day, Lilburn and Isham had the slaves hastily rebuild the fireplace, concealing the remainder of George inside. They likely would have gotten away with everything, but the following month another massive earthquake assaulted the area and the fireplace fell once more, exposing the unburned portions of poor George. When a neighbor's dog brought home George's skull, the brothers were indicted for murder. Realizing they stood little chance of being acquitted, Lilburn and Isham decided to commit joint suicide. Also apparently lacking any of their uncle's intelligence, Lilburn accidentally shot himself in the head while demonstrating how to carry out the suicide, leaving the even stupider Isham unable to kill himself before being arrested.

It seems that God was really committed to seeing the Lewis brothers receive their comeuppance, because the earthquakes that foiled their cover-up were part of what is now called the New Madrid earthquakes (named after New Madrid, Missouri, the town that received the hardest pounding), which remain the most powerful earthquakes to hit the eastern half of the United States. So strong was the seismic activity that the Mississippi River briefly ran backward, and the residents in New Madrid reported that the flat ground rippled in waves, like the ocean.

DUDE LOOKS LIKE A LADY

Deborah Sampson wanted to fight for colonial independence in the American Revolution, but there was just one insurmountable problem—she was a woman. Sampson didn't let that stop her though. In May 1782, she dressed herself as a man and enlisted in the Continental army under her deceased brother's name, Robert Shurtliff Sampson. In July that same year she was badly wounded by musket fire. Fearing that her true sex would be discovered, she asked her fellow soldiers to leave her to die. They did not, and instead carried her to the hospital. After some cursory treatment, Sampson quietly snuck out of the hospital to treat her wounds herself (a risky move that left her with a musket ball permanently lodged in her thigh).

She managed to keep her secret for over year—even receiving a promotion—until she contracted a fever so bad that it left her out of her senses. When Sampson's doctor removed her clothes, he discovered the heavy bindings she used to conceal her lady-ness. The doctor told no one, and instead took Sampson to his home where his wife and daughters treated her. By the time Sampson had fully recovered, the war was over, and she was honorably discharged.

Dual Duel Failure

In June 1836, Congressmen Daniel Jenifer of Maryland and Jesse Bynum of North Carolina met for a duel. Jenifer had said some unkind things about President Andrew Jackson's party and Bynum had taken exception. Satisfaction was demanded! Both men had reputations as a good shot, so death was in the air. The two men walked thirty paces apart, then turned and aimed. After a count of three, both men fired. Both men missed.

So they reloaded and tried again. And missed again. And again. And again. And again. On the sixth attempt Bynum's gun accidentally discharged before the count to three had been completed, but he missed Jenifer all the same. By the protocol of gentlemanly dueling, Jenifer's second had the right to shoot Bynum for firing early, but Jenifer stopped the man—not to be magnanimous, but because *he* wanted to shoot Bynum. So Jenifer steadied his gun and fired. And missed. In six attempts both men failed to even graze the other. Finally sensing that maybe the gods were trying to tell them something, Jenifer and Bynum agreed to a draw.

A LITTLE GUTS GO A LONG WAY

At the age of sixteen Audie Murphy stood just 5 feet 5 inches and weighed around 110 pounds, but he earnestly wanted to enlist in WWII. The marines and the air force turned him away due to his age and size before the army finally accepted him. And they wouldn't regret it. In 1944, while in southern France, a German soldier pretending to surrender shot and killed Murphy's best friend Lattie Tipton. Murphy flew into a berserker rage and single-handedly wiped out the German's machine gun crew, then used the German machine gun and grenades to wipe out several more German gun nests. For this he received the Distinguished Service Cross and, amazingly, this was hardly the most badass thing he did in the war.

In 1945, again fighting in France, Murphy's unit was reduced from 128 to nineteen men by German gunfire. Murphy sent all of the remaining men to the rear as he climbed aboard an abandoned and burning M10 tank destroyer. He used the M10's .50 caliber machine gun to annihilate the German infantry, some of whom were only 100 feet away. During all this—while the M10 was on fire and full of gas, and while Murphy was shot in the leg—he called in artillery fire using a landline telephone, pointing out where best to aim the incoming destruction. He did this for an hour until the Germans finally retreated. Later, when asked why he took on an entire German infantry by himself, he said, "They were killing my friends." Oh, and it should be mentioned that Murphy had malaria for almost the entire war.

Lil' Audie Murphy became one of the most decorated soldiers in US history, receiving the Medal of Honor, the Distinguished Service Cross, two Silver Stars, the Legion of Merit Medal, two Bronze Stars, and three Purple Hearts. He returned to America a national treasure. Hollywood even made a hit film about his astonishing bravery called *To Hell and Back* (based on Murphy's autobiography of the same name). And who better to star as Murphy than Murphy himself? Audie Murphy would go on to star in over forty films before dying in a plane crash in 1971.

 ## IMPEACHY KEEN

During the Constitutional Convention, when the groundwork of the US government was being constructed, Benjamin Franklin quipped that the removal of "obnoxious" chief executives had historically been accomplished by assassination. For the new America, Franklin felt that a procedural mechanism for removal would maybe be preferable: impeachment.

Since 1789, the House of Representatives has initiated impeachment proceedings only sixty-two times. Only two presidents have been impeached: Andrew Johnson and Bill Clinton. Both cases were acquitted. Many falsely assume Richard Nixon was impeached, but Nixon resigned before the House could vote on moving forward with an impeachment trial.

 ## COUNTERFEIT ART

Emanuel Ninger was a German immigrant who moved his family to New Jersey in 1882. He worked as a modest sign painter, so it surprised his neighbors when he soon bought a farm. Where did he get the money? Ninger told people he was receiving a pension from the Prussian army, but in reality he was receiving it from himself. Ninger was a master forger of a very unique variety. While most counterfeiters create presses to produce scores of fake bills, Ninger made his by hand, often spending weeks painstakingly producing a single $100 bill (in the 1880s that was the equivalent of over $2,000). His reproductions were near flawless, save for some cheeky omissions—Ninger would often omit the line crediting the Bureau of Engraving and Printing, as well as the counterfeiting warning. His forgery career proved short-lived though. The Secret Service busted him in 1896 after one of his $50 notes got wet and smudged in the presence of the bartender he gave it to.

Because only the rich could possess the bills he produced, the general public saw Ninger's crimes as relatively victimless, if not hilarious. And the rich saw him even differently yet. Since Ninger produced all his forgeries by hand, many viewed them as works of art. It was and is illegal to possess counterfeit money, which created a small black market for Ninger's bills among collectors. In the end, Ninger's fake bills became even more valuable than the currency they were pretending to be.

▦ THE NO-PARTY SYSTEM

The partisan back and forth of a two-party system has defined US politics from the very beginning. Yet that was never what the Founding Fathers intended. George Washington did not belong to a political party, because there weren't any political parties—just the patriots. But during Washington's first term, a divide was already forming between the young nation's political leaders. On one side blossomed the Federalist Party, led by Secretary of the Treasury Alexander Hamilton. The Federalists favored a strong central government, with a federal bank and close ties to Britain. Secretary of State Thomas Jefferson and James Madison strongly opposed these ideas, and thus grew the Democratic-Republican Party (whose adherents are often referred to as Jeffersonian Democrats). The Federalists burnt out in a few short decades, and for a too-brief period (1816–1824) America miraculously functioned as a nonpartisan country. Deservedly, this period is known as the Era of Good Feelings.

But paradise could only last so long. Soon the Democratic-Republican Party cleaved in two, forming into the Jacksonian Democrats (led by Andrew Jackson) and the Whig Party (American Whigs were another name for patriots during the Revolution). The Whigs eventually flamed out too, though the emerging antislavery Republican Party adopted many of their policies. Other third parties were to come and go along the way, but at the presidential level it has been the Democrats' and the Republicans' show ever since.

⬛ HEY, WHERE'S THE BIBLE?

The first presidential inauguration took place April 30, 1789, on the balcony of Federal Hall in New York City, which was the US capital at the time. Right before the ceremony was about to start, officiator Robert R. Livingston, who was chancellor of New York (a now defunct position), realized that no one had thought to bring a Bible for George Washington to swear his oath upon. Both Livingston and Washington were Freemasons, so Livingston had the Bible from nearby St. John's Masonic Lodge No.1 brought in. Since things were now running late, the Bible was opened in haste, randomly falling on Genesis 49:13: "Zebulun shall dwell at the haven of the sea; and he shall be for an haven of ships; and his border shall be unto Zidon." This same Bible was later used in the inaugurations of Warren Harding, Dwight D. Eisenhower, Jimmy Carter, and George H. W. Bush. It was to be used again for George W. Bush, but foul weather on the day of the ceremony prevented it.

GALVANIZED IRON JOE

US soldiers are commonly referred to as G.I.s, a satirical appropriation of the "government issue" stamp put on military equipment and supplies. But when the "G.I." stamp first came into use during WWI it actually stood for "galvanized iron." By WWII, the meaning had changed and soldiers were cynically identifying themselves as "government issue" too. The nickname grew less satirical and more affectionate as it became synony-

mous with being an American soldier. The Servicemen's Read-
justment Act of 1944, which provided a range of benefits for
returning veterans, was more commonly known as the G.I. Bill.

 ## PASSING THE BUCK

In classic poker terminology "the buck" was a marker showing which player was dealing. Often dealer duties would
rotate around the table and if a player did not want the
responsibility of dealing, he or she would "pass the buck."
The phrase was later used metaphorically to refer to shirk-
ing any kind of responsibility or duty.

The phrase also became an integral part of President
Harry Truman's legacy after photos emerged of a plaque
on his Oval Office desk reading, "The Buck Stops Here."
The plaque was a gift given to Truman by his friend Fred
Canfil, a federal marshal in Missouri. Canfil had seen the
plaque on the desk of El Reno, Oklahoma, prison warden
Clark Schilder. When Canfil inquired about the plaque,
Schilder revealed that it had been made for him at the
prison and could easily be replicated. And so it was. Canfil
gifted the replica to Truman shortly after Truman assumed
the presidency in 1945. After the plaque made national
news, Truman incorporated the motto into his public persona, making "buck" references in several speeches, notably: "The president, whoever he is, has to decide. He can't
pass the buck to anybody. No one else can do the deciding
for him. That's his job."

THE CONFEDERATES GET SILLY

In February of 1863, two back-to-back blizzards left 17
inches of snow on the Confederate army camps near Fredericksburg, Virginia. When twenty-six-year-old General
Robert Hoke woke to discover the snow, only one course
of action seemed fitting—an epic snowball fight. Hoke
gathered his North Carolina soldiers and, using his mili-

tary mind and his men's veteran skills, he staged an attack on the neighboring Georgian camp. Though armed with snowballs, the men nonetheless organized themselves as they would in a real skirmish, led by officers and utilizing cavalry and infantry in battle lines. The North Carolinians descended upon the Georgians, and a devastating pelting began.

After the snow-dust cleared, Georgia's Colonel William Stiles assembled a "council of war," and planned his counterattack. Stiles organized his soldiers into columns of companies, each man with a snowball in hand, and marched to Hoke's camp. But when they arrived, they discovered that the wily North Carolinians had filled their shoulder bags with snowballs—giving them great mobility, without needing to "reload." The Carolinians took many prisoners that day, "whitewashing" their captives before allowing them to leave. Nearly ten thousand Confederate soldiers participated in the "Great Snowball Battle."

★★★★★★★★★★★★★★★★★★

Robert MCNAMARA was the United States' longest-serving secretary of DEFENSE, serving under Presidents John F. Kennedy and Lyndon B. Johnson from 1961 to 1968. His full name is Robert STRANGE McNamara.

★★★★★★★★★★★★★★★★★★

A PATRIOTIC SPELLER

Noah Webster earned his place in history as the author of the American dictionary, first published in 1828 as *An American Dictionary of the English Language*. And he meant that title quite literally. Webster lived through the American Revolution and was a fervent patriot. He didn't just dislike the politics of Great Britain, he disliked their use of the English language too. He believed in the democracy of all things, including the democracy of words. In England, grammar, spelling, and pronunciation—much like everything else—were dictated by the aristocracy. Webster believed that an accurate dictionary must take into account how the common man uses language. While creating his dictionary (and his popular series of spelling tutorial books), Webster also took the opportunity to modify some spelling issues he objected to, Americanizing them. He replaced the *c* with an *s* in words like "defense," reversed the *re* at the end of words like "theater," and dropped the *u* from words like "color."

Of course, Brits still contend that we're using their language incorrectly.

WASHINGTON HOME

Mount Vernon, George Washington's home in Virginia, is one of America's most cherished historical landmarks. But it was originally known as Little Hunting Creek Plantation. When George's older half-brother Lawrence Washington inherited the estate, he changed its name to Mount Vernon in honor of British Vice Admiral Edward Vernon, whom Lawrence served under during the War of Jenkins' Ear. When Lawrence died of tuberculosis in 1752, George inherited the property and retained the name to honor his beloved brother, not Edward Vernon.

LEWIS AND WHAT'S-HIS-FACE

There may not be a more illustrious duo in American history than that of Lewis and Clark, who gained ground as permanent fixtures in both history books and the public imagination when they set off to explore the newly acquired Louisiana Purchase in 1804, searching for a river passage connecting the Missouri River with the Pacific

Ocean (which they didn't find, because it doesn't exist). Yet the Lewis and Clark Expedition could very easily have been called the Lewis Expedition...

President Thomas Jefferson, who dreamed up the expedition, had personally selected Meriwether Lewis as commander. But Lewis wanted a partner with more practical military experience, particularly experience with Native Americans. For this he selected an old acquaintance, William Clark. Lewis promised Clark that they would both receive a captain's commission and would have equal command of the expedition. But while in St. Louis, poised to begin their long journey, Lewis received a letter from Washington, D.C., informing him that Clark would only be receiving a lieutenant's commission. The letter did not explain the exact reasoning, other than to say that it was deemed "improper." Possibly President Jefferson felt that having co-commanders might cause problems, wanting Lewis to take sole command. Lewis immediately wrote to Clark (who was further down the river, stationed with their crew), apologizing and saying, "I think it will be best to let none of our party or any other persons know anything about the grade, you will observe that the grade has no effect upon your compensation, which by God, shall be equal to my own." And so it would be. As far as anyone on the expedition knew, Clark was a captain and was in dual command with Lewis.

In 2001, President Bill Clinton promoted Clark to the rank of captain in the US Army, posthumously. Better late than never.

A CLEAN SLATE

The United States went into debt to fund the Revolutionary War, and the country has carried a debt ever since. Some presidents have raised the debt, some have lowered it, but only one has ever paid it off—President Andrew Jackson. Before he was president, Jackson had been a land speculator and had a personal aversion to debt, which he saw as a moral failing. When he took office he began selling off Western land owned by the federal government and manically slashing the budget, blocking nearly every spending bill he could, including one to build national roadways. By January of 1835, Jackson had paid off America's $58 million debt ($1.2 trillion in today's dollars).

Jackson had killed the national bank as part of his budget war, so he divvied up the new surplus among the states. So of course the states started printing massive amounts of money. Soon the land bubble that had allowed Jackson to erase the debt was getting dangerously close to bursting. Jackson tried to remedy the problem by requiring all government land sales to be done in silver or gold, but this ended up creating a catastrophic deflationary backlash. The bubble then burst, leading to the Panic of 1837, one of the worst economic depressions in American history. But, hey, Jackson is still the only president to erase the debt, however temporarily.

One Final Expedition

The well-mannered, curious, and forthright Meriwether Lewis, who braved an arduous two-year expedition through the American Northwest, was not the kind of man you would expect to die under grim and mysterious circumstances. Yes, you might expect him to be taken by disease, starvation, or hostile Native Americans while on an expedition, but certainly not found with part of his head blown off, back in the civilized world. Yet...

On October 10, 1809, Lewis stayed at Grinder's Stand, an inn outside of Nashville, on his way to Washington, D.C., In the middle of the night, gunshots were heard, and Lewis was found barely alive on the floor of his room, bleeding from several gunshot wounds, including one to the head. He was dead by sunrise. The death was reported a suicide and immediately controversy arose. William Clark and President Thomas Jefferson, who both knew Lewis as well as any men could, accepted this sad fact. Jefferson confided in friends that Lewis had long suffered from "hypochondria," which is presumably how Jefferson viewed a yet-to-be-identified bipolar disorder. The Lewis family believed an assassin murdered him. But with no tangible motives or suspects, no formal legal inquiries were ever made.

A LADY OF A SPY

Rose O'Neal Greenhow was a member of Washington, D.C., high society who rubbed elbows with senators, generals, and presidents. When the Civil War broke out, the widowed Greenhow felt her loyalties divided. She ardently believed in the South's right to secession and was vocal enough on the subject that she was soon recruited as a spy by the Confederacy.

In the summer of 1861, she began passing secret messages to Confederate General P.G.T. Beauregard. Greenhow surprised even herself with the high-level information she was able to obtain. But it was not going unnoticed. By August, Allan Pinkerton, head of the Union Intelligence Service (and founder of the Pinkerton National Detective Agency), arrested Greenhow. Upon searching Greenhow's home he discovered notes on military movements and maps of Washington fortifications. The evidence was overwhelming. And Greenhow never denied it.

After serving a year in prison, Greenhow was deported to Virginia, where the Confederacy hailed her as a hero. Confederate president Jefferson Davis enlisted her for a diplomatic mission to bolster support for the Confederate cause in Europe. The Old World aristocracy, who by nature frowned upon the idea of an uppity government interfering with the rights of the ruling class, welcomed Greenhow with open arms. While in Britain she was received by Queen Victoria and even published a best-selling book,

My Imprisonment and the First Year of Abolition Rule at Washington.

In the fall of 1864, Greenhow returned to the Confederate states with dispatches from Europe and a sack of gold that she planned to donate to the Confederate Treasury (much of the gold is believed to have been royalties from her book). On October 1, 1864, her ship ran aground near Wilmington, North Carolina, after evading a pursuing Union gunboat. Fearing capture, Greenhow placed her gold sack around her neck and fled the ship in a rowboat. But when the rowboat capsized in the rough water, all that heavy gold did not do her any favors. Greenhow was pulled beneath the surface and drowned. Later, a Confederate soldier discovered her body—and her gold—when it washed ashore. Greenhow's grave marker simply reads: "Mrs. Rose O'N. Greenhow, a bearer of dispatches to the Confederate Government."

 ## CREEPY

The Committee for the Re-Election of the President (CRP), often mockingly abbreviated as CREEP, was a fundraising organization working toward the reelection of Richard Nixon. CRP earned its mocking nickname after it was implicated in the planning and funding of the 1972 Watergate scandal.

A LONG OVERDUE BOOK

Mark Twain's *Adventures of Huckleberry Finn* is considered one of the great American novels. After it was published in 1885, Twain gifted his original manuscript—full of notes and changes—to his friend James Fraser Gluck, a Buffalo lawyer and book collector. Gluck donated the manuscript to the Eerie County Public Library in New York, of which he was the primary benefactor. Yet, years later, when someone went looking for said manuscript, only the second half of *Finn* could be found. The first half was lost…until 1990.

The first half of the manuscript was located inside a trunk that once belonged to Gluck and had made a circuitous journey through inheritances to Los Angeles, California, where it was eventually discovered by one of Gluck's grandnieces. It seems that Gluck, who died very suddenly at the age of forty-five in 1897, had taken the first half of the manuscript home with him to read. As his family packed up his estate after his death, the manuscript was hastily put into the trunk that would be its home for one hundred years. Fortunately for Gluck's ancestors, the Eerie County Public Library wasn't charging any late fees.

EVERYBODY IS DOING IT

Most Americans associate the practice of scalping with Native Americans, but the gory haircut had been practiced in parts of ancient Eurasia, as well as medieval Europe. And only a few Native American tribes scalped as a custom prior to the arrival of the white man. European colonists were the ones with the true scalp fetish. During King William's War (1688–1697), Massachusetts offered a hefty fee for Indian scalps, and this practice continued in New England through pretty much every war the colony fought in up until the American Revolution. During the French and Indian War, Native Americans scalped their fair share of British colonists, but that was because the French offered them a similar scalp-for-money deal. Europeans were scalp crazy!

During the Civil War, William T. "Bloody Bill" Anderson was a pro-Confederate guerrilla who commanded a fearsome group of raiders that included future outlaw Jesse James. Anderson's gang carried out one of the most brutal guerrilla actions of the war, the Centralia Massacre, in which Anderson and his men killed over twenty unarmed Union soldiers they found aboard a captured train. The gang also had a penchant for scalping. Bloody Bill liked to adorn his horse's saddle with the scalps of Union soldiers.

TURTLE SOUP

In modern times, presidents have served traditional American food at the White House Fourth of July celebration, including barbecue classics such as hot dogs and hamburgers. The tenth president, John Tyler, had more unique tastes. For his 1841 Independence Day dinner, he served a 300-pound sea turtle cooked into a soup. Tyler was a lover of turtle soup.

Given the character of the American Revolution, you might presume that there are no ROYAL palaces in the United States. But America wound up with one when Hawaii became a state. Iolani Palace was the residence of HAWAIIAN kings and queens until the monarchy was overthrown in 1893, after which it was used as the capital building. The PALACE is now a museum.

YOU CAN JUDGE A MAN BY THE COMPANY HE KEEPS

At the age of twenty-five, Charles "Lucky Lindy" Lindbergh became world famous overnight when he piloted the *Spirit of St. Louis* in a solo flight from New York to Paris in May 1927 to claim a coveted prize of $25,000 ($310,000 now). Then he regrettably became even more famous in March of 1932 when his twenty-month-old son was kidnapped and murdered. The press dubbed the tragedy the

Crime of the Century, and in the aftermath of a very public investigation and an even more public criminal trial (in which immigrant laborer Bruno Richard Hauptmann was convicted and then executed in 1936), Lindbergh and his wife moved to England.

At the time, Adolph Hitler was building up his *Luftwaffe* (German air force), and the US military wished to use Lindbergh's international appeal to gain some insight into just what the Nazis were cooking up. Hermann Göring, founder of the Gestapo and commander of the *Luftwaffe*, was more than happy to pal around with Lindbergh, let him fly some planes, and generally impress him with the might of the Third Reich's engineering. And Lindbergh was certainly impressed—he reported that the Germans were years ahead of the United States as far as aviation technology was concerned.

Lindbergh quite liked Berlin and looked into purchasing a home there. In October 1938, on behalf of Hitler, Göring presented Lindbergh with a medal from of the Order of the German Eagle, an award given to prominent foreigners deemed sympathetic to Nazism. One month later the Night of Broken Glass pogrom occurred, which was a series of coordinated attacks against Jews throughout Germany. The American Jewish community thought that Lindbergh should return the medal as an international statement and show of support for Jews. Lindbergh thought differently, refusing. He also thought that America should steer far clear of the Nazis, becoming the spokesman of the antiwar America First Committee.

Some labeled Lindbergh a Nazi sympathizer. President Franklin D. Roosevelt called him a "defeatist and appeaser." American Jews thought he was anti-Semitic after he warned against the dangers of Jew's "large ownership and influence in our motion pictures, our press, our radio and our government," which he believed Jews were using to lead the US into war for personal reasons that ignored the best interests of the country. The anti-Semitism claims weren't helped by his views on eugenics and comments like, "Our bond with Europe is one of race and not of political ideology." Nor was his close friendship with automobile pioneer and eminent anti-Semite Henry Ford (who had also received an Order of the German Eagle medal).

After the attacks on Pearl Harbor, Lindbergh changed his tune, at least when it came to the Japanese. He became a technical representative in the Pacific Theater of Operations, teaching pilots special tricks and eventually partaking in combat missions.

THE OCCURRENCE OF AMBROSE BIERCE

"As to me, I leave here tomorrow for an unknown destination." So ended the last known letter of Ambrose Bierce, one of the most respected literary voices of his era. Bierce, best remember today for the satirical reference book *The Devil's Dictionary* and his short story "An Occurrence at Owl Creek Bridge," which is often required reading in high school English classes, was one of thirteen children— all given names that began with the letter "A." He fought in the Civil War and later became the most noted and influential columnist for William Randolph Hearst's *San Francisco Examiner*. In October 1913, at the age of seventy-one, Bierce put his affairs in order and then went off for a final adventure that started with a tour of his old Civil War battlefields and ended in Mexico, where he hoped to meet up with Pancho Villa's army to observe the Mexican Revolution. He was never heard from again.

The commonly accepted theory is that Bierce simply died as an unfortunate casualty in the incessant fighting in Mexico. Another popular version has him being executed by federal troops who discovered that he was looking for Villa. Yet another version has him finding Villa and dying on the battlefield. In *Born to Raise Hell,* Lowell Thomas's book about soldier-of-fortune Edward "Tex" O'Reilly, O'Reilly supported the theory that Bierce was executed by federal troops—though he did not witness the event, instead learning about it from local villagers. The locals supposedly told O'Reilly that the old gringo kept laughing, even after his executioners began to fire. More outlandish theories posited Bierce went to Mexico to steal an ancient Maya artifact called the Skull of Doom, or that he took up with a tribe of natives who believed he was a god.

PATTON'S SHELL-SHOCK SHOCKER

As a reward for his stellar success in WWII's North African campaign, in 1943 "Old Blood and Guts" General George S. Patton was given command of the Seventh Army in preparation for the invasion of Sicily. He had proven himself to be a formidable military tactician, but his career was nearly derailed by a single impulsive act... against one of his own men.

On August 3, while Patton was visiting wounded troops in a field hospital, he found Private Charles H. Kuhl huddled on a stool. Kuhl appeared unharmed, so Patton asked the man where his injuries were. Kuhl said that he wasn't wounded, he just didn't feel well; he couldn't "take it." Doctors informed Patton that Kuhl was suffering from battle fatigue, or what they had called "shell-shock" in WWI and what we now call *posttraumatic stress disorder* (PTSD). To a man who dreamed his whole life of getting the honor of fighting in a war, this was unacceptable. So the general slapped Kuhl across the face with his gloves and literally kicked him out of the tent, ordering him to return to the front line.

When US newspaper columnist Drew Pearson reported the incident, it became a media firestorm—members of Congress even demanded that Patton be stripped of command. According to Kuhl himself, when Patton returned on orders to apologize, Kuhl had already been readmitted to the hospital after the doctors discovered that his fatigue was actually malaria. Whether Patton thought that malaria was any more or less of an acceptable reason to miss a battle is unknown.

 ## JOB TITLE

After the colonists won their independence from Great Britain, they were left to figure out exactly how to run this new country of theirs. They had picked General George Washington to be their first leader, but how should they address him now that he was in charge? It was an issue Vice President John Adams took very seriously. He didn't think "president" quite cut it. It lacked splendor. "His Excellency" was suggested. As was "His High Mightiness." But most of the Founding Fathers did not agree with Adams's reasoning. After all, they'd just spent years and many lives ridding themselves of a monarch. As the debates grew heated, Benjamin Franklin snarkily suggested that Adams could be addressed as "His Superfluous Excellency." In the end it was decided that simply "Mr. President" would do just fine.

 ## MR. ZIP

The Zone Improvement Plan (or ZIP codes) was the brainchild of postal employee Robert Moon. Prior to the introduction of ZIP codes, the process of sorting and delivering mail was understandably slow. In the early 1940s, the United States Post Office Department (as the United States Postal Service was known from 1792 to 1971) had introduced two-digit postal zones for several large cities to help speed up the process, but Moon envisioned an entire country broken up into zones. By the 1960s, as the overall use of postal services reached a new high, the post office finally took action. In 1963, five-digit ZIP codes were introduced nationwide—though initially they were non-mandatory—and met with minor resistance.

The telephone company had recently switched to a number-only system and many Americans felt they were being inundated with too many damn numbers to remember. The post office went so far as to create a mascot named Mr. ZIP (informally "Zippy") to help convince reluctant mail users to try the system out. Fortunately the effectiveness of ZIP codes was immediately apparent to everyone, radically speeding up delivery times in an era when the old delivery systems were breaking down.

In 1983 the US Postal Service introduced four more digits to speed the process up even further, though the ZIP+4 system never became mandatory for general mail.

 ## A Casual Casualty

The first soldier to be killed in the Civil War was Private Daniel Hough. Following the declarations of secession by seven Southern states, South Carolina demanded that the US Army get the hell out of Fort Sumter near Charleston. Since the Union viewed secession as treason, it refused and the Battle of Fort Sumter ensued on April 12, 1861, kicking off the war. But the battle only lasted two days, and there were zero fatalities. As far as battles go, it was quite pleasant. The Union garrison surrendered the fort, and Confederate soldiers moved in. The Union only had one request before they vacated—they wanted to perform a one-hundred-gun salute to the US flag. In what must have seemed like a positive omen for the Confederates, midway through the salute a pile of cartridges exploded, injuring several Union soldiers and killing poor Private Hough. The Union was then escorted from the premises without finishing their salute.

Sharks Patrol These Waters

On July 26, 1945, the USS *Indianapolis* dropped off a very special cargo at the air base on Tinian Island near Guam. The cargo contained the enriched uranium for the atomic bomb *Little Boy*, which would be dropped on Hiroshima on August 6. Though the crew of the *Indianapolis* was entirely clueless as to the contents of their special cargo, they were regrettably to pay the karmic price for the devastation *Little Boy* brought to the citizens of Japan. On July 29, while the ship was reporting to new duties elsewhere, a Japanese torpedo sank the *Indianapolis* in the dark of night. Of the 1,196 men on board, roughly three hundred went down with the ship, leaving the rest floating in the oil-soaked water. It would be nearly five days before they were rescued, by which time there were only 317 survivors.

The story of the *Indianapolis* gained a high level of fame after it was featured in the 1975 movie *Jaws*, in a scene where actor Robert Shaw gives a sensational account of the tragedy that suggests sharks killed hundreds upon hundreds of the sailors. Sharks were indeed a daily presence, but they posed a much greater risk to the dead sailors than to the living ones. With an insufficient number of life vests and flotation devices, most of the deceased had simply drowned. The rest had to contend with exposure and dehydration and other sailors.

Captain Lewis L. Haynes, the ship's senior medical officer, gave a harrowing account of a madness that took hold of the group one evening, when the delirious men became convinced that there were Japanese sailors floating among them. "And then everybody started to fight. They were totally out of their minds. A lot of men were killed that night. A lot of men drowned. Overnight everybody untied themselves and got scattered in all directions." At first Haynes had set out to collect all the dog tags from the dead men, but with literally hundreds dying around him, the sheer weight of the dog tags threatened to submerge him, and Haynes had to let them go.

Though ultimately a very small percentage of men were likely killed by sharks, even if it were only six or seven, that would still make it the single worst shark attack episode in history.

John Adams was the FIRST president to live in the White House.

METER MADE

Park-O-Meter No. 1 was the world's first parking meter, and it was installed on the southeast corner of what was then First Street and Robinson Avenue in Oklahoma City, Oklahoma, in 1935. The meter was designed by newspaper publisher Carl Magee as a solution to the parking problem posed by the rapidly increasing number of automobiles in the city. The meter charged five cents for one hour of parking, and naturally citizens hated it, viewing it as a tax for owning a car. But retailers loved the meter, as it encouraged a quick turnover of customers. Just five years later there were 140,000 parking meters operating in the United States. As for Park-O-Meter No. 1, it now lives in the Statehood Gallery of the Oklahoma Historical Society.

 ## GENERATION GAP

Tenth president of the United States John Tyler was born in 1790 and died in 1862. At the time of this book's publishing, two of his grandchildren are still alive. How the hell is that possible, you surely ask? Well, Tyler men apparently have very impressive sperm. John Tyler fathered fifteen children—more than any other president. In 1853, at the age of sixty-three, John Tyler fathered Lyon Gardiner Tyler. Then in 1924, at the ripe old age of seventy-one, Lyon fathered Lyon Gardiner Tyler Jr. As if that wasn't virile enough, he fathered another son in 1928, Harrison Ruffin Tyler.

PEACE THROUGH MAD SCIENCE

Serbian American Nikola Tesla was one of the greatest scientific minds the United States has ever seen. Over the course of his impressive career he developed the alternating current (AC) electrical supply system and pioneered much of the work that went into wireless communication and the radio. Tesla's legacy was unfairly handicapped by the fact that many of his most practical innovations were credited to or owned by other men, like his former employer Thomas Edison. But during his own time he was renowned as a larger-than-life figure, an archetypal mad scientist.

Tesla's public persona was not an affected one to gain attention or business. He was in truth terrible at business and died penniless. No, Tesla was genuinely a bit mad. He had a photographic memory and did advanced calculations entirely in his head, making many of his most radical scientific concepts impossible to replicate because the damn lunatic didn't write down how he achieved them. He showed signs of obsessive–compulsive disorder, growing to hate round objects and touching human hair, and remained celibate his entire life (though he did claim to have developed an intense nonsexual love affair with a white female pigeon).

For every one of Tesla's practical ideas, he seemed to have two more totally batshit ones. In his Houston Street lab in New York, he maintained that he built an electromechanical oscillator, or "earthquake machine," that went out of control, violently shaking the building and threatening to level the whole neighborhood, forcing Tesla to destroy the machine with a sledgehammer. He also claimed that he discovered a way to split the Earth in two using similar controlled vibrations. But no idea better suits Tesla's mad scientist image than his "Peace Ray." A 1937 article in the *New York Times* explained that the Peace Ray would "send concentrated beams of particles through the free air, of such tremendous energy that they will bring down a fleet of 10,000 enemy airplanes at a distance of 250 miles from the defending nation's border and will cause armies of millions to drop dead in their tracks...." When put into operation, Dr. Tesla said this latest invention of his would make war impossible. "This death-beam," he asserted, "would surround each country like an invisible Chinese wall, only a million times more impenetrable. It would make every nation impregnable against attack by airplanes or by large invading armies."

As utterly bonkers as all that sounds, if any person ever could have conceivably built such a device, it would have been Nikola Tesla. He tried and failed to sell his Peace Ray to Great Britain and the League of Nations, but couldn't find anyone willing to pony up the amount of money it would cost to build and test it (or, presumably, anyone willing to take his idea seriously). Tesla died in 1943, at the age of eighty-six, taking the Peace Ray and many other insane, unrealized concepts with him.

THE HEADLESS HORSEMAN

When most people think of the Headless Horseman, they think of Washington Irving's classic short story "The Legend of Sleep Hollow" (published in the 1820 collection *The Sketch Book of Geoffrey Crayon*, which contains Irving's other classic tale "Rip Van Winkle" as well). But *The Headless Horseman* was also the title of a popular 1860s novel by adventure author Mayne Reid, who could count Arthur Conan Doyle, Vladimir Nabokov, and President Theodore Roosevelt as childhood fans. Irving's story was based on a popular German folktale, which he transposed to New York State. Reid's book claimed a much grislier origin.

Reid's titular creature was inspired by a story that may or may not be fictitious, but that inspired Reid all the same.

The alleged event stars real-life frontier hardass and legendary Texas Ranger William "Bigfoot" Wallace (1817–1899), who earned his nickname based on his considerable size. Wallace was born in Virginia, but headed to Texas in 1836 after learning that his brother had been killed by Mexican soldiers in the Goliad Massacre. After the Mexican-American War, Wallace claimed that his Mexican vendetta was over, but possibly that vendetta still simmered. For it was Wallace's time as a Texas Ranger that supposedly inspired Reid's story. Wallace was after a band of Mexican horse thieves led by a bandit named Vidal. When Wallace and his partner caught up with the thieves, he decided to set an example. So Bigfoot decapitated Vidal, strapped his headless corpse into his saddle, and set the horse galloping off into the desert. From that point forward residents of Texas reported sightings of a mysterious and terrifying headless rider roaming the desert, and the myth of El Muerto the Headless Horseman was born. True? Who knows. But it is a damn good ghost story origin.

A LONG, LONG VOYAGE

In 1977, NASA launched the *Voyager I* space probe with the primary mission of studying Jupiter and Saturn. *Voyager* successfully completed its mission in 1980. Since then it has been hurtling farther and farther away from Earth while remaining in contact with the Deep Space Network. In 1990, from a distance of 3.7 billion miles, the probe transmitted our solar system's first family portrait, in which Earth can be seen as a tiny blue speck alongside Venus, Jupiter, Saturn, Uranus, and Neptune (the remaining planets were either too dim to see or obscured by the sun). At the time of this book's publication, *Voyager* has reached the heliosphere at 11.1 billion miles from Earth, the farthest boundary of our cosmic neighborhood, which means it will soon become the first manmade object to leave the solar system and enter interstellar space. Barring a collision or malfunction, *Voyager* will continue to send back data until its battery dies sometime between 2025 and 2030.

As our emissary into deep space, *Voyager I* carries a gold-plated audio-visual disc in the off chance that some joyriding aliens should happen upon it. The disc contains photos of the Earth and its variety of life forms; a bevy of scientific and other relevant information; what amounts to a collection of soothing white-noise machine audio files, like whale songs and crashing waves; a greatest hits of Earth music, ranging from Mozart to Chuck Berry's "Johnny B. Goode;" and a message from President Jimmy Carter, saying, "This is a present from a small, distant world, a token of our sounds, our science, our images, our music, our thoughts, and our feelings. We are attempting to survive our time so we may live into yours."

Carter may not have been the most popular president, but he is now effectively Earth's representative to the cosmos.

 # A LITTLE PRE-GAMING

On March 4, 1865, when Abraham Lincoln and Andrew Johnson were inaugurated president and vice president of the country, Johnson was drunk out of his gourd. Johnson had decided to get plowed the evening before, and instead of getting sworn in with a hangover, he continued getting even more plowed that morning with Secretary of the United States Senate John W. Forney. Forney of course did not need to address a crowd. But Johnson did. And he gave a rambling, slurred speech. Those close to Johnson assured the press that the vice president did not normally booze it up so much, with Lincoln himself saying, "He made a bad slip the other day, but you need not be scared; Andy ain't a drunkard." Johnson claimed that he had been drinking whiskey to medicate himself for typhoid fever.

NOT A BAD DEAL

It is probably safe to say that the smartest decision US leaders ever made for the future of the United States was declaring independence from Great Britain. But after that, the savviest decision has to be the Louisiana Purchase, the 1803 acquisition from France of a whopping 828,000 square miles of land—an area that covers all of present-day Arkansas, Iowa, Kansas, Missouri, Nebraska, and Oklahoma, and parts of Louisiana, Minnesota, Montana, New Mexico, North Dakota, South Dakota, Texas, and Wyoming. The Louisiana Purchase accomplished two very important things: 1) it removed France as a competitor for American territory, and 2) with the US now laying claim to two-thirds of its present landmass, it became explicitly clear that the US was inevitably going to hog its way to the Pacific Ocean. In other words, America was not going to become New Europe. Most amazingly of all, not only was no war fought to acquire this land, but France gave us a screamin' deal to boot!

France had controlled the vast Louisiana Territory from 1699 until 1762, when they gave it over to Spain. When Napoleon Bonaparte rose to power, he reneged on that deal in 1800, hoping to build a French empire in North America. But an impending war in Europe caused Napoleon to forgo those plans. He also needed some cash, fast. President Thomas Jefferson's administration was able to close the acquisition deal for only $15 million, which is around $220 million today. Though $220 million is a lot of money, to put that figure into stark government spending perspective, that's about the same price as a single Boeing C-17 Globemaster III military transport aircraft. Or the budget of the movie *The Avengers*. For that low, low price Thomas Jefferson doubled the size of the country.

The US MOTTO, "In God We Trust," was not adopted as the national SLOGAN until 1956.

THE DATING WISDOM OF BENJAMIN FRANKLIN

In 1745, when Benjamin Franklin was thirty-nine years old, he wrote a letter of advice to his friend Cadwallader Colden, the lieutenant governor for the Province of New York. The greater purpose of the letter was to advise Colden to take a wife to cure his sexual urges, but the more entertaining section of the letter is a list of eight detailed arguments for why older women make better mistresses. Here is an abridged version of Franklin's sexy wisdom:

1. Because as they have more Knowledge of the World and their Minds are better stor'd with Observations, their Conversation is more improving and more lastingly agreable.

2. Because when Women cease to be handsome, they study to be good. And hence there is hardly such a thing to be found as an old Woman who is not a good Woman.

3. Because there is no hazard of Children, which irregularly produc'd may be attended with much Inconvenience.

4. Because thro' more Experience, they are more prudent and discreet in conducting an Intrigue to prevent Suspicion.

5. Because in every Animal that walks upright, the Deficiency of the Fluids that fill the Muscles appears first in the highest Part: The Face first grows lank and wrinkled; then the Neck; then the Breast and Arms; the lower Parts continuing to the last as plump as ever: So that covering all above with a Basket, and regarding only what is below the Girdle, it is impossible of two Women to know an old from a young one. And as in the dark all Cats are grey, the Pleasure of corporal Enjoyment with an old Woman is at least equal, and frequently superior, every Knack being by Practice capable of Improvement.

6. Because the Sin is less. The debauching a Virgin may be her Ruin, and make her for Life unhappy.

7. Because the Compunction is less. The having made a young Girl miserable may give you frequent bitter Reflections; none of which can attend the making an old Woman happy.

8. They are so grateful!!

MOTHER LODE

On January 24, 1848, a foreman named James Marshall was constructing a lumber mill on the American River near Coloma, California, when he made a curious discovery. In the tailrace of the mill's water wheel he found traces of shiny metal. Marshall brought the metal to the mill's owner, John Sutter, and the two men realized it was *gold!* Sutter asked Marshall to keep the news quiet, fearing what a swarm of gold-hungry prospectors might do for his own business interests in the area. But when Sutter's men began showing up in San Francisco purchasing items with pieces of gold, the secret didn't stay secret for very long. By August news had spread all the way to the Atlantic. When President James Polk confirmed the discovery in December, the floodgates were opened. America came down with gold fever.

An epic wave of people—around ninety thousand at a time when the total US population was twenty-three million—flocked to California the following year, earning themselves the nickname "forty-niners." Over 200,000 more hopefuls followed in the next six years, including an influx of immigrants from China and Latin America. San Francisco went from a Podunk town of two hundred citizens to one of the biggest cities in the country seemingly overnight. What was good for the California economy, however, wasn't so sublime for the Native Americans who lived in the Sierra Nevada mountain range, which contained the near mythically rich gold vein, or Mother Lode. Thousands of Indians were killed and even more displaced or stricken with illness.

The largest gold nugget found during the Gold Rush (and the second largest nugget found anywhere in the world, ever) was unearthed in 1854 and weighed in at 160 pounds.

A COMMON BOND

John Adams and Thomas Jefferson had been close friends during the American Revolution, but by the time Adams became the country's first vice president the two men were rivals. As a Federalist, Adams increasingly found Jefferson, a Democratic-Republican, insufferable. When Washington left the presidency after only two terms, the former buds battled bitterly to assume the empty throne. Adams defeated Jefferson by only a three-vote margin, and then four years later Jefferson defeated Adams. So bitter had their relationship become that Adams didn't even attend Jefferson's inauguration. But in retirement the two great minds couldn't quite stay away from each other, and a respectful mail correspondence eventually rekindled their respective admirations. Despite being seven years Jefferson's senior, Adams always claimed he would outlive Jefferson. When Adams died in 1826, his final words were, "Thomas Jefferson survives." Unbeknownst to Adams, in an amazing moment of synchronicity, Jefferson had also died—several hours earlier. So, technically, Adams had been correct.

But that wasn't the most bizarre synchronicity of the day. Both men died on July 4th, Independence Day, exactly fifty years from the ratification of the Declaration of Independence.

CALIFORNIA, LAND OF SUPER TREES

The ancient Egyptians finished construction of the Great Pyramid of Giza around 2560 BC. Halfway around the world, high up in what would someday be named the White Mountains of California, stood a Great Basin Bristlecone Pine tree that had already been alive for nearly three hundred years. Meet Methuselah, who, at the time of this book's publication, is still alive and well at the flabbergasting estimated age of 4,844. And if that doesn't make the human lifespan seem insignificant enough, the tree is named after Methuselah, a supernaturally elderly gentlemen from the Bible, who only lived to be a piddling 969 years old. Methuselah the tree used to have an older bristlecone pine brother in Nevada named Prometheus, but Forest Service personnel cut down Prometheus in 1964 for the purposes of research. It was only after the tree had been felled and tested that anyone realized they had just killed the oldest living individual organism on the planet.

California is also home to the tallest tree in the world, Hyperion, a coast redwood that tops out at 379 feet (roughly thirty-seven stories tall), as well as the largest tree by volume, General Sherman, a giant sequoia with a height of 275 feet and a diameter of 25 feet.

COLTER'S RUN

John Colter was a member of the Lewis and Clark Expedition. Unlike his two commanders, when the journey concluded in 1806, Colter hadn't had enough of the untamed frontier. Instead of returning home, he turned back west and the following year he became the first person of European descent to explore what is now Yellowstone National Park—a journey he made alone, which prompted some disbelief when he returned with stories of exploding geysers and steaming pools of bubbling water. Still not ready for civilization, Colter immediately ventured into the wilderness once again, this time into Montana with fellow Lewis and Clark Expedition veteran John Potts. But Colter's second adventure was not as enjoyable. Colter and Potts had already been having trouble with Blackfeet Indians when things came to a head sometime in 1809…

Colter and Potts were examining their beaver traps by canoe one morning when a large band of Blackfeet appeared on both sides of the creek. The Blackfeet, armed with arrows, beckoned them to come ashore. With little other choice, the two men consented. But once they'd pulled over, one of the Indians grabbed Potts's rifle. Colter wrestled the gun free and gave it back to Potts. Potts, panicking, pushed himself and the canoe back into the creek, leaving Colter on the shore. One of the Blackfeet shot an arrow at Potts, wounding him. Despite Colter's shouts to chill out and return with the canoe, Potts in turn shot the Indian dead with his rifle. This opened a full volley of Blackfeet arrows, which riddled Potts like a pincushion, killing him. Colter was now several degrees of totally screwed.

The Indians stripped Colter naked, then conversed with each other about what exactly to do with the white man. One of the Blackfeet asked Colter a rather suspicious question—could he run fast? Yes, Colter informed them, he was quick on his feet. With that the Blackfeet led him to a new location and gave him a simple instruction, which he understood immediately: *run*. Colter did as he was told, while the Blackfeet waited respectfully to give him a head start. But Colter wasn't lying. Despite having no shoes he was incredibly fast. He ran like the wind, so hard and so fast that the effort caused his nose to bleed. Stealing a glance, Colter discovered that only one of the Blackfeet warriors had been able to catch up to him. Sensing that he wasn't going to be able to keep this pace much longer, Colter suddenly spun around, startling the Indian, who fell and dropped his spear. Colter killed the man with his own spear and then continued on his way. Colter was saved only when he happened upon a beaver dam (or raft of driftwood, depending on the account), which he hid beneath until nightfall when all the Blackfeet had gone. Colter then floated down the river and eventually made it to safety.

Amazingly, Colter *still* didn't leave the frontier. Only after Blackfeet killed two more of his friends in 1810 did he determine that maybe there were benefits to living in a city. He then married and settled in New Haven, Missouri.

 ## NAME RECOGNITION

In the history of things named after people, Charles Lynch probably has the most dubious legacy. The term, if it wasn't obvious, is lynching. Born in 1736, Lynch was a Virginia planter and later a Virginia senator. During the American Revolution, Lynch served as a justice of the peace. When a Loyalist uprising in his territory threatened that peace, Lynch and his peers rounded up the suspects and, instead of putting them through proper trials, sentenced them in informal court. The punishments handed down mostly involved whippings and seizure of property, not the sickening tree-branch hangings that would later become associated with the Klu Klux Klan, but word of Lynch's vigilante actions got around. Such freestyle justice became known as "Lynch's Law." And the terminology stuck.

A DISMAL HIDEAWAY

"Maroon" was a name given to runaway slaves in North and South America who went wild in a geographical sense—escaping and forming independent settlements hidden away from the shackles and whips of Europeans.

The exact origin of the term is unknown, though it likely came from the Spanish *cimarron,* which had a similar usage. At the beginning of the eighteenth century (though possibly even as far back as the seventeenth century) a maroon community formed in the brutal conditions of the unwelcomingly named Great Dismal Swamp of Virginia and North Carolina. As oppressive as the Great Dismal Swamp marshlands were, freedom was worth the hardship. The inhabitants settled on the scarce high and dry parts of the marsh, obscured in the interior, braving insects, poisonous snakes, and foul terrain as they attempted to eke out an existence. The swamp also served as a hub for the Underground Railroad in the 1800s.

The reason for the Great Dismal Swamp's popularity among maroons is also why we do not know a lot about the community's history—it was an awful place and the swamp's forbidding conditions kept most sane people away. It is not like white settlers were clamoring for the land, and the sporadic attempts to clear the swamp of maroons always failed. It has only been in the past decade that archaeologists have begun to investigate the Great Dismal Swamp's secret civilization. It is unknown if the swamp was populated continuously or intermittently, though undoubtedly there were many who spent their entire lives, cradle to the grave, in the swamp. After the Civil War and the emancipation of the slaves, the maroon community disbanded.

Eli Whitney's cotton GIN revolutionized the cotton industry in America. Cotton gin is short for cotton ENGINE.

PRESIDENTIAL DISABILITY

In 1921, while Franklin D. Roosevelt was in New Brunswick, Canada, he contracted what most historians still believe was polio, resulting in paralysis from his waist down. Fearing how the disability could harm his political aspirations, Roosevelt invested a considerable amount of time and money into trying rehabilitation, founding both the Warm Springs Institute for Rehabilitation and the National Foundation for Infantile Paralysis (now known as the March of Dimes). He eventually trained himself to painfully stand upright using metal braces and a cane, and went to great lengths to prevent the public from seeing him as anything but a robust leader. Remarkably, only two known photographs exist of FDR in his wheelchair.

 # SEAGULL SAVIORS

The Mormon cricket isn't actually a cricket. It is a katydid, which is a relative of crickets and grasshoppers. The large, flightless bugs normally have a low population density, but every now and then an explosion in numbers can occur, leading to an infestation that blankets the landscape as they move forward eating everything in their path.

They earned their name due to just such an infestation, which befell the Utah Mormons in 1848. The bugs descended on the Latter-Day Saints' first harvest, devouring their crops and threatening to foil the settlement just as it was getting off the ground. According to Mormon folklore, the pioneers were miraculously saved by migrating seagulls that descended from the heavens like hungry little angels, gobbling up the katydids and saving the crops from total devastation. Ornithologists (those who study birds) don't think there was anything so miraculous about the event, as California gulls make a yearly presence on the Great Salt Lake and likely ate a relatively small portion of the insects. But regardless, in honor of the "Miracle of the Gulls," the California gull was made the state bird of Utah. The Seagull Monument of Temple Square in Salt Lake City also commemorates the event.

A Snug Fit

At 6 feet 2 inches and 330 pounds, William Howard Taft was the largest president in history. Despite his massive girth, he was said to be light-footed and a skilled dancer. But that did him little good contending with the small clawfoot White House bathtub, which Taft found himself stuck in one unfortunate evening. Rumor has it that a gallon of butter and four men were needed to pry the president from the tub. Whether that detail is true or not, Taft promptly had the clawfoot tub removed and installed a new 7-foot-long, 3-foot-wide bathtub. Now Taft could keep himself clean for all those dance parties.

The year after he left office, Taft lost nearly 100 pounds to cure himself of obstructive sleep apnea brought on by his obesity.

A Most Uncivil Body Count

Approximately 625,000 men died in the Civil War, which, to put that in perspective, is more American deaths than in World War I, World War II, the Korean War, and the Vietnam War combined. To put that into further perspective, the Vietnam War Memorial, which features the names of all the service members who died during the conflict, stretches 492 feet in length—if a similar memorial were constructed for the Civil War, it would be about 5,200 feet long. And rifles and cannon fire weren't the Civil War's deadliest weapons.

Disease was the most dangerous adversary for both Union and Confederate soldiers. The crowded camps and unventilated tents were breeding grounds for a host of

nasty things, including diseases such as mumps, chicken pox, and measles. Nearly one million Union soldiers contracted malaria. A recent study has even proposed that the long-accepted death estimate is *too small*; the death toll could be upward of 750,000.

BRIDGE FOR SALE

By the end of the eighteenth century, the six-hundred-year-old London Bridge, which spanned the Thames River in London, was in desperate need of replacement. It was just too narrow and too decrepit (you may recall a certain nursery rhyme regarding its stability). So they tore it down and built a new London Bridge, which officially opened for use in 1831. But time took its toll on this bridge too, and by the mid-twentieth century it was clear to London officials that the London Bridge needed to be rebooted once again. This time around, the Common Council of the City of London came up with an unorthodox idea. What if they sold the old bridge? Most people, including most of the council, thought the idea was idiotic. Who on Earth would buy the bridge? Well, God bless America. In 1968, entrepreneur Robert P. McCulloch, of McCulloch Oil, bought the London Bridge for $2.4 million and had it rebuilt in Lake Havasu City, Arizona, where it still stands.

 ## SUCCINCT SIGNAGE

In 1925, Arthur Heineman decided to build a hotel that capitalized on the increasing number of automobile drivers traveling between Los Angeles and San Francisco, selecting San Luis Obispo, California, as an ideal midpoint to appeal to weary motorists. He named his business the Milestone Motor Hotel, but when he discovered that he couldn't fit that entire name on the building's roof, he decided to conserve some space and stand out by calling it the Milestone Mo-Tel. The word "motel" was too catchy to be denied and was quickly adopted by other motor hotels around the country.

THE FOUNDING FOUNDING FATHER

The name James Otis Jr. probably doesn't ring too many bells, but he planted some of the first seeds for American independence. Born in 1725, Otis was a lawyer in colonial Massachusetts. In 1760, he represented colonists who were challenging the legality of the "writs of assistance," which enabled British authorities to enter any colonist's home with no advance notice or probable cause. Otis's orations during the case heavily influenced fellow Massachusetts lawyer John Adams, who would later say that it was Otis who first incited Adams's own revolutionary spirit. Otis continued to play a pivotal role in the years leading up to the colonial rebellion, but mental illness slowly pulled him from public life. He died in May of 1783, mere months before the Revolution officially ended with the signing of the Treaty of Paris. But at least he went out with a bang…

Otis died after being struck by lightning.

AMERICA'S FIRST GAY PRESIDENT?

The fifteenth president of the United States, James Buchanan, often referred to as the "bachelor president," may have been the first gay president too. There is no evidence that directly clarifies Buchanan's sexual orientation, but even during his era the gossip crowd bandied the theory about. Front and center was the fact that for fifteen years Buchanan shared a home with future vice president William R. King (who served with President Franklin Pierce). The two were often referred to as "Buchanan and his wife," and carried on with a steady correspondence after they stopped being roommates. After Buchanan's and King's deaths, the men's nieces somewhat suspiciously destroyed almost all their correspondence.

🇺🇸 AN EDGAR-WORTHY SETUP

Edgar Allan Poe is one of America's most important and influential literary figures, past and present. An early progenitor of the short story format, he is most directly associated with twisted tales of the macabre, like "The Raven" and "The Tell-Tale Heart," but Poe also pioneered the detective mystery subgenre—which is why the Mystery Writers of America named their annual awards the Edgars. Poe's life was fraught with misfortune and disappointment and, in an eerie case of life imitating art, his bizarre death at the age of 40 had all the hallmarks of one of his own stories.

Here are the facts. On September 27, 1849, Poe left Richmond, Virginia, to head home to New York. On October 3, Poe was found outside Ryan's Tavern in Baltimore, delirious and disheveled, wearing ill-fitting clothes that did not belong to him and in desperate need of medical attention. Poe was placed in a hospital and denied any visitors. His attending physician claims that, in his fevered and incoherent state, Poe repeatedly called out the name Reynolds, though no one has ever been able to determine exactly who this Reynolds was or why Poe was calling for him. In his brief moments of vague clarity, Poe was unable to explain how he had come to the city or the cause of his present condition. He died on October 7, his last words supposedly, "Lord, help my poor soul." Newspapers reported that Poe died from "congestion of the brain," which at the time was a common euphemism for deaths caused by alcoholism. But Dr. John Joseph Moran later claimed that Poe had not been drunk when admitted to the hospital. No medical records or death certificate exist for Poe, leaving his death entirely open for conjecture.

The theories of what killed the author are numerous, including hypoglycemia, suicide, rabies, diabetes, syphilis, influenza, and, of course, murder. An unlikely yet popular theory holds that Poe was a victim of cooping, a ballot-box-stuffing scam in which victims were drugged and forced to vote for a political party at multiple locations.

Alcoholism seems the most probably cause, given Poe's reputation as a dark, haunted genius whose perverted mind was fueled by booze and opium. Yet this image of Poe largely came from his obituary and a biographical article included in a posthumous collection of his work—both of which were authored by Rufus Wilmot Griswold, a bitter enemy of Poe in life and then far more so in death. Much of the dark picture Griswold painted of Poe was intentionally untrue and malicious. Poe's friends tried to debunk Griswold's pieces, but the unholy Poe created by Griswold excited readers. It's just more titillating to believe that stories like "Murders in the Rue Morgue" were written by a madman.

So the mystery remains.

THE NOT-SO ROMANTIC TALE OF POCAHONTAS

The storybook tale of Pocahontas, the beautiful daughter of Chief Powhatan, and her romance with handsome English settler John Smith is well known. But it is also a bunch of bull. The two never had a romance. She did indeed meet Smith in 1607 during his time at England's first successful colony, Jamestown, but at the time she was ten years old. It was another settler, John Rolfe, whom Pocahontas was to have a romance with. In the midst of a war between the settlers and her people, the young girl was captured and brought to Jamestown in 1612. During this period, Rolfe taught her to read and write, baptized her, renamed her Rebecca, and married her.

When Rebecca Rolfe journeyed to London in 1616 with her husband, she was surprised to find herself the darling of high society and called Lady Rebecca. She was even more surprised to discover that John Smith was still alive, having been falsely informed of his death years ago. As Smith described it in his journals, when they ran into each other it was somewhat awkward. It's possible that she did indeed harbor a crush for Smith, or possibly she just resented that he made promises to her father that were never kept. The romantic view would be the first option, as would the conspiracy theory that her sudden death at the age of twenty-one, just a month after her reunion with Smith, was the result of poisoning by a jealous John Rolfe. This is incredibly unlikely though, as she died on a return voyage to America—plus this was the 1600s, when people randomly dropped dead for a wide variety of mundane reasons all the time.

James Buchanan was the only president NEVER to MARRY.

AND THE GRAMMY GOES TO...

What do Presidents Jimmy Carter, Bill Clinton, and Barack Obama all have in common?

All three have won a Grammy Award for Best Spoken Word Album.

Even weirder, they all won over three consecutive years. Carter won in 2007 for the audiobook recording of his book, *Our Endangered Values: America's Moral Crisis*. Obama won in 2006 for reading his memoir, *Dreams from My Father*. And Clinton won in 2005 for reading his autobiography, *My Life*.

Richard Nixon was nominated in 1978 for the collected recordings of his landmark TV interviews with David Frost. Nixon lost to the recording of Julie Harris's performance in the one-woman play, *The Belle of Amherst*.

DON'T KISS THIS COOK

Mary Mallon emigrated from Ireland to the United States seeking employment as a cook. In 1900 she got a job in Mamaroneck, New York. Within two weeks, residents of the town came down with typhoid fever. The following year she took a job in Manhattan cooking for a wealthy family. Members of the family soon came down with typhoid. Then she got a job for another family. Seven out of the eight family members got typhoid. You might think that Mary would have sensed a pattern forming here, but apparently she did not. The same thing occurred again and again, family after family.

In 1906 she moved to Oyster Bay, Long Island, and the typhoid followed. The residents of Oyster Bay became suspicious, because typhoid had not been common in their area. George Soper, a civil engineer with typhoid experience, was hired to get to the bottom of things. After doing some investigating he realized that typhoid seemed to accompany Mary Mallon wherever she went. Yet Mary showed no symptoms of typhoid herself. Soper tried to get urine and fecal samples from Mary, but she refused— being perfectly healthy, Mary thought she was being unfairly accused.

Eventually, as typhoid continued infecting new victims, Mary was taken by police and forcibly contained in isolation for three years. As it turned out, Mary was the first asymptomatic carrier of typhoid that anyone in America had ever seen. Throughout it all, Mary still did not believe she was to blame. Since Mary had technically broken no specific law, in 1910 the New York State Commissioner of Health agreed to free her as long as she promised to stop working as a cook. She promised. Then she adopted the pseudonym Mary Brown and continued working as a cook. Surprising no one other than Mary, she infected some more people with typhoid. In March 1915, determining that Mary could not be trusted, public heath authorities placed her in permanent quarantine. In custody Mary became a minor celebrity, referred to in the press as "Typhoid Mary." She died in 1938, still in quarantine.

FIGHTING DIRTY

During the American Revolution, colonial soldiers needed any and every advantage they could think of to best the better-equipped and better-trained Red Coats. The British found many of the American tactics dishonorable. Aside from hiding in foliage and wearing common clothes that made combatants indistinguishable from civilians, some rebels developed a unique trick to enhance their musket balls. They would chew on them, roughing the otherwise smooth surface in the hopes of creating a jagged wound that would prove harder for British medics to heal.

GOING OUT ON TOP

Eight presidents have died while in office. Four were assassinated: Abraham Lincoln, James Garfield, William McKinley, and John F. Kennedy. And four died of natural causes: William Henry Harrison, Zachary Taylor, Warren Harding, and Franklin D. Roosevelt.

Harrison has the lame distinction of dying only one month into his term, giving him the shortest presidency in history (a statistic likely never to be beat). It is important to note that, at sixty-eight years old, Harrison also held the record for oldest president until Ronald Reagan was elected. The problem was that apparently Harrison was all about setting presidential records. Despite being old as all hell for the time period and March 4, 1841, being an extremely cold and wet day, in an attempt to show Americans that he was still a scrappy tough guy, Harrison delivered the longest inaugural address in history (nearly two hours). Some modern scholars don't believe that the inauguration day weather contributed to the severe cold

Harrison contracted several weeks later, but it surely didn't help. After being bedridden for over a week, he died on April 4 from a host of maladies, including pneumonia, jaundice, and septicemia.

THE SAD, STRANGE, AND HORRIBLE FATES OF THE STAYNER BROTHERS

Cary Stayner was born in 1961. Steven Stayner was born in 1965.

On the afternoon of December 4, 1972, Steven was walking home from school in Merced, California, when he was approached by forty-one-year-old Kenneth Parnell and an associate, who were posing as church representatives seeking donations. Steven said his mother might give a donation, so Parnell offered to give him a ride home. Instead of taking Steven home, Parnell took the boy to a cabin and molested him. Parnell then claimed that he had been granted legal custody of Steven, because Steven's parents could not afford him and did not want him anymore. Steven remained with Parnell until 1980, at which point he had entered puberty and started to lose Parnell's affections. When Parnell kidnapped five-year-old Timmy White, Steven realized he could not allow another boy to succumb to his fate. So Steven took Timmy and successfully escaped.

Because of limitations in California law at the time, Kenneth Parnell only served five years in prison. In 1989, Steven died at the age of twenty-four in a motorcycle crash. In 1999, the city of Merced planned to rename one of their parks Stayner Park in Steven's honor, but the plan was scrapped when Cary Stayner suddenly made the papers...

Cary had been forced to live in the shadow of his little brother Steven. First, for seven years while his parents grieved over Steven's disappearance, and then in a whole new way when Steven's return became a media hoopla, spawning a book and TV movie, both titled *I Know My First Name Is Steven* (a quote taken from Steven's original police statement). But Cary stated that he had fantasized about murdering women before Steven was abducted. Whatever it was that led to Cary's mental malformations, in 1999 he murdered two women and two teenager girls in Yosemite National Park.

A statue of Steven Stayner and Timmy White stands in Applegate Park in Merced. Cary Stayner was sentenced to death and is currently housed on death row at San Quentin Penitentiary in California.

 # SOME UNWANTED PROPERTY MODIFICATIONS

As the Civil War broke out, Confederate General Robert E. Lee and his wife, Mary, fled from their Virginia estate, known as Arlington. The joint had a great view overlooking Washington, D.C., so unsurprisingly the US government confiscated the property shortly thereafter (technically for $92 in unpaid taxes). In an uncharacteristically harsh move, President Lincoln had a cemetery built on the property with the idea that after the war—win or lose—Lee would have to stare at the graves of men the South had killed. Needless to say, Lee never tried to reclaim Arlington. Years later, his oldest son George Washington Custis Lee sued the federal government and successfully reclaimed the property. Not wanting to exhume the graves or be the owner of a cemetery, George sold Arlington back to the government for $150,000.

More than 300,000 soldiers are buried in what is now called the Arlington National Cemetery.

JOHN PAUL JONESOVICH

John Paul was born in 1747. He began a seafaring career in his native Scotland before later venturing to America around the time of the American Revolution, where he slapped "Jones" to the end of his name (there is no definitive evidence on exactly why he opted for this name alteration). With his snazzy new name, John Paul Jones became the United States' first naval hero, terrorizing the British fleet as a captain and privateer in the Continental navy.

He is best remembered today not for his ballsy 1779 sea battle with the HMS *Serapis*, but for what he said when the *Serapis* demanded that Jones surrender—"I have not yet begun to fight!" Yet Jones was not always popular with his commanders or his own men. Many of his contemporaries felt that Jones was far more concerned with personal glory than anything else. After the war ended, the federal government decided to sell most of the Continental navy's ships to help pay off debts. Which meant there weren't as many jobs to go around. When Jones was not offered his desired rank of admiral, a change in both his name and geography occurred once again.

In 1788, after living briefly in Paris, Jones accepted an offer from the Empress Catherine II of Russia to join the Russian Navy, taking on the name Pavel Dzhones. As rear admiral, Jones helped repel Ottoman forces in the Russo-Turkish War (1787–1792). Whether deserved or not, Jones entered the crosshairs of his fellow Russian commanders, who had him recalled to St. Petersburg. After getting caught up in accusations of sexual misconduct, Jones eventually returned to Paris, embittered, where he died in 1792.

WHAT WINE PAIRS WELL WITH SOUR GRAPES?

Ninety percent of American wine is produced in California. If California were its own country, it would be the fourth largest wine producer in the world, behind Italy, France, and Spain. The state's varied range of climates and terrains makes it one of the most diverse wine-producing regions anywhere on Earth. But just as the California wine industry was getting off the ground in the early twentieth century, the 18th Amendment ushered in Prohibition and killed the party. Because the production of fine wine is such a slow process, it wasn't until the 1960s that California wine had gotten back into the swing of things. Now there was only one obstacle standing in the way of California vintners—they were American.

America may have been the most powerful country in the world, but it was still Europe's little brother. The idea that the state that produced Hollywood and The Beach Boys could also produce wine as good as France's was laughable, especially to the French. This inspired Steven Spurrier, a British wine expert and wine merchant living in Paris, to stage the Paris Wine Tasting of 1976 (or the Judgment of Paris).

The idea was to pit the Old World against the New World in a blind taste test, where judges could not be influenced by subjective preconceptions. Eleven judges, almost entirely French, comprised the panel, and when the marks were all tallied up, a California wine came in first place in both categories (red and white wines). French winemakers dismissed the results, claiming they meant nothing, and the French press barely touched the story. But the victory, however statistically meaningless, started to change deep-rooted popular opinion about the supremacy of European wine, opening the door for other current fine wine producers like Argentina, Australia, New Zealand, South Africa, and Chile.

 ## PRESIDENTIAL PATENT

In 1849, Abraham Lincoln received a patent for a device he designed to lift boats over shoals and other obstructions in shallow rivers. He conceived his invention after twice getting hung up by shallow water obstacles during river travels. Lincoln's device was never commercialized, but he remains the only president to hold a patent.

As recently as the 1990s, WOMEN were not allowed to wear PANTS on the Senate floor.

SUPER CHICKEN

Chickens have been known to aimlessly run around for a spell after having their heads cut off. Mike, also known as Miracle Mike and Mike the Headless Chicken, did so for almost two years. In September 1945, farmer Lloyd Olsen of Fruita, Colorado, set out to prepare a chicken for dinner. He selected a cockerel named Mike to have the honor, but Olsen's decapitating blow was slightly off its mark, removing Mike's head but leaving most of the brainstem. Much to Olsen's surprise, Mike survived. Either from sheer amusement or a respectful sense of wonder, Olsen spared Mike and continued caring for the chicken. Mike was fed through his neck hole with an eye-dropper and eventually learned to live without a head, strutting around the yard, climbing on perches, and even attempting (and failing) to crow. Olsen accurately assessed Mike's curiosity appeal and began touring the country, displaying the bird at fairs and in sideshows, until death finally caught up with Mike the Headless Chicken in March 1947.

GOOD SAVE

Stephen Pleasonton was a clerk working in President James Monroe's administration during the War of 1812. In 1814, with the British close to Washington, D.C., Monroe gave Pleasonton the task of removing important State Department books and documents from the White House in the event that the Brits should take the city. So Pleasonton procured several large bags and had them filled with the Department's records, including the US Constitution and the correspondence of George Washington, among other records. He then had the bags stashed at a nearby mill. With the British now closing in, Pleasonton prepared to evacuate the White House, but as he was leaving the building he happened to spot something that apparently no one else had—the Declaration of Independence was still hanging on the wall in its frame. He removed the Declaration and personally carried it away. As he thought about the significance of the document he carried in his arms, he also began to second-guess his selected storage location. Pleasonton quickly had all the other documents removed from the nearby mill, loaded onto wagons, and carted 35 miles away to Leesburg, Virginia. That very same night the British arrived and burnt down the White House and several other government buildings.

As a reward for his powers of observation, in 1817 Pleasonton was given a new position, the first "fifth auditor" in the Treasury Department. He would hold the position until his death in 1855.

 ## GO FOR BROKE

In 1942, the US government, still reeling with paranoia after the Pearl Harbor attacks, rounded up nearly 110,000 Japanese Americans and placed them into internment camps. But by 1943, due to the increasing demand for fresh soldiers—plus petitioning by Hawaiian-born Japanese soldiers who had been discharged from the military after Pearl Harbor—the Army formed the 442nd Regimental Combat Team, made up entirely of Japanese Americans. Known as "Buddhaheads," the 442nd came to kick some serious ass for America, despite the fact that most of the soldiers' parents were being held as prisoners in their own country. Their motto was "Go for broke," and by the end of the war the 442nd had become the most decorated unit for its size and length of service in US military history.

In total, about fourteen thousand men rotated in and out the 442nd, racking up a staggering 18,143 awards, including fifty-two Distinguished Service Crosses, 560 Silver Stars, twenty-two Legion of Merit Medals, four thousand Bronze Stars, 9,486 Purple Hearts, twenty-one Medals of Honor, and an unprecedented eight Presidential Unit Citations. Go for broke, indeed.

NAMELESS TRIBUTE

The Battle of Saratoga (two battles actually, on September 19 and October 7, 1777) was a turning point in the Revolutionary War, and its hero was General Benedict Arnold. In the years after Saratoga, Arnold became dissatisfied with the Continental army. He adamantly opposed the decision to accept military assistance from France, but more than that, he often felt slighted by the Continental Congress, believing he was deserving of greater recognition than he received. So he opened a series of negotiations with British agents, exploring the possibility of switching sides. In September 1780, while commander of West Point, Arnold made a botched attempt to hand over the key fortification to the British. Before he could be captured, Arnold escaped and joined British forces, where he was given the rank of a British brigadier general.

Considering that Benedict Arnold's name became a synonym for traitor, this put John Watts de Peyster, a philanthropist and military historian, in something of a pickle decades later. De Peyster had written extensively about the Battle of Saratoga, and wished to donate a monument commemorating Arnold's heroism in said battle. Erected in what is now the Saratoga National Historical Park in New York, the monument features no image of Arnold, nor does it mention him by name. Known as the Boot Monument, the statue features only a single military boot, in honor of the foot injury Arnold received defending the country he ended up betraying. The dedication on the back of the monument reads in part, "In memory of the most brilliant soldier of the Continental Army, who was desperately wounded on this spot…"

KEEPING IT IN THE FAMILY

We have had two father and son president combos (John Adams and John Quincy Adams and George H. W. Bush and George W. Bush), as well as a grandfather and grandson combo (William Henry Harrison and Benjamin Harrison). But the familial relations don't stop there. James Madison was a second cousin of both Zachary Taylor and James Polk, who were also second cousins themselves through different family members. Things start getting ridiculous if you expand out to third and fourth cousins. Franklin D. Roosevelt was related to eleven other presidents through blood or marriage. Though Franklin and Theodore Roosevelt shared a surname, they were only fifth cousins. Theodore was more closely related to Franklin's wife, Eleanor, who was Theodore's niece. As it happens, Franklin and Eleanor were also fifth cousins.

I'LL FLIP YOU FOR IT

In 1843, William Overton and Asa Lovejoy filed a claim on a piece of land near the confluence of the Willamette and Columbia Rivers in the Oregon Country. At the time the area was known simply as "the clearing." Before the two men could get around to giving it a proper name, Overton sold his half of the claim to Francis Pettygrove. Lovejoy had wanted to name the settlement after his hometown, Boston. Pettygrove was of a similar mind, though he wanted to name it after his own hometown, Portland, Maine. Neither would budge, so they decided to settle the dispute like fancy gentlemen—with a coin toss. Using a copper one-cent piece, they played best two out of three, and Pettygrove won.

The "Portland Penny" is now on display in the Oregon Historical Society Museum.

NOW THAT'S DEDICATION TO DEMOCRACY

During the 1948 Democratic primary in Texas, Lyndon B. Johnson was running for the Senate against former governor Coke Stevenson. Stevenson came in first but lacked a majority, so a runoff was held. When the runoff was tallied, Johnson won by just eighty-seven votes. Curiously, 202 ballots from a single precinct had been cast in alphabetical order and just moments before the polls closed. Oh, and all 202 voters were dead at the time. Despite angry claims of fraud from the Stevenson camp, the Democratic convention upheld Johnson's victory.

JULY 2, INDEPENDENCE DAY

"The Second Day of July 1776, will be the most memorable Epocha, in the History of America. I am apt to believe that it will be celebrated, by succeeding Generations, as the great anniversary Festival." John Adams excitedly wrote those words to his wife Abigail about America's great turning point. A month earlier, Richard Henry Lee of Virginia addressed the Continental Congress and proposed a clean break from Great Britain.

It was an audacious and not particularly popular idea, as most of the delegates wanted peace, not independence. But over the course of June the British had been particularly exasperating, so when Congress convened again on July 2, the independence movement was now in the majority and the representatives voted for separation. Having sensed this likelihood, Congress had already assigned Thomas Jefferson to draft up a little thing called the Declaration of Independence. July 2 was the day independence was declared. July 4 was simply the day the details of the declaration document were approved for printing.

WATCH OUT BELOW!

Skylab was the United States' first space station. It orbited Earth from 1973 to 1979, hosting three different three-person crews. The station was damaged when it was first launched, which gave NASA an excuse to perform its first ever major in-space repair. Overall, Skylab was a success, and as the station wore down, NASA made plans to refurbish it using the new Space Shuttle program. Skylab was in need of repairs, and more pressingly in need of a boost to correct its decaying orbit. When development of the space shuttle was delayed, NASA suddenly had a problem. Left unattended, Skylab was going to drift back into Earth's atmosphere and crash...somewhere. This did not seem like a good thing. NASA weighed their options, such as trying to destroy Skylab with missiles, but considering that the station was the size of a house, this hardly seemed a foolproof plan to eliminate debris. In the end, they decided to let the pieces fall where they may. Literally.

Skylab's fiery return to Earth was an international news event. Newspapers offered rewards for pieces of the wreckage. Comedian John Belushi joked about the crash on *Saturday Night Live*. People threw Skylab parties and bought T-shirts with targets printed on the front. NASA, for their part, tried to guide Skylab's reentry to minimize the risk of hitting a populated area. They aimed for the Indian Ocean, but the station did not break up as fast as they had calculated. Sections of debris landed in eastern Australia, southeast of Perth where, luckily, few people live.

Drolly, the local Australian government fined NASA $400 for littering. NASA did not pay it.

LAST WORDS OF THE DAMNED

Most famous last words were not literally the last thing a man or woman said before passing out of this world, but instead just the last interesting thing they said while someone was around to hear it. Realistically speaking, it is hard for the sick and dying to be pithy or witty moments before death claims them. This puts those sentenced to execution in a rare spot, for they know with great certainty that their last chance for words is approaching. And it is interesting what words some choose…

John Wayne Gacy, known as the Killer Clown because he performed as a clown as a side-job, was convicted of killing thirty-three young men and boys in suburban Chicago between 1972 and 1978. His last words were directed at a prison guard: "Kiss my ass."

Aileen Wuornos was a prostitute convicted of killing seven men while hitchhiking in Florida in 1989 and 1990. Actress Charlize Theron won an Academy Award for portraying Wuornos in 2003's *Monster*. Oddly enough, her last words involved a Hollywood movie: "I'd just like to say I'm sailing with the rock, and I'll be back like *Independence Day*, with Jesus June 6. Like the movie, big mother ship and all, I'll be back."

Gary Gilmore was convicted of killing a motel manager in Utah and executed by firing squad in 1977. Norman Mailer wrote a Pulitzer Prize–winning true crime book about Gilmore called *The Executioner's Song*. Gilmore's last words were, "Let's do it."

Robert Alton Harris was convicted of murdering two teenage boys in California and executed in 1992. His last words were, "You can be a king or a street sweeper, but everyone dances with the grim reaper."

So Close

Four presidential nominees have won the popular vote but ultimately lost the presidency due to the quirky nature of the electoral college: Andrew Jackson lost to John Quincy Adams in 1824, Samuel J. Tilden lost to Rutherford B. Hayes in 1876, Grover Cleveland lost to Benjamin Harrison in 1888, and most recently Al Gore lost to George W. Bush in 2000.

SCROOGETTE

Hetty Green was known as the Witch of Wall Street. Born in 1834, she had amassed an enormous fortune by the end of nineteenth century by buying and selling real estate, railroads, mines, and mortgages. She is considered America's first female tycoon. She also holds a record in a different kind of history book—*The Guinness Book of World Records* anointed her the world's "greatest miser." Though surely exaggerated, in her time the stories of her stinginess were legendary. Despite dying with somewhere between $100 million to $200 million ($1.9 to $3.9 billion today), Green conducted all of her business out of the offices of a New York bank, not wanting to spring for the cost of her own office. She would wear a single dress until it wore out, telling her maid to only wash the dirtiest portions of the dress to save on soap. She ate only the cheapest food and was rumored to carry a metal pail of dry oatmeal with her to save on restaurant costs. Her scroogiest moment may have been when her young son Ned broke his leg and Green brought him to a free clinic for the poor. At the time, it was reported that, when discovered, Green became embarrassed and withdrew Ned, proclaiming that she would treat him at home. Then the boy needed to have his leg amputated because of gangrene. But modern historians point out that Ned's leg was amputated years after the free clinic incident, and then Green did in fact bring him to other doctors.

Though he lost a leg, Ned learned a lot about saving money from his mother. When Ned and his sister Sylvia inherited Hetty's fortune in 1916, they were able to pass through the Great Depression unscathed by following Hetty's example. But Ned and Sylvia were also freer with their money—Ned was an avid supporter of the Massachusetts Institute of Technology, and when Sylvia died in 1951, she left almost the entirety of the family fortune to charity.

Woodrow Wilson is the only president with a PhD. He received his degree from Johns Hopkins University in history and political science.

OLYMPIC ART

At the 1912 Summer Olympics in Stockholm, Sweden, American Walter Winans took home two medals—a silver medal for his marksmanship in the shooting competition and a gold medal for his 20-inch-tall sculpture of a horse pulling a small chariot, titled *An American Trotter*. You read that correctly. Winans took home the first-ever Olympic gold medal for a sculpture. And he wouldn't be the last. Alongside honoring athletic achievements, from 1912 to 1952, the Olympics awarded 151 medals to works in the fine arts, including sculpture, painting, architecture, literature, and music. And it was also an American who killed the practice. Avery Brundage became president of the International Olympic Committee (IOC) after WWII and wanted to promote the purity of the Olympic Games. He felt that art had no place. Brundage had entered a piece of literature in the 1932 competition, but only earned an honorable mention.

THE MELTING POT

The United States has always been a nation of immigrants. The Civil War, fought to preserve the Union the Founding Fathers went to so much trouble to establish, only reaffirmed this fact. During the Civil War, one third of the Union army was comprised of immigrants. Ten percent of the army was made up of German soldiers, 7.5 percent Irish soldiers, and after 1863, one in ten soldiers was African American. Overall, one in four regiments had a majority of foreigners, including English, French, Italian, Polish, and Scottish. This was not the case in the South. And they lost.

MR. PEANUT

In 1896, Booker T. Washington, the president of the Tuskegee Institute (a school for African Americans), invited botanist and inventor George Washington Carver to head its agriculture department. Carver taught there for forty-seven years and gained national notoriety from a series of bulletins for farmers, through which he encouraged African Americans to shift away from cotton by promoting alternative crops, such as peanuts, soybeans, and sweet potatoes. His most popular bulletin was published in 1916 and titled *How to Grow the Peanut and 105 Ways of Preparing it for Human Consumption*. He discovered ways to turn peanuts into cloth dyes, leather dyes, insulating boards, wood stains, and wallboards.

Carver is often credited with inventing peanut butter. This is not true, as forms of peanut butter date back to the fifteenth century, but he devised many recipes and was most certainly the man responsible for bringing peanut butter to public and commercial attention. He was also responsible for helping to dispel the myth that black people were not intelligent enough of succeed in the sciences. By the time Carver was in his seventies, he had become so renown for his multitude of creations that in 1941 *Time* magazine dubbed him the Black Leonardo.

SELECTED BIBLIOGRAPHY

★ ★ ★ ★ ★ ★ ★ ★ ★

A full list of resources is available upon request.

PRINT RESOURCES

Ambrose, Stephen E. *Nothing Like It In the World: The Men Who Built the Transcontinental Railroad 1863–1869*. New York: Simon & Schuster, 2001.

Ambrose, Stephen E. *Undaunted Courage: Meriwether Lewis, Thomas Jefferson, and the Opening of the American West*. New York: Simon & Schuster, 1996.

Ayres, Thomas. *That's Not My American History Book: A Compilation of Little Known Events and Forgotten Heroes*. Lanham, MD: Taylor Trade, 2000.

Beyer, Rick. *The Greatest Presidential Stories Never Told: 100 Tales from History to Astonish, Bewilder, and Stupefy*. New York: HarperCollins, 2007.

Blum, Howard. *American Lightning: Terror, Mystery, the Birth of Hollywood, and the Crime of the Century*. New York: Crown, 2008.

Edwards, Owen. "Cut and Paste." *Smithsonian Magazine*, January 2012, 24.

Fox, Don M. *Patton's Vanguard: The United States Army Fourth Armored Division*. Jefferson, NC: McFarland, 2003.

Horwitz, Tony. "Remember the Raisin." *Smithsonian Magazine*, June 2012, 26.

Lucas, Marion Brunson. *A History of Blacks in Kentucky: From Slavery to Segregation, 1760–1891*. Frankfort, KY: Kentucky Historical Society, 1992.

McCullough, David. *1776*. New York: Simon & Schuster, 2005.

McCullough, David. *John Adams*. New York: Simon & Schuster, 2001.

Millard, Candice. *The River of Doubt: Theodore Roosevelt's Darkest Journey*. New York: Anchor Books, 2005.

Minnesota Law Review 95 (December 2010): 347–423.

New Mexican (Santa FE, NM). January 12, 1982.

Paine, Albert Bigelow. *Mark Twain: A Biography, Volumes 3–4*. New York: Harper & Brothers, 1912.

Parrish, William E. *David Rice Atchison of Missouri: Border Politician*. Columbia, MO: University of Missouri Press, 1961.

Staples, Arthur G. *The Letters of John Fairfield*. Augusta, ME: Lewiston Journal Company, 1922.

Toll, Ian W. *Pacific Crucible: War at Sea in the Pacific, 1941–1942*. New York: W. W. Norton, 2011.

WEB RESOURCES

The Atlantic: Rebecca J. Rosen, "Get Ready, Because Voyager I Is *This* Close to Leaving Our Solar System," June 13, 2012, http://www.theatlantic.com/technology/archive/2012/06/get-ready-because-voyager-i-is-this-close-to-leaving-our-solar-system/258456.

BBC News Magazine: Daniel Wasaw, "Who, What, Why: How many soldiers died in the US Civil War?" April 3, 2012, http://www.bbc.co.uk/news/magazine-17604991.

Boing Boing: Cory Doctorow, "Bailout costs more than Marshall Plan, Louisiana Purchase, moonshot, S&L bailout, Korean War, New Deal, Iraq war, Vietnam war, and NASA's lifetime budget—combined!" November 25, 2008, http://boingboing.net/2008/11/25/bailout-costs-more-t.html.

CNN: Jim Spellman, "Vietnamese businessmen scoop up smallest U.S. town for $900,000," April 5, 2012, http://articles.cnn.com/2012-04-05/us/us_wyoming-town-auction_1_buford-town-cheyenne.

The Daily Mail: Robert Hardman, "The Queen Mother: She loved owls, fairies and the miners. She hated oysters, LibDems and being kissed by a U.S. president. And she lived every day as if it were her last," September 17, 2009, http://www.dailymail.co.uk/news/article-1214041/The-Queen-Mother-She-loved-owls-fairies-miners-She-hated-oysters-LibDems-kissed-U-S-president-And-lived-day-last.html.

Des Moines Register: Tom Longden, "Sampson, Francis L.," February 4, 2008, http://www.desmoinesregister.com/article/99999999/FAMOUSIOWANS/712160326/Sampson-Francis-L.

Digital History: Mintz, S., and McNeil, S. (2012). *Digital History*. Retrieved October 5, 2012 from http://www.digitalhistory.uh.edu.

Discover Magazine: Stephen Ornes, "Whatever Happened To… Mind Control?: The CIA's Experimentation with LSD Led to

Disastrous Results," August 4, 2008, http://discovermagazine.com/2008/aug/04-whatever-happened-to-mind-control.

Examiner.com: Mike Radinsky, "Trading muskets for snowballs—The great Confederate snowball battle of Rappahannock," February 14, 2010, http://www.examiner.com/article/trading-muskets-for-snowballs-the-great-confederate-snowball-battle-of-rappahannock.

The Guardian: Vanessa Heggie, "Sports doping, Victorian Style," *Notes and Theories: Dispatches from the Science Desk* (blog), June 19, 2012, http://www.guardian.co.uk/science/blog/2012/jun/19/sports-doping-victorian-style.

History.com:

"10 Surprising Civil War Facts," May 10, 2012, http://www.history.com/news/10-surprising-civil-war-facts.

"Castro Visits the United States," *This Day in History* (blog), http://www.history.com/this-day-in-history/castro-visits-the-united-states.

"First national memorial is ordered by Congress," *This Day in History* (blog), http://www.history.com/this-day-in-history/first-national-memorial-is-ordered-by-congress.

"Jackson holds 'open house' at the White House," *This Day in History* (blog), http://www.history.com/this-day-in-history/jackson-holds-open-house-at-the-white-house.

"President Cleveland marries in White House," *This Day in History* (blog), http://www.history.com/this-day-in-history/president-cleveland-marries-in-white-house.

"Secretariat wins Triple Crown," *This Day in History* (blog), http://www.history.com/this-day-in-history/secretariat-wins-the-triple-crown.

"Toy company Wham-O produces first Frisbees," *This Day in History* (blog), http://www.history.com/this-day-in-history/toy-company-wham-o-produces-first-frisbees.

"World's first parking meter installed," *This Day in History* (blog), http://www.history.com/this-day-in-history/worlds-first-parking-meter-installed.

"Zimmerman Note presented to U.S. ambassador," *This Day in History* (blog), http://www.history.com/this-day-in-history/zimmermann-note-presented-to-us-ambassador.

Elizabeth Hanes, "9 Tales of Broken Arrows: Thermonuclear Misses Throughout History," May 22, 2012, http://www.history.com/news/9-tales-of-broken-arrows-thermonuclear-near-misses-throughout-history.

Elizabeth Hanes, "Independence Day at the White House: 5 Fourth of July Tales," July 3, 2012, http://www.history.com/news/independence-day-at-the-white-house-5-fourth-of-july-tales.

Elizabeth Hanes, "What Happened to Amelia?: 9 Tantalizing Theories about the Earhart Disappearance," July , 2012, http://www.history.com/news/what-happened-to-amelia-9-tantalizing-theories-about-the-earhart-disappearance.

Jennie Cohen, "10 Things You Didn't Know About the Penny," March 30, 2012, http://www.history.com/news/10-things-you-didnt-know-about-the-penny.

The Huffington Post: "Pres. John Tyler's Grandchildren Are Still Alive," January 25, 2012, http://www.huffingtonpost.com/2012/01/25/pres-john-tylers-grandchildren-still-alive_n_1232430.html.

Los Angeles Times:

Rene Lynch, "'Unabomber' Ted Kaczynski: Proud Harvard alumnus—or taunter?" *Nation Now* (blog), May 24, 2012, http://www.latimes.com/news/nation/nationnow/la-na-nn-unabomber-ted-kaczynski-harvard-20120524,0,4498725.story.

John Flesher, "A military victory few can imagine," May 20, 2009, http://articles.latimes.com/2009/may/10/news/adna-horse-soldiers10.

Mental Floss:

Matt Soniak, "FUSAG: The Ghost Army of World War II," April 13, 2012, http://www.mentalfloss.com/blogs/archives/118080.

Matt Soniak, "How Aunt Jemima Changed U.S. Trademark Law," June 15, 2012, http://www.mentalfloss.com/blogs/archives/111340.

National Archives: "Pieces of History: General Robert E. Lee's Parole and Citizenship," *Prologue Magazine*, Spring 2005 37(1), http://www.archives.gov/publications/prologue/2005/spring/piece-lee.html.

National Public Radio:

Robert Smith, "When The U.S. Paid Off The Entire National Debt (And Why It Didn't Last), *Planet Money* (blog), April 15, 2011, http://www.npr.org/blogs/money/2011/04/15/135423586/when-the-u-s-paid-off-the-entire-national-debt-and-why-it-didnt-last.

Larry Abramson, "50 Years After A Cold War Drama, A Silver Star," June 15, 2012, http://www.npr.org/2012/06/15/155111355/50-years-after-a-cold-war-drama-a-silver-star.

New York Times:

Scott James, "On the Golden Gate Bridge, a Year of Rising Suicides," August 26, 2011, http://www.nytimes.com/2011/08/26/us/26bcjames.html.

Carol Pogash, "Colma, Calif., Is a Town of 2.2 Square Miles, Most of It 6 Feet Deep," December 9, 2006, http://www.nytimes.com/2006/12/09/us/09cemetery.html.

"National News Briefs; Second Flaw Found In Grand Canyon Stamp," February 3, 2000, http://www.nytimes.com/2000/02/03/us/national-news-briefs-second-flaw-found-in-grand-canyon-stamp.html.

Rita Reif, "First Half of 'Huck Finn,' in Twain's Hand, Is Found," February 14, 1991, http://www.nytimes.com/1991/02/14/books/first-half-of-huck-finn-in-twain-s-hand-is-found.html.

Douglas Martin, "Robert Moon, an Inventor of the ZIP Code, Dies at 83," April 14, 2001, http://www.nytimes.com/2001/04/14/us/robert-moon-an-inventor-of-the-zip-code-dies-at-83.html

Kenneth Change, "Satellite's Fall Becomes Phenomenon," September 22, 2011, http://www.nytimes.com/2011/09/23/science/space/23satellite.html.

Constance Rosenblum, "'Hetty': Scrooge in Hoboken," December 19, 2004, http://www.nytimes.com/2004/12/19/books/review/19ROSENBL.html.

NewYorker.com: Mikhail Iossel, "Ray Bradbury in the U.S.S.R." *Page Turner* (blog), June 8, 2012, http://www.newyorker.com/online/blogs/books/2012/06/ray-bradbury-soviet-union.html

Public Broadcasting Service:

"The Story of…Smallpox—and Other Deadly Eurasian Germs," *Guns, Germs, and Steel* website, http://www.pbs.org/gunsgermssteel/variables/smallpox.html.

"Hell on Wheels," *American Experience* website, http://www.pbs.org/wgbh/americanexperience/features/general-article/tcrr-hell.

Salon.com: J. A. Getzlaff, "Mike the Headless Chicken Day," January 6, 2012, http://www.salon.com/2000/01/06/chicken.

Salt Lake Tribune: Utah Is No. 1—For Online Pornography Consumption, March 2, 2009, http://www.sltrib.com/business/ci_11821265.

SFGate: Susan Sward, Stacy Finz. Meredith May, Torri Minton, "Overshadowed All His Life / Low-key Cary Stayner took back seat to kidnapped brother," July 30, 1999, http://www.

sfgate.com/news/article/Overshadowed-All-His-Life-Low-
key-Cary-Stayner-2915936.php.

Slate.com: Ruth Graham, "Shopaholic at the White House: Was
President Lincoln's wife bipolar or just ahead of her time?"
February 14, 2010, http://www.slate.com/articles/double_x/
doublex/2010/02/shopaholic_at_the_white_house.2.html.

Smithsonian.com:

Megan Gambino, "The Monuments That Were Never Built,"
November 23, 2011, http://www.smithsonianmag.com/history-
archaeology/The-Monuments-That-Were-Never-Built.html.

Steve Twomey, Phineas Gage: Neuroscience's Most Famous
Patient," January 2010, http://www.smithsonianmag.com/
history-archaeology/Phineas-Gage-Neurosciences-Most-
Famous-Patient.html.

"The 'Latin Lover' and His Enemies," *Past Imperfect* (blog), June
13, 2012, http://blogs.smithsonianmag.com/history/2012/06/
the-latin-lover-and-his-enemies.

Richard Conniff, "Mammoths and Mastodons: All American
Monsters," April 2010, http://www.smithsonianmag.com/
science-nature/Mammoths-and-Mastodons-All-American-
Monsters.html.

"The 1959 Plan to Turn Ellis Island into a Vacation Resort,"
Paleofuture (blog), June 18, 2012, http://blogs.smithsonianmag.
com/paleofuture/2012/06/the-1958-plan-to-turn-ellis-island-
into-a-vacation-resort.

Tony Horowitz and Brian Wolly, "The 10 Things You Didn't
Know About the War of 1812," May 22, 2012, http://www.
smithsonianmag.com/history-archaeology/The-10-Things-
You-Didnt-Know-About-the-War-of-1812.html.

Greg Daugherty, "Seven Famous People Who Missed the *Titanic*,"
March 2012, http://www.smithsonianmag.com/history-
archaeology/Seven-Famous-People-Who-Missed-the-Titanic.
html.

"The Ax Murderer Who Got Away," *Past Imperfect* (blog), June 8,
2012, http://blogs.smithsonianmag.com/history/2012/06/the-
ax-murderer-who-got-away.

Joseph Stromberg, "When the Olympics Gave Out Medals
for Art," July 25, 2012, http://www.smithsonianmag.com/
arts-culture/When-the-Olympics-Gave-Out-Medals-for-
Art-163705106.html#ixzz21lNXlxqn.